UNTHINKING MASTERY

UNTHINKING MASTERY

Dehumanism and Decolonial Entanglements

JULIETTA SINGH

DUKE UNIVERSITY PRESS

Durham and London

2018

© 2018 Duke University Press
All rights reserved
Printed in the United States of America on acid-free
paper ∞
Cover designed by Courtney Leigh Baker
Typeset in Minion Pro and Gill Sans Std
by Graphic Composition, Inc., Bogart, Georgia

Library of Congress Cataloging-in-Publication Data
Names: Singh, Julietta, [date] author.
Title: Unthinking mastery : dehumanism and decolonial
entanglements / Julietta Singh.
Description: Durham : Duke University Press, 2017. | Includes
bibliographical references and index.
Identifiers: LCCN 2017019894 (print)
LCCN 2017021286 (ebook)
ISBN 9780822372363 (ebook)
ISBN 9780822369226 (hardcover : alk. paper)
ISBN 9780822369394 (pbk. : alk. paper)
Subjects: LCSH: Postcolonialism in literature. | Power (Social
sciences) in literature. | Coetzee, J. M., 1940– —Criticism and
interpretation. | Mahāśvetā Debī, 1926–2016—Criticism and
interpretation. | Sinha, Indra—Criticism and interpretation. |
Kincaid, Jamaica—Criticism and interpretation.
Classification: LCC PN56.P555 (ebook) | LCC PN56.P555 S55 2017
(print) | DDC 809/.93358—dc23
LC record available at https://lccn.loc.gov/2017019894

Cover art: Sarah Anne Johnson, *Party Boat*, 2011.
Scratched chromogenic print, photospotting and acrylic
inks, gouache and marker, 28 × 42 in. Image courtesy of
the artist.

CONTENTS

ACKNOWLEDGMENTS

A beloved mentor once told me that all books are in some sense auto-biographical. While writing *Unthinking Mastery*, I began to see the book as an intimate engagement with my own struggles and desires, perhaps most poignantly because it came into being during a time of life when I was made to understand that I was a profoundly vulnerable yet enduring thing. The birth of a child, the untimely death of a close friend and colleague, the sudden loss of a beloved parent, the onset of intense and abiding pain, a precarious emergency surgery, a slow and disorienting rehabilitation—these particular events coalesced to insist on the need to become myself differently, to read myself otherwise, to learn myself as a radically dependent, immeasurably porous bodymind. *Unthinking Mastery* developed through this particular and resonating temporality, and in crafting it I have become vitally reshaped by the futures it dreams.

There is nowhere else to begin the beautiful work of thanks than by turning to Nathan Snaza, whose intellectual brilliance is incalculably embedded across these pages. I thank him for thinking and unthinking mastery with me, and for letting these acts become a vital part of everyday life. I remain forever bewildered by his friendship and by the ways of living he makes possible.

This book was living a rather quiet life until Jack Halberstam saw promise in the manuscript and opened a world to me. I thank him (eternally) for his stunning engagements with this work, for his visionary sense of how to give shape to its antimasterful politics, and for offering me the promises of failure and solidarity. Christopher Breu's insight and ethical reach have made him almost mythical to me. For urging me to embrace the messiness of utopia and pressing me toward the political futures of unthinking mastery (which I will always be mulling over), I am intensely grateful to him. Parama Roy read a very early version of the manuscript and recognized therein a potential I had not yet made manifest. Her meticulous readings and unbelievably generous commentary were instrumental to what the book would become and indeed to my own understanding of what I was trying to accomplish. Ann Pellegrini read the manuscript with the keenest editorial eyes and offered critical insights, psychoanalytic finesse, and inexhaustible energy and enthusiasm.

At Duke University Press, Courtney Berger has made having an editor feel akin to winning a jackpot; I can imagine no better fortune for a writer than the opportunity to work with her. Sandra Korn kept me on task while sustaining my jubilance, and Liz Smith expertly ushered the book through production and into the world of objects. To all those behind the scenes at Duke, my most sincere thanks for your work on this book.

Unthinking Mastery benefited from my participation at several events over the years. As a fellow at the New School's Institute for Critical Social Inquiry, I had the fortune of immersion in Judith Butler's Freud/Klein seminar. Her breathtaking psychoanalytic readings helped to inspire currents of this work. The students in Ann Pellegrini's "Queer Humanimalities" graduate seminar at New York University read this book in its late stages with keen and critical eyes. In particular, Troizel Carr, Justin Linds, and Wendy Lotterman enlivened aspects of the work for me in smart and surprising ways. I am thankful to the organizers and participants of various conferences at which I delivered early chapter drafts, snippets, or tangential ideas from this book: "The War on the Human" conference in Athens, Greece; "Cosmopolitan Animals" in London, England; the workshop in honor of Lisa Smirl at the International Studies Association Conference in Toronto, Canada; and the American Comparative Literature Association in Vancouver. Versions of two chapters have appeared in journals: chapter 3 appeared as "Post-Humanitarian Fictions" in *Symploke* 23, nos. 1–2 (2015), and chapter 4 appeared as "The Tail End of Disciplinarity" in *Journal of Postcolonial Writing* 49, no. 4 (2013).

Those indispensable figures of my graduate education hold my enduring love and gratitude. My doctoral advisor, John Mowitt, listened intently to my earliest brainstorms on mastery, commented on sketchy drafts, and punned his way through prospective titles for this book. For a history of committed thinking with and toward me, and for seeing promise that I often failed to see, I remain abidingly thankful to him. Simona Sawnhey taught me theory's relation to political and intimate life. Her unwavering care and refusal to let up on me during my graduate years ushered me toward a life of feminist deconstruction that has been so endlessly sustaining. Ajay Skaria offered me Gandhi and mentioned almost happenstance that whatever else I was trying to think about, I was latently preoccupied with the problem of mastery. Shaden Tageldin taught me what I needed to know—the stakes of my own disciplinary training—and created a pedagogical space that made all the difference in the world. My early years in the United States would have been radically diminished without the intelligence, wit, and laughter of the "South Asia Girls"—beloved friends and fellow graduate students among whom I learned and unlearned so much: Aditi Chandra, Emily Rook-Koepsel, and Pritipuspa Mishra. In Canada, I could not have done without the early mentorship of Susie O'Brien and Imre Szeman. Susie introduced me to so many of my abiding intellectual passions, and Imre steered me toward a future in comparative literature I could not have dreamed up for myself.

I am thankful to all my students at Richmond who keep surprising me, especially Phoebe Krumich, who found me early in my teaching career and taught me the intimacies of teaching, and Kerry Boland, who came out of nowhere and stunned me with her magnificent ability to think queerly. For showing me the joys and differences of pedagogy, I am also especially grateful to Joyce Garner (for her endless, bolstering energy), Harleen Bal, Michael Doss, Jo Gehlbach, Mariah Gruner, Diego Leal, Alex Rooke, and Jen Swegan.

The University of Richmond has been a most generous supporter of my work, and I thank the institution for its many research fellowships during the years I was writing this book. In my home department in English, I have been embraced by wonderful friends and colleagues. I am especially beholden to Suzanne Jones and Louis Schwartz, who as department chairs kept me sound, steady, and supported across the years. Emily Tarchokov guided me through the day-to-day work of institutional life and remains an invaluable support. Monika Seibert and Elizabeth Outka read my earliest attempts at articulating mastery and asked me tough foundational questions. Bert Ashe watched with a keen and humorous eye as I paced the halls pre-tenure and offered support of many kinds across the years. Libby Gruner's generosity and savvy continue to be invaluable to me. I am so grateful for the friendship and collegiality of Laura Browder, Abigail

Cheever, Daryl Dance, Joe Essid, Terryl Givens, Brian Henry, Ray Hilliard, Peter Lurie, Joyce MacAllister, Reingard Nethersole, Kevin Pelletier, Anthony Russell, and David Stevens.

I have found a great deal of inspiration in the Women, Gender, and Sexuality Studies Program at Richmond. Deepest thanks to my friends Holly Blake, Crystal Hoyt, Erika Zimmermann Damer, Dorothy Holland, Glyn Hughes, Lázaro Lima, Lucretia McCulley, Ladelle McWhorter, Mariela Méndez, MariLee Mifsud, Melissa Ooten, Nancy Propst, Andrea Simpson, Kathleen Skerrett, and Sydney Watts.

For keeping me intact, I am immeasurably indebted to Allyson Rainer, for spectacular grace and wisdom across crucial years of recovering, writing, and waiting; Art Bryant, for orchestrating the future; Jeremy Arthur Sawyer, for years of unrelenting patience so long ago; Susan Wolver, for recognizing the sound of pain and responding by moving mountains; and John Reavey-Cantwell, for the steadiest hands under pressure.

In the world at large, my sincere thanks to Nadim Asrar, Lisa Balabuk Myrl Beam, Cara Benedetto, Neil Besner, Barbara Browning, Thomas Cannavino, Aaron Carico, Cesare Casarino, Sonja Common, Sarah Dadush, Sneha Desai, Sapana Doshi, Kate Eubank, Molly Fair, Arran Gaunt, Jesse Goldstein, Macarena Gómez-Barris, Christian Haines, Alistar Harris, Silas Howard, Catherine Hunter, Dave Johnson, Keir Johnson, Mina Karavanta, Andrew Knighton, Derek Kornelsen, Rob Krause, Laurie Kyle, Cecily Marcus, Susan McHugh, Fleur McLaughlan, Rick Monture, Carla Mundwiler, Leslie Orlikow, Tracey Osborne, Lucas Penner, Aly Pennucci, Thomas Pepper, Rebecca Ponder, Ricardo Rebolledo, Frank Achim Schmidt, Barbara Schott, Karen Shimakawa, Matt Stoddard, Ben Stork, and John Erik Troyer (from the department). Clare van Loenen and Peter, Marcie, and Juno Taffs have been hilarious and exceptionally generous friends. Among other things, I thank them for offering me crucial hours of quiet writing time at critical moments.

Very special thanks to Sarah Anne Johnson for her extraordinary generosity now and way back when, for her stunning art, and for her permission to reproduce it in this book. And to Lorne Roberts, who invited me into the Canadian clear-cut long ago, and who more recently returned me to the political stakes of that way of life. I thank him for this past and for how it keeps feeling its way into the future.

The enduring love and friendship of my dearest friend, Julie Penner, has been so inexpressibly vital to me. It is with her I keep learning—even from afar—that being sensitive is a style of living in the world to be embraced rather than eschewed. Lisa Smirl, my beautiful friend and colleague who did not live to see this book come to life, is nevertheless loved and remembered in its pages.

For sharing with me the intimacies of history, I thank my siblings: Renate Singh, Robert Singh, and Meera Singh. David Common—for whom the filial term "cousin" will never suffice—has been a lifelong supporter and beloved friend. I thank him for his unwavering commitment to me across the most blissful and the most bewildering times, and for endless piggyback rides.

The profound kindness and care of my stepparents has meant the world to me: Giovanni Geremia has shown me a style of calm being that I adore and has provided me with the biggest and best hugs of my life. Renate Singh has been a loving support, and I am grateful for the memories she holds and keeps sharing with me.

Unthinking Mastery is a love letter to my parents, whose embodiments of history and unconventional forms of mentorship have given rise to the unanswerable questions that continue to drive my thought: in loving memory of my father, Jagat Narain Singh, whose pride in his wayward youngest daughter is still and always felt, and whose transformations across the years have been profoundly pedagogical for me; and for my stunning mother, Christine Common, a woman for whom trees, old buildings, creatures, and offspring all begin to blur, and in so doing suture the maternal to the ethical. This book is yours.

At last, for queer cohabitation and its utopian horizons: to Cassie, who remained willfully entangled with me for so long, and who taught me how to become communal; to the unflappable Nathan, for always dreaming up the world with me; and to the magical Isadora, who angles us all toward enchantment.

Introduction

Reading against Mastery

Everywhere I see the battle for mastery that rages between classes, peoples, etc., reproducing itself on an individual scale. Is the system flawless? Impossible to bypass?
On the basis of my desire, I imagine that other desires like mine exist. If my desire is
possible, it means the system is already letting something else through.

—HÉLÈNE CIXOUS, *Sorties* (1986)

What different modalities of the human come to light if we do not take the liberal
humanist figure of Man as the master-subject but focus on how humanity has been
imagined and lived by those subjects excluded from this domain?

—ALEXANDER WEHELIYE, *Habeas Viscus* (2014)

"Mastery," Hélène Cixous laments, is "everywhere." In our world, "the battle
for mastery . . . rages between classes, peoples, etc., reproducing itself on an
individual scale" (1986, 78). Ubiquitous, reproductive, and beyond enumer-
ation, mastery appears inescapable. And yet, Cixous declares, the very existence of her desire to live beyond mastery suggests that others too might
share this desire. What she learns from her desire is that resistant collectivities are in reach, that in fact a seemingly impenetrable "system" of mastery
has *already* been breached. Through my solidarity with Cixous's desire and
through my own desire for forms of what I call *dehumanist solidarity*, this
book reaches toward other modes of relational being that may not yet be
recognizable.

Precisely because mastery is "everywhere," mine is an impossible project
whose impossibility is what has made it inescapable for me. I attempt to
unfold mastery rather than to foreclose it, and to dwell on its emergence
where it is least expected. Rather than to define mastery (and in so doing to
reproduce it), I aim across these pages to trace some of mastery's qualities,

drives, corollaries, and repetitions across two crucially entangled moments of decolonization: the anticolonial and the postcolonial. *Unthinking Mastery* is a summons to postcolonial studies and its interlocutors to attend to the persistence of mastery at the foundations of the field. I argue that mastery's obdurate presence necessarily affects how scholars within and beyond the postcolonial project envision their intellectual pursuits today. More expansively, it is an appeal to begin not simply to repudiate practices of mastery but, to borrow from Donna Haraway (2016), to "stay with the trouble" that is produced through attention to where, how, between whom, and toward what futures mastery is engaged. In this sense, I am interested in mastery not as something to be overcome but rather as an inheritance that we might (yet) survive.

Across anticolonial discourse the mastery of the colonizer over the colonies was a practice that was explicitly disavowed, and yet, in their efforts to decolonize, anticolonial thinkers in turn advocated practices of mastery—corporeal, linguistic, and intellectual—toward their own liberation. Within anticolonial movements, practices of countermastery were aimed explicitly at defeating colonial mastery, in effect pitting mastery against mastery toward the production of thoroughly decolonized subjectivities. For thinkers as diverse as Mohandas K. Gandhi and Frantz Fanon—key players in the first two chapters of this book—decolonization was an act of undoing colonial mastery by producing new masterful subjects. I argue that this discourse of anticolonialism, which was geared toward the future, did not interrogate thoroughly enough its own masterful engagements. It did not dwell enough, in other words, on how its complex entanglements with mastery would come to resonate in the postcolonial future it so passionately anticipated. Precisely because mastery served as a motive for revolutionary action *and* as an antidote for colonial domination, it is a vital site from which to analyze the work of mastery in "globalized" life today. Through discourses of decolonization that have sought to undo the dynamics of colonial mastery, we can begin to understand how pervasive and intimately ingrained mastery is in the fabric of modern thought, subjectivity, and politics. The task of this book is to begin—simply to begin—to trace some of the desires and aims of mastery across decolonization movements of the twentieth century through the intimately sutured discourses of anticolonialism and postcolonialism. My desire is to engage with revolutionary and literary texts in ways that can reorient our masterful pursuits, ones that characterize global relations and continue to threaten our survival. The outright repudiations and reinscriptions of mastery across anticolonial and postcolonial discourses are vital places from which we can begin to address how drives toward mastery inform and underlie the major crises of our times—acts of intrahuman violence across the globe, the radical disparities in resources and rights between the Global North and Global South, innumerable forms of human and nonhuman extinction, and escalating threats of ecological disaster.

For anticolonial thinkers, engaging the logic of mastery that had long since governed over the colonies was critical to restoring a full sense of humanity to the colonized subject, to building a thoroughly decolonized postcolonial nation-state, and to envisioning less coercive futures among human collectivities. In the anticolonial moment, mastery largely assumed a Hegelian form in which anticolonial actors were working through a desire or demand for recognition by another. The mastery at work in this project was one whose political resonance resided in national sovereignty and the legal principle of self-determination, one that approached the dismantling of mastery through an inverted binary that aimed to defeat colonial mastery through other masterful forms. In postcolonial studies—which takes a decisively cultural turn in its attention to colonialism's lasting legacies— these Hegelian valences continue to dwell in articulations of mastery. The postcolonial literary texts to which I turn midway through this book represent mastery through an oscillation between the dialectical Hegelian mode and a deconstructive one. While these texts rehearse recognizably masterful forms of relation and practice, they also urge us—through their messy narrative play—toward mastery's undoing. Through my close attention to the possibilities entangled in the complexities of decolonial discourses both political and literary, I identify, in the company of Cixous, "something else" being let through the abiding and proliferating force of mastery. Within these discourses, these modes of articulation that often (as we shall see) betray themselves, we can begin to imagine—even to feel, and in feeling be transformed by—what Alexander Weheliye calls other possible "modalities of the human" (2014, 8). Weheliye turns us, through his black studies critique of the racial blinders of biopolitics, toward a critical engagement with the forms of humanity envisioned and practiced by those excluded from the domain of Man as "the master-subject."[1] Alongside Sylvia Wynter, he signals "different genres of the human" that require us to attend to the always enfleshed alterities of being human (Weheliye 2014, 2–3).

Dehumanism

I am eager to dwell alongside these other humanities, to explore as well how such dwellings might enable us to become exiled from subjectivities founded on and through mastery. This is a practice I call *dehumanism*: a practice of recuperation, of stripping away the violent foundations (always structural and ideological) of colonial and neocolonial mastery that continue to render some beings more human than others. Dehumanism requires not an easy repudiation and renunciation of dehumanization but a form of radical dwelling in and with dehumanization through the narrative excesses and insufficiencies of the "good" human—a cohabitation that acts on and through us in order to imagine other forms of political allegiance. To read the human otherwise, I draw from the interdisciplinary discourses of posthumanism and queer inhumanisms even while my dehumanist aims depart in more and less crucial ways from these projects.

Within the broad reach of posthumanism, two intellectual branches are essential to *Unthinking Mastery*. The first takes up questions of the animal, including the animality of the human, which will come into sharp focus in chapter 4.[2] The second falls under the heading of new materialisms, which, as I elaborate in chapter 5, emphasizes how matter actively contributes to and shapes environments, communities, and politics.[3] These trajectories of posthumanism insist that "the dominant constructivist orientation to social analysis is inadequate for thinking about matter, materiality, and politics in ways that do justice to the contemporary context of biopolitics and global political economy" (Coole and Frost 2010, 6). They also call attention to how humanism is structured by a separation between the ideological fantasies of the human's unique agency and the disavowed materialities that underlie it. While I am drawn to these particular trajectories of posthumanism, little attention is paid in its discourses to the specificity of neocolonial relations of power and materiality. Dehumanism, then, aims to bring the posthuman into critical conversation with the decolonial.

Posthumanism begins with a querying of the human through its most privileged points of departure, generally focusing on the philosophers and techno-scientific innovations that allow us to trouble the category of the human as such. Following Wynter's insistence on the difference between the human and Man, we can say that Man has been the subject/object of posthumanist inquiry. Departing from posthumanism, queer inhumanisms aim to query the human from the position of some of its least privileged forms and designations of life.[4] Tavia Nyong'o, for instance, calls attention to the "continued liberal enchantment" in intellectual discourse with a subject that remains "transparent," unmarked by various categories of difference. He argues that in collusion with this liberalism, "posthumanist theory has tended to present the decentering of the human as both salutary and largely innocent of history" (2015, 266). Drawing on black studies, Nyong'o queries how such subjects can then work to decenter the human while remaining committed to the political projects articulated from these positions of (in)human exclusion. How, in other words, might the project of remaking the human happen from its outside?

In the hopeful spirit of queer inhumanisms, dehumanism begins with the dehumanized—"humans" and their others—as its critical point of departure. José Esteban Muñoz has summoned us toward the necessary labor of "attempting to touch inhumanity" (2015, 209), and Nyong'o insists that we pressure history in the making and unmaking of the subject. Indebted to queer inhumanism's ethical reach, I modify the concept of inhumanism, which (despite the desires of those committed to its potentialities) loses track in its own grammatical formulation of the histories, practices, and narratives that make some human and cast others outside its orbit. The prefix "in" of inhumanism points to a privation that does not intuitively signal the history of the making of nonhuman subjects and forms of being. Shifting *in*humanism to *de*humanism, I move away from a seemingly ontological formulation of Man and its others toward a more pointed formulation that implicates in its very utterance the processes of dehumanization through a term that signals clearly the imperial work of making humans and worlds. Dehumanism, then, is united with queer inhumanisms as it presses us toward an overtly global, imperial critique of the making and mapping of Man and its proliferating remnants.

The "de" of dehumanism also and vitally articulates the "de" of deconstruction, crucially foregrounding the particular force of narrative in the making and unmaking of subjects, and the "de" of decolonial ethico-politics. Dehumanism is driven by the promises of vulnerability with the aim of forming other less masterful subjectivities. As I argue across *Unthinking Mastery*, the act of reading is vital to this process of imagining otherwise and dwelling elsewhere, to the relentless exercise of unearthing and envisioning new human forms and conceptualizations of agency. Reading becomes not a humanizing process that rehearses the largely anthropocentric discourses of decolonization but a much more radical process of opening us to the possibility of becoming ourselves promisingly dehumanized. What possibilities live in these other "modalities" of the human? What vital hope is (still) lingering in exile when we are ready to open our borders? Even to become, ourselves, hopefully dispossessed of mastery?

Locating Mastery

Existing critiques of postcolonial studies have thus far not taken seriously enough the position of mastery at its foundations. Since its inception in the 1980s, subaltern studies (which holds a foundational role in the more diffuse intellectual body known as postcolonial studies) has been taken to task from within and by scholars outside its project. A central critique of postcolonial studies charges it with being an elitist intellectual fantasy removed from the Realpolitik of capital.[5] This critique accuses postcolonial theory of a blindness toward or a misrecognition of Marxism and calls for a turn from bourgeois nationalism toward a true proletarian nationalism (or internationalism). This turn necessarily requires a pruning back of the "excesses" of poststructuralist approaches to postcolonial history and political theory. My concern with this line of critique is that, while it attempts to become grounded in the facts of class struggle, it advocates a return to Hegelian Marxism and implicitly concedes to an ongoing dialectic of "mastering mastery." In effect, it returns us to a formulation of the master and slave in which the only way to undo their relation is through an overcoming, a mastering of that which masters. This logic of mastery superseding mastery remains continuous across Georg W. F. Hegel and Karl Marx, and, as I argue in chapters 1 and 2, resonates in anticolonial thinking through revolutionary figures such as Fanon and Gandhi. Mastery has likewise made its way, often unthinkingly, into the discourse of postcolonial studies and its critiques. It is the task of this book to signal this inheritance of mastery and to illustrate that, by continuing to abide by the formulation of "mastering mastery," we remain bound to relations founded on and through domination. In so doing, we concede to the inescapability of mastery as a way of life.

In contrast to other predominant critiques of the field that take aim at the postcolonial project for its treatment of Marxist theory or assail it as a bourgeois project riddled by too much intellectual jargon,[6] I approach post-colonial studies with an intimacy and enduring attachment to some of its most rudimentary aims: to explore how the cultural politics of colonialism remain intact and to trace the entanglements of ideological practice and material fact as they signal the legacies of colonialism. My own critique of the field returns to the inaugural problematic of mastery in anticolo-nial discourse in order to attend to its status therein and its legacies there-after. This is not a gesture of repudiation but an invitation to approach the project of postcolonial studies with a new vitality. In complex and often unthinking ways, colonial mastery became politically disassociated from other masterful acts in anticolonial thought. The continuities among pur-suits of mastery have, I argue, carried forward unreflexively into postcolo-nial studies and have crucial consequences for the intellectual project. In order simultaneously to tarry with mastery and to unhinge ourselves from its hold, I turn toward some of the major voices of anticolonial politics before giving sustained attention to readings of postcolonial literary texts. These literary texts take up masterful trajectories in thought, language, and practice that remain if not extolled then largely ignored and unchallenged within the dominant modes of knowledge production today. They com-plicate claims to goodness, civility, stewardship, and humanitarianism by emphasizing subjectivities that are, to quote Talal Asad, "beset with con-tradictions" (2007, 2). Asad's aim is to show these contradictions at work in relation to suicide bombings, in which the desire to distinguish between "morally good" and "evil" forms of killing reveals contradiction as "a fragile part of our modern subjectivity" (2). This fragile subjectivity emerges not only through extreme claims of good and evil killing but also and critically through practices of the quotidian "good" through which debilitating force is often concealed. In the second half of this book, when I turn explicitly to an exemplary archive of postcolonial literary texts, I aim to show how engaging with these texts can open us to finding mastery where it is least expected. In order to loosen the hold of mastery, we must learn to *read* for it. If we can do so, these texts, while in no sense offering guidelines for proscriptive future politics, ask us to open ourselves to reimagining ways of relating to each other—to others human, nonhuman, and inhuman to which (even when disavowed) we are mutually bound.

As with so many of life's most abiding preoccupations, my interest in the status of mastery across anticolonial and postcolonial discourses began indirectly, with a discomfort I did not yet understand. While pursuing my doctoral degree in comparative literature in the United States, I was seeped in anticolonial and postcolonial critique and began to notice the uncritical reproduction of mastery within texts otherwise overtly critical of its colonial forms. In Edward Said's *Orientalism* (1979), a foundational work in postcolonial studies, he critiqued early Orientalist intellectuals "whose unremitting ambition was to master *all* of a world, not some easily delimited part of it such as an author or a collection of texts" (109). Said insisted not on the need to redress mastery altogether but on the need to *limit* its reach, to pursue mastery within reasonable, delineated parts. In turn, from those geopolitical regions of the world that have been marginalized by the Eurocentricism of intellectual practice, mastery continues to echo as a mode of inclusion. Ferial Ghazoul's vision of a future comparative literary practice for the Arab world, for instance, is one in which scholars will be "equally at home" in their native and foreign languages. She wishes that "a generation of comparatists be inspired who can master several literary traditions and speak about each of them with authority. It is only then that comparative literature will come into its own as an academic discipline that is credible and viable" (2006, 123). I sympathize with Ghazoul's refusal of disciplinary marginalization, with the desire to find oneself "at home" within disciplinary knowledge production and within languages intimate and once foreign to us. And yet one of the claims of *Unthinking Mastery* is that we must begin to exile ourselves from feeling comfortable at home (which so often involves opaque forms of mastery), turning instead toward forms of queer dispossession that reach for different ways of inhabiting our scholarly domains—and more primordially, of inhabiting ourselves. The intellectual authority of literary and area studies, its "credibility" and "viability," continuously relies on mastery as its target, as that which will produce authoritative, legitimate knowledge and in so doing resist the power of Eurocentrism.

Some may balk at my emphasis on the *language* of mastery that recurs in crucial postcolonial texts, insisting that this particular evocation of mastery should be cordoned off from the more overtly violent aspects of colonial mastery. But let us not forget that these are each scholars for whom language and its resonances are absolutely critical to their intellectual pursuits, and for whom language speaks and acts through its connectivities and refractions. Although its history can be traced back to classical Latin forms, a perusal of the *Oxford English Dictionary* suggests that the word "mastery" and its morphemes ("master" as noun, verb, and adjective) took hold during the period of early modernity. In its oldest meanings, a master is someone who had bested an opponent or competitor, or someone who had achieved a level of competence at a particular skill to become a teacher of it. It is, of course, this last valence that is being signaled and advocated by these leading intellectuals. Yet what postcolonial thinking has taught us (perhaps even most cogently through Said himself and through the extraordinary wealth of critical projects that have been informed by his work) is precisely that the mastery of colonization reveals the tightly bound connections between these two seemingly distinct registers: to "best" someone, to beat them and in so doing become master over them on the one hand, and to reach a level of competence in which one becomes rightfully pedagogical on the other hand. To put it crudely, a colonial master understands his superiority over others by virtue of his ability to have conquered them materially *and* by his insistence on the supremacy of his practices and worldviews over theirs, which renders "legitimate" the forceful imposition of his worldviews. The material and ideological, as postcolonial studies has time and again shown us so convincingly, cannot be easily parsed. The conscious and unconscious choices we make in relation to language (perhaps especially as scholars of languages and literatures) begin to reveal to and for us the ways that—often despite ourselves and our desired politics—we remain bound to structures of violence we wish to disavow. Conceiving of ourselves as intellectual masters over those bodies of knowledge (broad or discrete) that we have tasked ourselves to engage connects us to historical practices of mastery that our work seeks to explore and redress. We must with increasing urgency revise the very idea of (and the languages we use to describe) our work as intellectuals—with what resonances, and toward what possibilities.

The most contentious claim of this book, then, and the one that cuts to its core, is that there is an intimate link between the mastery enacted through colonization and other forms of mastery that we often believe today to be harmless, worthwhile, even virtuous. To be characterized as the master of a language, or a literary tradition, or an instrument, for instance, is widely understood to be laudable. Yet as a pursuit, mastery invariably and relentlessly reaches toward the indiscriminate control over something—whether human or inhuman, animate or inanimate. It aims for the full submission of an object—or something *objectified*—whether it be external or internal to oneself. In so doing, mastery requires a rupturing of the object being mastered, because to be mastered means to be weakened to a point of fracture. Mastery is in this sense a splitting of the object that is mastered from itself, a way of estranging the mastered object from its previous state of being. Michel Serres insists upon this work of mastery when he writes that "he who likes to command can do so, but on one condition: the eyes of the producers, of the energetic and the strong, have to be poked out" (2007, 36). For Serres, the "condition" of mastery is precisely that the master must maim the formerly "energetic" and "strong"—he must debilitate in order to be master. Whether we desire mastery over a slave, an environment, or a body of texts, we are always returning to this primordial fracture—to the partial destruction of the object that the would-be master yearns to govern over completely. Mastery, as we will see across anticolonial discourse and postcolonial literary texts, also turns inward to become a form of self-maiming, one that involves the denial of the master's own dependency on other bodies.

The Particularities of Mastery

I conceptualize mastery as a violent problematic that includes but remains critically distinct from the more particular versions of sovereignty and dominion. As such, I will dwell here briefly on the entanglements and distinctions between these categories. Sovereignty, a concept that functions in the discourse of political theory, is primarily concerned with the state. As such, and unlike mastery, it depends on the state for its action and proliferation. "Sovereign is he," writes Carl Schmitt, "who decides on the exception" (2005, 5). While there is a great deal of literature written on Schmitt's notion of the exception,[7] what is important to my argument here is that Schmitt links sovereignty to the production and security of state borders. Although power has long-since mutated from the sovereign, Michel Foucault reminds us that within political thought and analysis we "still have not cut off the head of the king" (1990, 89). In Foucault's inaugural formulation of biopolitics, he argues that it "focused on the species body, the body imbued with the mechanics of life and serving as the basis of the biological processes: propagation, births and mortality, the level of health, life expectancy and longevity, with all the conditions that can cause these to vary" (139). Returning to the earliest meanings of mastery, we could say that the politics of mastery shift from a focus on overcoming an opponent or adversary toward skillful management of the self and its others. At the surface a less violent and coercive set of practices, skillful management becomes mastery's dominant mode in the biopolitical moment. Through the emergence of biopolitics, mastery ceases to be localized in a sovereign power, instead becoming a network that is diffused and dispersed across a range of sites, institutions, and actors.

For Michael Hardt and Antonio Negri, "the concept of sovereignty dominates the tradition of political philosophy and serves as the foundation of all that is political precisely because it requires that one must always rule and decide. Only the one can be sovereign, the tradition tells us, and there can be no politics without sovereignty. . . . The choice is absolute: either sovereignty or anarchy!" (2004, 329). This unremitting reliance on "the one" who must rule and decide (whether this singular entity is king or a ruling collective) is for Hardt and Negri a fallacy that limits a thinking and practice of contemporary politics. To supplant this notion of the one, they introduce the "multitude," which is not a social body precisely because "the multitude cannot be reduced to a unity and does not submit to the rule of one. The multitude cannot be sovereign" (330). While this formulation of the multitude intervenes in the dominant discourse of political philosophy and holds promise for less coercive forms of relational politics, it does not necessarily dismantle or escape practices of mastery that can and do continue to circulate and proliferate within the political formation of the multitude and "beyond" it. Mastery is always political but cannot be situated only within the realm of political governance. Even within collectives that refuse sovereign power, mastery can come into play through dispersed, impersonal forms of power that operate masterfully on and within particular bodies within the multitude. As Judith Butler (2015) reminds us, even when "the people" gather in protest, there can be forms of violence operational within and in relation to the collective. If the multitude promises alternative forms of political action, it is not immune to masterful dynamics within and beyond the multitude itself.

Similarly, the concept of dominion, which situates "man" in relation to the natural world, has entailed an interpretive practice of mastery over the earth. In Genesis, dominion becomes a particular human mode of relating to the world—indeed of caring for it—through practices of management and expertise that hinge on the human goal of mastering nature in order to let it flourish, to cultivate it, to submit it with the aim of maximum prosperity. When God gives Adam and Eve dominion "over the fish of the sea, over the birds of the air, and over every living thing that moves on the earth" (Genesis 1:28), their first task is to name all that they will have dominion over. The question of language and naming recurs across *Unthinking Mastery*, specifically in chapter 2, where I dwell on the anticolonial language debates, and again in chapter 5, where the Antiguan writer Jamaica Kincaid wades through the colonial stakes of naming and possession. The concept of dominion clarifies how mastery is tied to language, and how in its power to name the human also gains authorization to particular forms of masterful consumption: because I have named you, I can consume you. I take up this relation between logic, mastery, and consumption in chapter 4 through my analysis of the South African writer J. M. Coetzee's *The Lives of Animals* (1999). Dominion is, as Mick Smith (2011) reminds us, certainly a relation where mastery plays out explicitly through the care of resources, land management, and animal husbandry. Both sovereignty as a state problematic and dominion as an ecological one are iterations of mastery—ones that reveal crucial aspects of mastery but without exhausting its machinations.

I have suggested that to define mastery would be a gesture toward mastering it. It would also risk foreclosing mastery in such a way that disables attention to the gaps and fissures of such a definition, where mastery may leak out and take forms that are not contained within its definitive script. I am concerned with instances in which mastery is reinscribed as another kind of act, appearing untethered from its origin. I approach mastery, then, not by defining the act but through tracing some of its enduring characteristics. At least three features of mastery circulate throughout my readings, offering us not a definition but *qualities* by which we can begin to think with mastery and against it—in the sense not merely of opposition but of dwelling alongside. First, mastery involves splitting in either the sense of carving a boundary or an infliction of mutilation—or, often, both at the same time. Consider the 1947 Partition of India, when the splitting of India to create an independent Islamic nation-state in the form of Pakistan was entangled with the mass migrations and mutilations of various religiously coded bodies. Mastery in this political context illustrates other distinct histories of colonization, histories that likewise can be traced via the enforced creation of political spaces and the mutilation of bodies.

A second quality of mastery that follows from the first is that it involves the subordination of what is on one side of a border to the power of what is on the other. In the Hegelian formulation of the master/slave dialectic, to which I will turn in detail below, this means that by splitting the slave, and by splitting off from the slave, the master comes to hold (at least a fantasmatic notion of) an enduring mastery. The splitting that is inherent to mastery, the fracturing that confirms and inaugurates it, and the ongoing practices of subordination that drive it forward are inescapable in the foundational thinking of the subject of modern political thought. Therein, the very notion of the human relies on and is totally unthinkable without mastery. In the *Second Treatise on Civil Government* (1689), John Locke grounds the modern subject, the subject of the emergent nation-state and capitalist economy, on a mastery that confirms the subject as such. In a famous passage linking "Man" to private property, Locke writes: "From all which it is evident, that though the things of Nature are given in common, yet Man (by being Master of himself, and *Proprietor of his Person*, and the Actions or Labour of it), had still in himself the great foundation of Property; and that which made up the great part of what he allayed to the Support or Comfort of his being, when Invention and Arts had improved the conveniences of Life, was perfectly his own, and did not belong in common to others" (qtd. in Esposito 2008, 66). Man here is defined as the being who is, or who can be, "Master of himself." He is not thinkable without this practice of mastery that inaugurates him as "proprietor" of himself, who as Man becomes master of himself *as* property. This would mean that before "Man" can mark himself out and become master/proprietor of himself, there has to be something ("himself") more primary, more diffuse, that enables the mastering but cannot be reduced to it. For Locke, then, Man as the masterful modern subject is a privatization and appropriation of something *else*, something that precedes and perhaps always escapes or exceeds mastery— something within and around Man that, in fact, Man has to "master" in order to become himself, which is to say, in order to become free. While mastery here becomes totalizing and inescapable (one is either mastered by another or is master of oneself), its very emergence presupposes that

Handwritten marginalia (left margin): Challenging borders

Handwritten marginalia (right margin): How do schools hold on to mastery? · curricula · structure · policing there is something outside of mastery, something that mastery feeds on but disavows. To unthink mastery therefore requires either a radically different understanding of what it could mean to be human or perhaps a thinking of the human that would not be human at all. Foucault reminds us, "Man is an invention of recent date" (1994, 387), and as such I am keen to imagine a subject or person who would not be human *in this way*, in this *style* of masterful Man articulated through political philosophy.

Finally, mastery requires that this split and hierarchized relation be extended in time. Hegel's conception of the master/slave dialectic so dominant in modern political thought is one that unfolds across time. That is, Hegel's account of mastery is fundamentally narrative.[8] A life and death battle for recognition (always, for Hegel, one that unfolds between masculine gendered subjects) produces a master who is willing to die for an ideal and a slave who wants to preserve his life and thus submits to another. In the beginning, there are "two self-conscious individuals" who face a "life-and-death struggle" (Hegel 1977, 113). At the end of the struggle, "one is the independent consciousness whose essential nature is to be for itself, the other is the dependent consciousness whose essential nature is simply to live or to be for another. The former is lord, the other is bondsman" (115). Hegel will come to show us that the lord-as-master is in fact dependent on the slave's recognition of him, "a recognition that is one-sided and unequal" (116) because one is "recognized" and one "recognizing" (113).[9] What is crucial to my argument here is the narrative form of this dialectic: what Hegel calls the "essential nature" of the master and slave are in fact the outcomes of a struggle that must unfold in time and come to be *recognized as permanent*.[10] In Alexandre Kojève's highly influential reading of the master/slave dialectic, man is never merely man but "always, necessarily, and essentially, either Master or Slave" (1980, 8). Kojève's reading presents a contingent outcome as a question of necessity and essence, in effect transforming history into myth.

And yet, as Marx would come to insist, like Fanon and Paulo Freire after him, the material labor of the slave—his work that transforms reality (Hegel 1977, 117–19)—holds the active potentiality of other relations of power not beholden to mastery. Joining Marx and Fanon toward a postcolonial pedagogy, Freire insists that the task of the oppressed is "to liberate themselves and their oppressors as well. The oppressors, who oppress, exploit, and rape by virtue of their power, cannot find in this power the strength to liberate either the oppressed or themselves" (2000, 44). While Freire envisions this critical pedagogy as an urgent "humanistic" task, I would recast this liberatory politics as precisely a *dehumanist* necessity. If the masterful work of global imperialism functions through the dehumanization of those it aims to conquer, and if we can now argue that the human to which we have been aspiring is intimately bound to a logic of mastery, then looking toward those "other genres of being human" that have been lived and will be lived by those subjected by imperial force might offer us other performances of the human that allow us to begin to practice nonmasterful forms of politics. This dehumanist practice of "beginning" to unfold the human from its outsides necessarily takes place in a queer temporality, one that José Esteban Muñoz (2009) and Elizabeth Freeman (2010) insist has already been happening, and has yet to come.

Postcolonial Hegel

If the Hegelian dialectic of lordship and bondage has been cast and accepted across much of modern thought as mythical, as that which can account for relations across time and space, it has been the task of decolonial thinkers to contextualize it historically. Examining Hegel's use of source materials in the making of his notorious claims about Africa as a place "outside" history,[11] Robert Bernasconi (1998) argues that Hegel was in no sense formulating a reading of Africans (as proper subjects of slavery) that was free from the colonial mode of thinking of his day. Rather, Hegel embellished and culled selectively from his source materials, producing claims he *desired* to make about Africans. Such desire, Bernasconi shows us, is tied to the philosophical production of a certain conception of the subject (and of subjectivity) in which the European must be thought by and through the European philosopher in dialectical relation to its others. Africa therefore had to be cast by Hegel in terms that would enforce its unintelligibility in relation to Europe.[12]

Caroline Rooney follows this critique of Hegel to argue that "Western philosophical and critical thought serves, in the first place, to prevent a reception of the thought in question. Most seriously, there are ways—be they crudely obvious, subtly muted or genuinely perplexed—in which a thinking of Africa becomes that which is given as unthinkable" (2000, 15). Unlike Said's notion of Orientalism, Africa emerges not as Europe's antithesis but as something so unthinkable as to be beyond the frame. Hegel's own contradictory claims *about* Africans, and his assertions about Africans *as* contradiction, begin for Rooney to blur the lines between the self and the other, between the subject who produces knowledge and the objects of that knowledge production. Colonial thought, within which both Bernasconi and Rooney firmly situate Hegel, has relied on certain fabulous and fabricated (and sometimes geographically distinct) conceptions of others, conceptions that come to reveal less about the "objects" of its control and much more about colonial subjectivity and the production of its alterities.

In "Hegel and Haiti" (2000), Susan Buck-Morss offers a historically grounded answer to a question that has long occupied scholars of Hegel: From where did the philosopher's conception of lordship and bondage originate? Buck-Morss locates Hegel's "struggle to death" between master and slave squarely within the facts of the Haitian revolution led by François-Dominique Toussaint Louverture that was taking place during the period of Hegel's formulating this seemingly ahistorical relation.[13] Hegel specifically discussed reading the newspaper during that historical period, even describing how the press "orients one's attitude against the world and towards God [in one case], or toward that which the world is [in the other]. The former gives the same security as the latter, in that one knows where one stands" (Buck-Morss 2000, 844). Hegel all but confesses to being "oriented" by the world events of his day, allowing Buck-Morss to declare that "Hegel knew—knew about real slaves revolting successfully against real masters, and he elaborated his dialectic of lordship and bondage deliberately within this contemporary context" (852). Why, then, had scholars not picked up on the influence that Buck-Morss proposes is inescapable in Hegel's orientation, in the very formulation of the relation between the master and the slave?

I am especially compelled by the frame within which Buck-Morss situates her examination of Hegel and Haiti, bringing at the beginning and ends of her text the problem of disciplinary thinking through which we have inherited the past, and through which we safeguard ourselves against the threat of other modes of thinking, other possible forms of inheritance (2000, 822). Recalling how years after his shaping of the master/slave dialectic, Hegel would come to study Africa with more concrete, scholarly intention, Buck-Morss argues: "What *is* clear is that in an effort to become more erudite in African studies during the 1820s, Hegel was in fact becoming dumber" (863). Beyond soliciting a chuckle from her readers (at least this reader), Buck-Morss shows us a Hegel who never understood Africa, who projected his desires onto it, and who would come paradoxically to know it less as he studied it more: "It is sadly ironic that the more faithfully his lectures reflected Europe's conventional scholarly wisdom on African society, the less enlightened and more bigoted they became" (846). And here, Hegel comes to reflect us back to ourselves in our own pursuits to master the worlds we study. Disciplinary thinking is practical: it enables us to frame ourselves as masters of particular discourses, histories, and bodies of knowledge. It safeguards us against the incursions of oppositional frames, or methods of understanding that might unhinge us from our own masterful frames. Concluding her study of Hegel and Haiti, Buck-Morss asks us: "What if every time that the consciousness of individuals surpassed the confines of present constellations of power in perceiving the concrete meaning of freedom, *this* were valued as a moment, however transitory, of the realization of absolute spirit? What other silences would need to be broken? What *un*-disciplined stories would be told?" (865). From a queer methodological standpoint, Jack Halberstam likewise echoes this deep concern with disciplinary knowledge production and its erasures when he argues that "disciplines actually get in the way of answers and theorems precisely because they offer maps of thought where intuition and blind fumbling might yield better results" (2011, 6).

Narrative and Matter

Mastery is a concept that is situated at the threshold of matter and narrative. As a fundamentally narrative problematic, mastery assigns particular roles (the master, the slave) and holds those roles in place (it "characterizes" them) in a temporal, narrative structure. To win a fight is not to become the master, unless both the master and the slave *recognize* that in the future, the outcome will be the same. The master is envisioned as the winner, then, whose winning comes to be taken for granted in a proleptic narrative account of the world that authorizes future action. Once instantiated, the narrative has to elicit the participation of both characters, master and slave, in ways that allow and disallow particular *material* actions (labor first and foremost in the Marxist-Hegelian version). This calls for a renewed attention to the material effects of narrative at stake in what has been called recognition (in Hegelian terms), interpellation (in Marxist terms), and identification (in psychoanalytic terms). Through these material changes in a subject who "finds" him or herself in a narrative (either as master or slave), the subject's actions and affects are informed by narrative, even as these subjects must continually reproduce it. In other words, narrative and materiality are entangled in ways that cannot possibly be reduced to a unidirectional causality.

Once mastery is understood as an entanglement between narrative and matter, or "matter and meaning" (Barad 2007), it becomes crucial to recognize how the narratives of mastery are always fragile, threatened, and impossible. Indeed, the most basic lesson of new materialist thinking is that matter *itself* is aleatory, surprising, and "vibrant" (Bennett 2010). Matter is not stable and cannot be mastered, despite the narrative fictions that enable us to imagine and engage it as such. It is not inert in time; it evolves, shifts, mutates, surprises. What is true of matter is true of those forms of matter called humans, who come to resist the narratives of mastery that shaped their subjectivities in surprising and excessive ways.

What gets bestowed with agency and rights is a question central to both new materialisms and postcolonial studies, although the two fields have yet to join forces explicitly. Because postcolonial studies has been primarily centered on the urgency of policies and practices of dehumanization among peoples, it has been slower to see how the practices of dehumanization at the heart of its politics cannot be extricated from a deep concern with a broader ecological thinking. It is not merely that the subjugation of environments is intimately linked to the subjugation of peoples; rather, it is that the logic that drives the modern world cannot formulate the non-human world as one invested with meaningful, dynamic life. Equating colonization with the "thingification" of colonized peoples, Aimé Césaire (2001) argues that the processes of colonization require the commodification and objectification of other cultures and the people who comprised them.[14] To extend Césaire, I also argue that "thingification" vitally names a limit to our dialectical thinking of life itself: to be rendered a thing is to be placed into a whole world of other things that are not designated as valued life forms. Postcolonial studies needs to think with infinitely more care through its anticolonial foundations so as to approach the commonality of being among all these "things," however proximate or distant they may appear to the "properly" human subject.

Dipesh Chakrabarty's recent attention to climate change and the emergence of the human's "geological force" is among the most ecologically inclusive turns for the field of postcolonial studies to date. Chakrabarty explains, building on scientific research, that in the aftermath of the Industrial Revolution, humans have emerged as "geological actors" to the extent that we are now "a force on the same scale as that released at other times when there has been a mass extinction of species" (2009, 207). While as a species and as individuals humans have always been "biological actors"—creatures whose presence affected their environments—we have now emerged as a geological force that is changing the basic functions of the planet. The subject that has formed modern Western thought, the one inherited by postcolonial thinking, is one whose unequivocal goal of mastery has fractured the earth to the point of threatening destruction of its environment and itself. There can be no more urgent reason to rethink the subject and its desires than this. It is our charge, then, to explore the foundations of decolonial resistance to this subject, to see where such resistance remains entangled in its own inherited legacies, and to turn toward evocations of subjectivities no longer wed to an uncritical politics of worldly mastery. Indeed, such politics hinge on a fantasy and relentless enforcement of human distinctiveness, and a new subjectivity that is not beholden to mastery necessitates calling into question the very notion of the human that has been produced and enforced across modernity.

This is a moment in which human-induced ecological catastrophe is both in effect and imminent, in which human population displacement and species extinctions have become normative expectations. It is a moment, in other words, when human practices of mastery fold over onto themselves and collapse.[15] Mastery as the logic of a certain form of human being needs urgently therefore to be unthought and replaced by new performances of humanity. Dominic Pettman, urging us to recognize the "human error" implicit in our own self-conception as species, argues: "Considering ourselves as the source of that-which-we-call-human, and viewing animals or technics as mere conduits—as a means to that end—is a fallacy. It is to see mastery where a vital, complex, ahuman dynamic reigns" (2011, 127). Working through Agamben's (2003) notion of the "anthropological machine"—that logic that produces the human for itself—Pettman argues that the human is revealed to be nothing more than a provincial right to "conspicuous consumption." By now, every devoted environmentalist, every activist for humans and animals, and everyone who attempts to tread the earth with more care has confronted the systemic monstrosity of human mastery over the earth. Staring at ourselves as a conquering force, our mass destructive tendencies appear unstoppable. The act of unthinking mastery is in response a vehicle through which we can begin to change fundamentally our thinking and practices of this style of being human.

I am curious about how anticolonial thought and postcolonial literature can lead toward a radical engagement with forms of worldly living that do not entail mastery at the center of human subjectivity. My critique of mastery dovetails with ecologically motivated discourses such as posthumanism and new materialism, discourses that seek urgently to displace the anthropocentricism of the human. In these discourses, "things" come to *matter*—objects we ordinarily consider lifeless are positioned as vitally linked to our selves, our species, our individual and collective well-being, and our ability to sustain ourselves on the planet. Jane Bennett's call to "enliven" matter, to see life where we have failed to recognize it, is a means of chastening her own "fantasies of human mastery" by emphasizing the materiality of being itself. By seeing matter as lively rather than inanimate, and as therefore intimately connected to us, we can "expose a wider distribution of agency, and reshape the self and its interests" (Bennett 2010, 122). Likewise, Mel Y. Chen's (2012) aim toward "animating" the world we ordinarily conceive as inanimate is similarly preoccupied with a distribution of agency that exceeds the human in order to queer our own subject positions. We can see clearly how the discourse of new materialism has, among other things, poignantly ecological stakes that aim to extend drastically the rights and agencies that have long since been guarded as essentially and exclusively human (even as new materialism and biopolitics would push us to seek forms of politics not dependent on humanist rights). Like other discourses positioned on the intellectual left, new materialisms name mastery as a deleterious aim but have yet to engage a theoretical formulation and analysis of mastery as such.

New materialisms have also tended to eschew literature as its object of study. If new materialism has been in part a response to and against the linguistic turn (Coole and Frost 2010), this perhaps accounts for why scholars in the field have in their attentions to corporeality overwhelmingly avoided an emphasis on language, literature, and their complex and contradictory relations to materiality. A critical exception is Christopher Breu's *Insistence of the Material* (2014), which reads the late capitalist literature of materiality, attending to precisely the ways that materiality and language cannot be parsed. Engaging directly with new materialist discourse as a literary scholar, Breu argues that "in order for us to fully attend to the materialities of our bodies, we need to insist on the ways in which the materiality of language (as well as the forms of subjectivity shaped by language) and the materiality of the body not only interpenetrate and merge but also remain importantly distinct and sometimes form in contradiction to each other" (9). Breu's insistence is precisely that both language and bodies are material and have material effects that are interpenetrating and divergent. While the linguistic turn emphasized how language and discourse crucially shape our conceptualization of materiality, new materialisms have sought instead to attune to how materiality affects discourse, and how there are material relations that exceed what we can capture through language. These ideas are crucial to *Unthinking Mastery*, which braids together theories from the linguistic turn with the materialist turn in order to trace relations between forms of narrative and material politics across discourses of decolonization.

Vulnerable Reading

Unthinking Mastery engages the politics of decolonization through deconstructive, feminist, and queer readings. If, as I have suggested, mine is an impossible project, it is also a profoundly hopeful one that gazes toward a future it still cannot see. Failure is absolutely crucial to my attempts, and to the ways that the texts I engage across this book invite practices of reading that confront and question our subjectivities. Following Halberstam's suggestion that we read failure as a queer refusal of mastery (2011, 11), I attend to mastery's recurring failures in postcolonial literature as promising, hopeful, even utopian. In failing to master, in confronting our own desires for mastery where we least expect or recognize these desires, we become vulnerable to other possibilities for living, for being together in common, for *feeling* injustice and refusing it without the need to engage it through forms of conquest. I am compelled by R. Radhakrishnan's argument that far from being a sign of the instability or weakness of the postcolonial project, ambivalence is its vitality. Radhakrishnan argues that "postcoloniality is always already marked by ambivalence and that the task is to politicize this given ambivalence and produce it agentially" (2000, 37).[16] To repudiate the ambivalence of postcolonial studies is to disavow its full potential as a mobilizing system of resistant thinking. If our very subjectivities have emerged through modern legacies of mastery, how could we not in fine Freudian style play out the *fort-da* of refusing mastery and calling it back? From within the logic of mastery, I dwell on ambivalence across the pages of this book, and I attend to the productive ways in which failure across anticolonial discourse and postcolonial literature is absolutely vital to the project of shaping a dehumanist politics to come.

What I call *vulnerable reading* is a dehumanist methodology that inherits two crucial deconstructive formulations of reading as a politics: Derrida's (1988) insistence that one cannot simply reverse binaries but must displace them is vital to the task of disentangling mastery. Gayatri Chakravorty Spivak's attention to the essential unmasterability of literature allows for a reframing of reading and teaching that foregrounds "othering . . . as an end in itself" (2003, 13). Reading encounters can for Spivak "rearrange" our desires in ways that are not anticipatable, and thus are vitally antimasterful and lead us toward our vulnerabilities. Working within this deconstructive tradition, Sarah Wood, in her attempt to read "without mastery," summons a future reader who would not be beholden to mastery, one who can "be ready for all the things that happen to someone who doesn't read as if they belonged with, or to, the right side, the side of the master" (2014, 20).

Building on these deconstructive reading practices, and following Judith Butler's (2004) work on "collective vulnerability" as a mode of redressing sudden violence, I advance vulnerable reading as an open, continuous practice that resists foreclosures by remaining unremittingly susceptible to new world configurations that reading texts—literary, artistic, philosophical, and political—can begin to produce. Vulnerable readings resist disciplinary enclosure, refusing to restrict in advance how and where one might wander through textual engagement. Across *Unthinking Mastery*, I engage closely with thinkers and texts that I love. We might call this a queer love, following Elizabeth Freeman, who writes beautifully in *Time Binds* of her "queerest commitment" to close reading, to "the decision to unfold, slowly, a small number of imaginative texts rather than amass a weighty archive of or around texts" (2010, xvii). Like Freeman, my own book stays close to those thinkers and texts I cannot do without, and finds in them the messy utopian promises of dehumanism.

Vulnerability brings to the fore subjectivities that are shaped by the intimate awareness of relations of dependency. Dwelling on how the attacks on the World Trade Center and the Pentagon on September 11, 2001, exposed America's own vulnerability in relation to the "outside" world, Butler theorizes vulnerability as a mode of resisting ongoing cycles of violence and retribution. The sociopolitical response of America at this moment revealed a particular and particularly American subject, one that sought to "maintain its mastery through the systematic destruction of its multilateral relations, its ties to the international community" (Butler 2004, 41). Instantiated at the national level, this subject "seeks to reconstitute its imagined wholeness, but only at the price of denying its own vulnerability, its dependency, its exposure, where it exploits those very features in others, thereby making those features 'other to' itself" (41). Urging us to move away from this dialectical formulation of identity, Butler pressures a thinking of dependency that can produce alternative forms of subjective being and collectivity that do not remain hinged to a politics of vengeance against and disempowerment of others.

Although in this text Butler is committed to a thinking of human relations in particular, her work exceeds the human realm since it reveals a mode of praxis in which the subject recognizes that every aspect of itself is dependent on every*body* and every*thing* around it. Even while the discourse of modernity has disavowed this vital dependency through its desire to render the human master of everything, the fragility of the human in the wake and anticipation of so many intercultural and ecological catastrophes can no longer afford to pretend that it is not dependent materially, bodily, and psychically on others, both human and nonhuman. Reading as a practice of unmasterful vulnerability can challenge the very foundations of being human that make possible everyday life in the "globalized" world, opening up other modes of performing humanity that can become habitual. The practice of vulnerable reading can move us "beyond" mastery, not in the sense of exceeding it but in the sense of *surviving* it in order to envision being otherwise in and for the world. By reading literature vulnerably—with a willingness toward undoing the very logic that constitutes our own subjectivities—postcolonial literary texts can open us to other earthly relations and assemblages.

While I devote considerable energy to a critical reading of how mastery is unthinkingly reproduced within those very discourses that aim to reject its more overtly colonial forms, I do so precisely because of a haunting awareness that my own thinking, prose, and practices are riddled with forms of mastery I still cannot identify. Through vulnerable reading, I turn back to myself to let narratives (and my readings of them) unearth me as a desiring, historical subject. Vulnerable reading rewrites me. A critical engagement with texts that shape my own ethical, political, and artistic imagination is a way of also becoming other to myself, of becoming myself differently. Aligned with Cixous, who posits the fact of her desire for unmasterful life as pointing to a system that is despite itself "letting something else through," my critique of the limits of the thinkers and texts with whom I write is driven by an aim to unearth the (other) ethico-political possibilities that remain active within their thought—and within my own.

The Form of *Unthinking Mastery*

The first two chapters of *Unthinking Mastery* dwell within anticolonial discourse to flesh out the complex ways by which it aimed to undo colonial mastery through other masterful forms. In these chapters, I elucidate how colonial mastery becomes bound to other masterful practices of decolonization through the submission of both physical bodies and less tangible bodies of knowledge. In chapter 1, I examine the work of Frantz Fanon and Mohandas K. Gandhi to situate mastery in the theory and practice of decolonization according to two of its most discerning thinkers. While Fanon formulated corporeal violence against the master as a necessary act that would restore the humanity of the slave, Gandhi insisted on nonviolence as essential to the emergence of a truly liberated subject. Although Gandhi and Fanon appear to be diametrically opposed in their theories of decolonization, their strategies for liberation similarly employed mastery as a concept and practice that was vital to the emergence of a fully decolonized subject. Through a feminist-materialist reading practice, I argue that this reliance on mastery remains bound to dialectical thinking and produces within Gandhian and Fanonian thought a series of sacrificial figures—women, animals, the disabled, and outcasts, for instance—that haunt anticolonial discourse as its "remainders" and have a critical resonance for the politics and practices of decolonization in the present.

Forms of corporeal mastery that were so crucial to colonization and its undoing were likewise echoed through anticolonial formulations of less tangible linguistic bodies. In chapter 2, I dwell on the valences of mastery in the anticolonial language debates. Decolonization necessitated critical considerations of colonial and native languages in envisioning liberation struggles and postcolonial education and governance. Like the physical bodies mastered through colonization, so too were languages—both colonial and native—envisioned as bodies that needed either to be mastered or repudiated in the passage toward national independence. Tracing the discourse of language mastery in anticolonial thought through Gandhi, Fanon, Aimé Césaire, and Albert Memmi, I then turn to how postcolonial studies and world literature have in turn claimed language mastery as an intellectual necessity. Language mastery, I argue, travels across intellectual currents and unites them through an indiscrete drive toward conquest. Across various discursive fields, these rehearsals of linguistic mastery are intimately tied to practices of mastery over other more tangible bodies.

In the final three chapters, mastery is supplanted by my emphasis on the potentialities of dehumanism through engagements with postcolonial literary texts. I turn to texts that traverse multiple genres—the novel, the short story, the lecture-narrative, and the garden and travel memoir. The progression of these chapters is marked by a widening frame through which to read the human and its hopeful reconfigurations. Moving from intrahuman relations to human/animal relations and finally to the relation between humans and their ecological habitats, *Unthinking Mastery* glides toward increasingly expansive frames for (re)situating the human. Across genres and geographies, subjects repeatedly emerge as those in contest and compliance with forms, desires, and practices of mastery in and beyond the postcolony. These characters struggle with the tensions between how they live and who they imagine themselves to be, with their material and psychic lives that come into unwanted conflict with the disavowed lives of others. I read these characters critically and sympathetically—not with a will to point out their weaknesses and contradictions but to see how narrative prose elucidates the complexities of postcolonial subjectivity and the possibilities for other psychic and affective forms of being that are mobilized when we abide by literary language and representation.

In chapter 3, I analyze representations of humanitarian workers in conflict with their putative objects through readings of J. M. Coetzee's novel

Life & Times of Michael K (1983) and Mahasweta Devi's short story "Little Ones" (1998). These texts play with what I call *humanitarian fetishism*—the process of obscuring the complicity of humanitarian agents with those systems of inequality they seek to redress. In these texts, the desire and practice of humanitarian workers to offer aid is revealed to be inextricable with a simultaneous desire to hold mastery over their objects of aid. They also emphasize the forceful work of narrative in the confirmation of the humanitarian subject as "innocent" or removed from politics. Pressing on how particular forms of aid remain inscribed by and complicit with colonialism, these texts usher readers toward a critique of liberal subjectivity itself. In so doing, they edge us toward a dehumanist ethics through which we, along with the protagonists, tarry with the fictions that have produced and enforced our own subjectivities.

Chapter 4 takes up readings of Indra Sinha's novel *Animal's People* (2007) and Coetzee's "lecture-narrative" *The Lives of Animals* (1999), texts that in very different but intimately sutured ways refuse an easy division between the human and the animal. By emphasizing the double valence of "dispossession," I look to these texts as ways of both moving toward those beings dispossessed by the current global order and toward a dispossession of our own masterful subjectivities. I begin with a reading of Sinha's novel, based loosely on the 1984 Union Carbide disaster in Bhopal, India. The novel's dehumanized protagonist Animal, whose body is crippled by toxic exposure, claims his animality and comes to mobilize a dehumanist, humanimal ethics by the end of the novel. In Coetzee's lecture-narrative, his protagonist, Elizabeth Costello, an aging white female fiction writer, wishes to claim her animality and to convince, against Western reason, her academic audience to radically rethink their disciplinary refusals of animal subjectivity. Costello's failure in the face of reason becomes a call to imaginative horizons and to ethical possibilities of humanimal collective living. She presents us with a contingent ethics based on feeling, on ambivalence, and on the critical, even hopeful, necessity of human failure.

I return to failure and complicity in chapter 5, where I explore the garden as an ecological site rooted in (and uprooted by) histories of violence and promise. Through evocations of my own ecological pasts, and readings of Jamaica Kincaid's garden prose, I summon the productive potential of discomfort and entanglement in rethinking how we might re-earth ourselves as planetary beings. I examine what I call Kincaid's *vital ambivalence* in the production of her American garden, in which we discover a sub-ject that is at times blatantly contradictory, at times violent in her desires to master her garden, at others projecting on postcolonial subjects of the Himalayan region the same kinds of Orientalist configurations that she disavows explicitly in her critique of colonial mastery. These contradictory, disturbing, and provocative ways of writing the postcolonial subject are, I argue, a most promising gesture toward an earthing of human subjectivity in the wake of ecological disaster. Precisely by exposing the radical incongruities and "seedy" underbelly of the subject, Kincaid compels us to tend to our less masterful potentialities.

While mastery emerges somewhat differently across each chapter of this book, it does so in ways that are essential to think together. My readings of revolutionary discourse and literary prose repeatedly confront the ways that "coherent" narratives of self and mastery are always based on far more fragile materialities and psychic displacements than their narratives enable. In so doing, they urge us toward dehumanism as a political practice that can produce profound psychic and material effects. These texts, as though anticipating Halberstam, recuperate failure as a necessary condition of resistance, collectivity, and utopian promise in unmasterful relations among life forms. In the coda, I begin to think expressly about what it might mean to *survive* mastery, to live with mastery in such a way that lets other worldly forms of engagement resound. Through a brief reading of the final scene in Aimé Césaire's *A Tempest* (2002), the anticolonial rewriting of Shakespeare's *The Tempest*, I dwell on listening as a critical mode of becoming vulnerable to the voices—human and nonhuman, audible and muted—that are always sounding even when we have not been trained or allowed ourselves to listen: Listening, as opposed to voicing that which we "know." Listening, as an act that might let each other in—psychically, physically—to another's ways of inhabiting the world; to being entities that are always touching and being touched by others, even when we are not aware of this touching, even when this touching is entirely unpredictable.

I once shied away from the critical charge of being "utopian," as though utopia had nothing to do with the politics of the present. In fact, utopic desire materializes in tactile and corporeal ways, and it does so in particular places—even while it reaches toward an elsewhere that is not yet at hand. The desire for utopia is always and already a failed desire, but the real and contextual effects of its failure are precisely where we can find mastery's interstices. Now, in the face so many ongoing, firmly entrenched, and unthinking forms of mastery—over each other and over other worldly forms—it is a charge that *Unthinking Mastery* and its author will love to embrace.

CHAPTER I

Decolonizing Mastery

Love can fight; often, it is obliged to.
—MOHANDAS K. GANDHI (1976)

I am a master and I am advised to adopt the humility of the cripple.
—FRANTZ FANON, *Black Skin, White Masks* (1967)

At a quick historical glance, it would be easy to cast two of the twentieth century's most radical anticolonial thinkers—Mohandas K. Gandhi and Frantz Fanon—as politically antithetical. While indeed there is much to distinguish their thinking, postcolonial theorists have pointed to the foundational role that both thinkers have played in the emergence of postcolonial theory as a mode of critical inquiry. Leela Gandhi, for instance, has argued that Gandhi and Fanon are "united in their proposal of a radical style of total resistance to the totalising political and cultural offensive of the colonial civilizing mission" (1998, 19). She follows Gyan Prakash, who positions Gandhian and Fanonian thought as "theoretical events" that situate their work squarely within the emergence of postcolonial theory (1995, 5). Against the common historicization of postcolonial theory's emergence in the 1980s when it swept the academic scene, these scholars enable us to see postcolonial theory's longer critical history. Returning to Gandhi and Fanon as early iterations of postcolonial theory, then, is vital to the task of revisiting the postcolonial project today in the efforts to reinvigorate and to mobilize it toward new world dynamics.

In this chapter, I dwell on the works of these two central figures of twentieth-century decolonization in order to query their mappings of thoroughly decolonized subjectivities. For both Gandhi and Fanon, decolonization hinged on the necessity of a fundamental reconstitution of the self in the shaping of a postcolonial world. And yet, to achieve this end, the subjection of other bodies appeared almost necessary to anticolonial self-recovery. I trace the intertwined and overlapping circuits of love and violence across Gandhi and Fanon and attend to forms of anticolonial embodiment that each thinker advanced. In particular, I am interested in how two such distinct thinkers reveal within their accounts of decolonization seemingly inescapable sacrificial frames, ones in which particular bodies come repeatedly under masterful subjection in the narrative accounts of psychic, bodily, and socio-structural liberation. While they aimed in utopic gestures toward masterful practices that could lead to a liberation of the "whole," I argue, Gandhi and Fanon could not adequately account for the *remainders* of mastery—for those figures of abjection that were reproduced through the liberatory horizons of anticolonial discourse.

My critique of Gandhi and Fanon is born from the haunting knowledge that my own thinking is, like theirs, always producing remainders I cannot yet identify. To look back at Gandhi and Fanon critically is in effect to reflect on how those of us positioned on the intellectual left are also (and often despite ourselves) creating outsides to our own desiring inclusivities. Far from disciplining anticolonial politics and current critical thinking, I want to mobilize their messiness. Perhaps embedded within the knotty contradictions of decolonizing discourse lies the very possibility of unmasterful styles of being. Attending to the remainders that could not be enfolded into the unifying efforts of Gandhian and Fanonian politics is thus a way of bringing history forward to meet our own political projects. Sifting through the mess of utopian anticolonial politics is an act of becoming more sensitive to those remainders we continue to produce in the present moment. José Esteban Muñoz describes this as a melancholic politics that can become "a mechanism that helps us (re)construct identity and take our dead with us to the various battles we must wage in their names—and in our names" (1999, 74). My critique of these monumental figures of decolonization is thus based not on an ungenerous desire to expose the contradictions of those to whom I am so undeniably indebted but to bring Gandhi and Fanon with me into the present. Doing so, I aim to listen to the haunting legacies and inspirational force that continue to resonate through them in the service of those who have been forced out of ethico-political movements, and those we might yet come to embrace.

Returning to Gandhi and Fanon toward a revitalized thinking of postcolonial theory, we can begin to see how anticolonial solidarities are forged by way of mastery even while particular forms of colonial mastery are rebuked. Critically, we can also identify how the pursuit of mastery produces remnants of the social body that come to be employed by and excised from the rhetoric of a decolonizing body politic. Within Gandhian and Fanonian narrative accounts of decolonization, there is a continuous way in which particular figures—colonized women, indigenous peoples, the "uncivilized" groups of the emergent nation-state, the animal, the cripple, and nature itself—must be subjected by the emergent master who is himself the embodiment of the new nation-state and who maneuvers away from colonial domination toward freedom. As a literary scholar, I emphasize here *narrative*—how Gandhi and Fanon craft their emergent politics through political discourses that tell stories of becoming psychically and corporeally decolonized. What careful attention to these narratives reveals are figures of difference that are exiled from and subjected by masterful anticolonial movements, ones that linger at the margins of its discourses as exclusions that betray the purportedly inclusive aims of anticolonial futures. Within this anticolonial discourse, I read for and toward the most vulnerable subjects of decolonization. Attending to the slips and sacrifices of "other" bodies within this discourse becomes critical to the making, shaping, and reading of our own psychic, bodily, and relational selves.

For Gandhi, "love can fight," and it can do so both through the self-mastering body that resists external forms of violence and through the body that enacts physical violence against others in the service of less violent futures. What we see through careful attention to Gandhian ethico-politics is that these forms of "fighting" are never as separable as they appear. Acts of self-mastery can and do also entail forms of violence against other bodies. As I look to Gandhi's work on self-mastery as the antidote to holding mastery over others, and to becoming self-governing and free from the hold of the colonial master, I attend to how his narratives of *swaraj* (self-rule), *satyagraha* (truth-force), *brahmacharya* (celibacy/abstinence), and *ahimsa* (nonviolence) often involve the subjugation of other bodies. Women, indigenous peoples, animals (both human and nonhuman), and "uncivilized" groups who do not properly conform to the struggle for Indian national unity are all figures that reveal the contingencies, remainders, and dominance of Gandhi's masterful politics. Such bodies, I argue, become *subjects of* and *subjected to* a Gandhian ethico-politics of self-mastery. Decolonization was likewise an embodied process of self-making for Fanon, whose psychoanalytic practice led him to advocate for collective violence against the colonial forces that restricted the (masculine) colonized body. Fanon framed himself explicitly as a "master," one that had been "crippled" through the colonial relation. For him, decolonization was an act of reclaiming this lost, masterful humanity that had been stripped from him through the racist dehumanization of colonialism. He articulated this through the language of humanism and universal love, even while he cast his anticolonial humanist politics in tension with women, the disabled, and, more subtly, the natural world.

These admittedly crude summations of Gandhi and Fanon's masterful anticolonialisms illustrate how tightly linked they are, despite one being lauded as a nonviolent activist and the other criticized as a thinker who promoted violent action. Both popular formulations selectively pluck from the oeuvre of their political writings, abandoning, for instance, the often perplexing necessities of violence in Gandhian thought, or the explicit calls to love and orientation toward the Other across Fanon's writing. Following their narrative paths, I aim to consider their resonances through their mutual calls for new forms of embodiment in the process of decolonization and to attend to what such forms of masterful self-practice and embodiment shape and efface in collective struggle for liberation. In the narrative accounts of each thinker, the decolonizing body aims toward more loving relations and more peaceful forms of sociality. Both Gandhi and Fanon make clear that the domain of love is not dissociable from violence, and that violence is at stake in every act of remaking the self and is always embedded in the engagements of love toward oneself and others. Attending to the messy entanglements of love and violence in these thinkers allows us to move past the overly simplified versions of Gandhian and Fanonian politics in order both to offer more nuanced and generative accounts of their foundational contributions to anticolonial thought and postcolonial theory and to loosen some of the knots of their political thought so as to develop through and alongside them different political possibilities for the present.

Fanon's Sacrificial Women

Feminist readings have already stressed women as glaring figures of difference and subjection across anticolonial writing. Kalpana Sheshadri-Crooks, for example, refers to "the now over-familiar feminist contention that most national liberation movements and thought tend to be masculinist in their orientation and rhetoric" (2002, 93). I will trace some of these critiques here both because they bear repeating and because they are related to the other figures of alterity that remain outside Fanon's political purview and to which I turn later in this chapter. Feminist scholarship has aptly pointed to the crucial fact that liberation was mobilized in these discourses through practices of control over female bodies in the remaking and restaging of specifically masculine ones. Women often emerge in the discourses of liberation as self-masters par excellence, subjects that without pause remain steadfast in the face of danger. Yet they are also the weak links in the trajectories of national freedom—freedom that remains bound to new visions, performances, and embodiments of masculinity. If women are both instrumental and sacrificial in the creation of anticolonial masculinities, this does not mark a paradox but signals instead a logic of anticolonialism. Within this logic, bodies marked as feminine are abjured in the recuperation and transformation of masculine bodies in the act of liberation.

Fanon, whose anticolonial politics were shaped by and through psychoanalysis, insisted on the primacy of race in the processes of identification. In *Identification Papers*, Diana Fuss locates identification within a particularly colonial history (1995, 141). She explains that identification "is itself an imperial process, a form of violent appropriation in which the Other is deposed and assimilated into the lordly domain of Self. Through a psychical process of colonization, the imperial subject builds an Empire of the Same and installs at its center a tyrannical dictator, 'His Majesty the Ego'" (145). As Fuss and feminist scholars after her have argued, however, the woman of color in particular disappears in Fanon's framing of identification.[1] For Fuss, identification has a genealogy that is rooted in colonial history. Yet she argues that while Fanon situates race as central to identification, he "does not think beyond the presuppositions of colonial discourse to examine how colonial domination itself works partially through the social institutionalization of misogyny and homophobia" (160). In effect, Fanon *races* identification while he *erases* the woman of color from its purview. Fanon could write of the psychosexual lives of white women (1967e) and dwell at length on Algerian women's heroic psychic and bodily sacrifices toward the revolution (1965), but on the psychosexuality of the woman of color, he declared outright (in an echo of Freud): "I know nothing about her" (1967g, 180). Hegel and Fanon make funny bedfellows here: While Africa was, as I discussed in the introduction, absolutely unknowable for Hegel, he nevertheless fabricated and produced decisive readings of it that contributed to the imperial project on the continent.[2] Fanon produced psychoanalytic readings of Algerian women in the struggle for decolonization even while he professed that he "knows nothing" of black women, whose sexual desires and psychic constitutions appear too inconsequential and confounding to be folded into his larger narrative of decolonization.[3]

In "Algeria Unveiled" (1965), Fanon illustrates how the "liberation" of women's bodies in the colonies became central to the colonial enterprise through a process of domination that Spivak would famously come to formulate as "white men . . . seeking to save brown women from brown men" (1988, 305). Fanon argues that the figure of the veiled woman became for the colonizer both the symbol of cultural savagery in the colonies and the most effective tool for controlling the colonized body politic. If the veil was the most glaring sign of the Algerian woman's oppression, it became the unrelenting task of the colonial administration "to defend this woman, pictured as humiliated, sequestered, cloistered" and in urgent need of liberation from the barbaric Algerian man (1965, 38). She became a means by which the colonizer could gain full control over Algerian culture: "In the colonialist program, it was the woman who was given the historic mission of shaking up the Algerian man. Converting the woman, winning her over to the foreign values, wrenching her free from her status, was at the same time achieving a real power over the man and attaining a practical, effective means of destructuring Algerian culture" (39). Here we see the "civilizing mission" of colonial practice framed precisely and most effectively through the mastering of the female body. This body reflected for the colonizer a barbarous patriarchy that itself needed to be brought to full submission. Unveiling the Algerian woman would thus not only "liberate" her but would perversely bring her into a pseudomasterful role (always under the authority of the white man) by empowering her to hold a "real power" over Algerian men. By being laid bare, brought into the fold of Western femininity, she would become able to emasculate the Algerian man who had enslaved her. This emasculation would in turn make the Algerian man more easily dominated by colonial power, "destructured" by his woman into a form ripe for full submission to the "real" (white) Man. In his reading of colonial logic's confounding contradictions, Fanon emphasizes how the

Algerian woman emerged all at once as absolute victim, weapon of imperial conquest, and gateway to conquering the Algerian man and "delivering" him into colonial submission.

While Fanon "unveils" colonial logic, he also cannot help but to affirm the Algerian woman as a threat to Algerian masculinity even as he is determined to defend her honor. His aim is to illustrate how the colonial imagination of the Algerian woman has been a radical mischaracterization. In fact, for Fanon she is selfless in relation to the revolution and, even more strikingly, she is one who best performs self-mastery: "This revolutionary activity has been carried on by the Algerian woman with exemplary constancy, self-mastery, and success. Despite the inherent, subjective difficulties and notwithstanding the sometimes violent incomprehension of a part of the family, the Algerian woman assumes all the tasks entrusted to her" (1965, 53–54). Although she is "sometimes" subjected to the "violent incomprehension" of parts of the patriarchal family unit, the Algerian woman remains undeterred by this violence and is steadfastly committed to "the tasks entrusted to her" (54). Her agency in Fanon's narrative is here limited to a masculine revolution that decides to "entrust" her, that makes use of her body and her determination in carrying out revolutionary acts. She is an agent but not *agential*: she follows the orders of the revolution because she remains so devoutly committed to the embodied masculinity of the anticolonial men whose bodies and psyches will, unlike her own, be positively reshaped and humanized by the revolution.

In contrast to Diana Fuss, who argues that in Fanon's thought "the colonial other remains an undifferentiated, homogenized male, and subjectivity is ultimately claimed for men alone" (1995, 160), Kalpana Seshadri-Crooks insists that "a sympathetic understanding of Fanon's masculinist politics forces us to confront the contradictions in a simple feminist position that privileges women's issues and well-being first (even if it is because women otherwise always come last) and in isolation from other overlapping and extenuating concerns. In the 'suicide' and rebirth of the 'new man' envisioned by Fanon perhaps lies 'our' salvation as (women and as) human beings" (2002, 94). For Seshadri-Crooks, Fanon's "political masculinism" folds into a broader struggle of decolonization that gives way to inclusion, to a politics of decolonization that is dehumanizing to *all* humans. She thus historicizes Fanon by arguing that "what Fanon makes clear is that at the moment of his writing, political struggle and national sovereignty were unimaginable without a rehabilitation of masculinity" (96). I remain compelled by Seshadri-Crooks's commitment to the promise of more inclusive futures that can be shaped through politics that themselves hinged on particular forms of exclusion. Other accounts of Fanon's masculine politics, however, explicitly pressure the idea that such political discourses might give way to an increasingly expansive and inclusive politics to come.[4] Gwen Bergner signals how Fanon's "universal" subject is specifically male, indicating that "racial identities intersect with sexual difference" (2005, 3). She aims to examine the role of gender in *Black Skin, White Masks* in order to "broaden Fanon's outline of black women's subjectivity and to work toward delineating the interdependence of race and gender" (3). Feminine subjectivity is both crucial to and absent from *Black Skin, White Masks*, and this slippage becomes vital to understanding Fanon's own account of racialized masculine subject formation (9). For Bergner, then, the parsing of race and gender in Fanon's psychoanalytic formulation of the "universal" is imperative to mobilizing his anticolonialism, to recognizing what Fanon overlooked—namely, how colonial society "perpetuates racial inequality through structures of sexual difference" (13).

In "The Woman of Color and the White Man" (1967h), Fanon famously engages an extended, wholly unsympathetic reading of Mayotte Capécia's autobiography, *Je suis Martiniquaise* (1948). Introducing this text as "cut-rate merchandise, a sermon in praise of corruption," Fanon embarks on a psychoanalytic reading of black Antillean female subjectivity through a narrative account of a woman's desire to be married to a white man (1967h, 42). In an interesting move, Fanon narrativizes Capécia's own narrative account by beginning his discussion of her text as follows: "One day a woman named Mayotte Capécia, obeying a motivation whose elements are difficult to detect, sat down to write 202 pages—her life—in which the most ridiculous ideas proliferated at random. The enthusiastic reception that greeted this book in certain circles forces us to analyze it" (42). Fanon's introduction to this text, which he proceeds to rail against, is cast as a story—"one day a woman . . ."—that represents a black woman's desire to self-represent as not only absurd but incomprehensible. Like so many other gendered and sexed slippages and continuities across Fanon, here his telling of Capécia's own story becomes a story in itself, one in which Fanon as narrator tells us that the motivations of his black, female antihero are "difficult to detect." It is she, after all, who extends out to all women of color, of whom Fanon "knows nothing." (I will turn in the following chapters to the crucial importance of writing ourselves as impossibly split subjects, and to the gendered, raced, and hybrid possibilities of such writing.) Given Fanon's own psychoanalytic frame, one in which the black male body is "universal," Capécia's writing is always already indecipherable to him. Within Fanon's own narrative of decolonization, the woman of color's narration must be proleptically dismissed.

Gandhian (Ef)feminism

Instrumental and disposable. Allies and excesses. What becomes clear is that in the formation of Fanon's own masterfully embodied emergent subjectivity—a subjectivity that for him is necessary to decolonization—other specifically gendered and sexualized figures must be eschewed in its making. Likewise, in Gandhi's own narrative accounts and pursuits of swaraj (self-rule)—a state of being produced by and through practices of mastery—women play a tricky role. As Madhu Kishwar (1985) has illustrated, Gandhi was inclusive of women in the movement toward national liberation and saw them as critical constituents to producing social change. For Gandhi, accounting for women was in fact instrumental to the transformation of the body politic at large, and he was quick to see the relations between the personal (the home) and the political, especially in terms of the embodied politics of ahimsa (nonviolence) as a devotional practice. He persistently situated women in the home as wives and mothers even while he created social change that sought to alleviate gender oppression. As progressive as Gandhi's inclusivity of women appeared, as Kishwar argues, he failed to understand that gender oppression was a historically grounded and social experience that could not simply be overcome through the moral dedication of women.

If the proper place of women for Gandhi was as devoted homemakers, he also selectively employed the figure of the improper woman to frame British life and its illnesses. In *Hind Swaraj*, a narrative framed as a discussion between an inquisitive, well-educated "Reader" and an "Editor" (the loosely veiled figure of Gandhi himself), the Editor argues that the British Parliament, hailed "the Mother of Parliaments," is like a "sterile woman and a prostitute" (1997, 32). While Gandhi-as-Editor acknowledges that these are "harsh terms," he also abides by them, affirming that the British Parliament is a "sterile woman" insofar as it "has not yet of its own accord done a single good thing" and is like a prostitute because "it is under the control of ministers who change from time to time" (32). Gandhi later declared that he stood by every word of *Hind Swaraj* with the exception of his use of the term "prostitute"—a word that offended the "fine taste" of a female English friend and that he therefore regretted using (Skaria 2007, 219).

The link here between sterility and prostitution is fascinating in its own right, not merely because it reveals a striking (but not altogether unexpected) patriarchy at work in Gandhian metaphorics but because it links the biological capacity for reproduction with the social production and function of sex labor. If the corporeal is tied to the social in Gandhi's masculinist politics, the female slides between the biological and the social, but she does so as an errant subject.

Gandhi proceeds from this unabashed evocation of the British Parliament as a failed or fallen woman to a declaration that the fundamental problem of the Parliament is that it is one "without a real master" (1997, 32). Perceived as the height of civilization, the Editor explains that Britain is in fact diseased and suffering from its commitment to the pursuit of modern civilization, a commitment that lends itself directly to colonization. Following Gandhi's logic, the colonial master is one born from an improper, masterless nation-state, and his actions are the actions of a master who himself has not been subjected to a "proper" form of state mastery.[5] The development of a properly masterful governing body in Gandhian terms would thus necessitate a rescue from its thoroughly gendered insufficiencies.

Over the course of his autobiography, Gandhi's anticolonial politics are crystalized through the transformation of his own anticolonial masculinity. Parama Roy (2010) offers a rich and persuasive account of Gandhi's complex staging of anticolonial masculinity, particularly through the lens of the mahatma's alimentary politics.[6] As a youth, Gandhi believed that India's freedom from British colonial rule would happen through the embodied transformation of Indian subjects. According to his early logic, because large constituents of Indian subjects were vegetarian, they had bodies that were too weak to fight their carnivorous masters. The young Gandhi held firmly to the belief that meat eating was the gateway to national liberation, to literally overthrowing the British through what Roy calls "culinary masculinity" (2010, 81), and to claiming India as a self-ruled nation-state.[7] He would famously come to reverse this logic, believing instead that nonviolent practice was vital to true liberation. This meant, as Roy aptly illustrates, that Gandhi's own body and its self-staging would become vital to his projection of an explicitly anticolonial masculinity. While Fanon's masculine colonized body was one always tensed by and against the force of colonization, and in need of release from that tension, Gandhi's own slim, scantily clad figure—one that leans toward effeminacy—would come to signal a no less embodied but very different representation of masculinity positioned against colonial force.

If Gandhi's body has become emblematic of "passive resistance" to colonial rule (a term that Gandhi himself renounced because in fact the practice of satyagraha was better translated as "love-force" or "truth-force," which was in no sense "passive"), it remains a body that recasts the "look" and register of masculinity itself.[8] Indeed, as Roy argues, Gandhi's own adoption of a nearly naked aesthetic aligned him with debates about respectable women's attire in public places (2010, 85–86). As both Kishwar and Roy illustrate, Gandhi was in so many respects aligned with women's issues and saw women as vital allies in his movement toward a mass mobilization of anticolonial social transformation. But within the practices of self-mastery that Gandhi saw as so vital to the production of truly liberated subjectivities, women play an odd role. Gandhi's commitment to brahmacharya—a term that translates as "celibacy" but exceeds the sexual connotations of this term—necessitated for him practices of testing his self-control. Somewhat scandalously, such tests included lying in bed beside female followers and ashram inmates to ensure that he would not become aroused by them. Joseph Alter begins an essay on celibacy and sexuality in North Indian nationalism by declaring, "It is well known that Mahatma Gandhi felt that sexuality and desire were intimately connected to social life and politics, and that self-control translated directly into power of various kinds, both public and private" (1994, 45). But if Gandhi could claim to have mastered his sexual desire, he certainly struggled across his life with its alimentary corollary, struggles that Roy reveals cannot be extricated from the female figures that in his autobiography appeared never to waver in their practices of abstinence.

Drawing on Derrida's reading of the biblical story of Abraham and Isaac,[9] Roy turns to the figure of Sarah as mother who is explicitly absented from the story. Thinking through the gendered valences of sacrifice in *The Gift of Death*, Derrida asks: "Does the system of this sacrificial responsibility . . . imply at its very basis an exclusion or sacrifice of woman?" (1995, 76). Roy illustrates how women were complexly situated within the sacrificial frame of Gandhian ethico-politics. In her reading, Gandhi's vegetarianism is bound to self-subjection and sacrifice in the service of refusing harm to others. I will return expressly to the figure of the animal in Gandhian thought below, but first I want to dwell on Roy's argument for how Gandhian ethics hinges on a sacrificial exclusion of women: "If the vegetarian is one who is willing to sacrifice himself rather than sacrificing the other that is the nonhuman animal, what is indeed properly his own to sacrifice? Who is it who can undertake the responsibility of sacrifice? If sacrifice is a burden it is surely also an entitlement and an assertion of one's rights over one's body and one's actions and those of others. Can a woman be a sacrificer?" (2010, 109). Here Roy asks us to consider the fascinating figure of Gandhi's wife, Kasturba, who across the autobiography repeatedly emerges as more devout and less conflicted in her unfailing religious commitment. Unlike Gandhi, who struggles relentlessly with his alimentary desires (much more so than with his sexual desires), Kasturba appears—just as Gandhi's mother did early in the autobiography—steadfast and unwavering in her religious devotion. Mothers and wives are thus the unflagging keepers of proper practice in Gandhian ethics, ones that he looks to as models for his own desired purity and as figures that often exceed his own devotional capacities.

Yet Kasturba in particular reveals what Roy calls the "gendered contours" of Gandhi's parables of alimentary crisis, parables that illustrate "the complex character of women's (non-)sacrifice" (2010, 109) as Gandhi holds the position of "vegetarian patriarch" (106). In one parable, Gandhi falls gravely ill at a moment when he has vowed to abstain from cow's milk. Kasturba, herself an abstainer, persuades her husband to drink goat's milk to restore him to health. Roy writes: "Gandhi's response to this instance of apad dharma, a paradoxical act that preserves life and undermines ethics at the same time, is an acknowledgement of his human frailty" (112). While Gandhi confronts his frailty, he also breaks (or compromises) the vow in order to carry on the fight for national independence. On the one hand, the political becomes a realm that makes this particular sacrifice necessary, for Gandhi must live in order to stay the course of the fight for satyagraha. On the other hand, Gandhi describes himself as having "succumbed" to his wife's insistence, here making clear the relation between sexual and alimentary seduction. Roy writes: "This tale stages the question . . . of what or who is sacrificed in sacrificing oneself to an ideal of vegetarian purity. How is one to assess, for instance, the vegetarian sacrifice of the public man or mahatma in relation to the vegetarian sacrifice of the child or the woman/wife/mother?" (113). Gandhi characterizes woman as "the embodiment of sacrifice and *ahimsa*" (114). But in this narrative (as in others), Kasturba comes clearly to lack the "heroic status and purity of sacrifice" (114). Here she serves as a proper figure of the Hindu wife's dharma in sustaining the life of her husband, all the while confirming "her status as one who is not entitled to offer sacrifice in her own right. Sacrifice is ... an entitlement, even a property right, so that the sacrificer proper is ready not just to sacrifice himself but, perhaps just as importantly, to sacrifice others" (114). Roy's reading of Gandhi's gendered embodiment and sacrifice emphasizes how within his thought women play an absolutely vital role in his self-staging and vision for political mobilization, while revealing that sacrifice is a properly masculine realm, one through which female agency is concurrently sacrificed.

The Potential of Self-Mastery

Fanonian and Gandhian thought—as divergent as they appear—rely, then, on particularly gendered alliances, exclusions, and erasures in order to stage their political projects. Women emerge in the narrative accounts of these anticolonial leaders as indispensable supporters and as subjects that need to be cast off from the properly male realm of decolonization. The scholarship that has taken up the status of women in anticolonial thought paves the way toward a thinking of other less explored figures of anticolonial discourse that are similarly caught up in and refused by the masterful aims and practices of decolonization. I will turn to some such figures— the indigene, "uncivilized" groups, the animal, the cripple, and nature—to dwell on the relations between anticolonial masteries and colonial violence in the making of particularly masculine decolonized subjectivities.

As Ashis Nandy argues, in Gandhian thought "freedom is indivisible, not only in the popular sense that the oppressed of the world are one but also in the unpopular sense that the oppressor too is caught in the culture of oppression" (1983, 63). Gandhi wrote at length about how modern civilization created sick societies from which colonization was born. Throughout *Hind Swaraj*, he dwells extensively on how his path toward freedom would liberate Indian subjects not only from colonial rule but from its reliance on the more primordial disease of modern civilization. Swaraj was thus critically also an invitation to freedom for India's English masters. The pursuit of self-rule was therefore not merely targeted toward the liberation of Indians and other global subjects living under colonial rule but was an act of utopic mobilization in which both colonizers and colonized would become liberated. The gateway to true liberation was, for Gandhi, absolute discipline over oneself, and he sought "complete independence" not merely from British rule but from any external power whose influence could lead him away from the proper path of "truth." Elaborating this notion of "truth" at the center of Gandhian thought, Partha Chatterjee writes: "To Gandhi . . . truth did not lie in history, nor did science have any privileged access to it. Truth was moral: unified, unchanging and transcendental. It was not an object of critical inquiry or philosophical speculation. It could only be found in the experience of one's life, by the unflinching practice of moral living" (1986, 97). If truth was that which one discovered for oneself through a relentless pursuit of moral living, this meant also that it could not be squared with "the dominant thematic of post-Enlightenment thought" (97). Gandhi's truth, then, resided in a politics of experimentation that could never be foreclosed, and that was thus fundamentally incompatible with dialectical reason. This formulation of truth, founded on an uncertain practice of experimentation, might offer us the most powerful method by which to exceed mastery's hold in the everyday production of the human through neocolonial politics today.[10]

While Gandhi's formulation of his practice remains structured by logics of (self-) mastery, his experimental practice in fact functions against mastery's definitive foreclosures. This is most apparent—perhaps paradoxically—in his attempts to explain brahmacharya, a practice of self-mastery in which one "controls his organs of sense in thought, word, and deed" (1998, 24). Gandhi took the vow of brahmacharya in his pursuit of truth, and confesses that its definition is one that he himself does not understand completely: "The meaning of this definition became somewhat clear after I had kept the observance for some time, but it is not quite clear even now, for I do not claim to be a perfect *brahmachari*, evil thoughts having been held in restraint but not eradicated. When they are eradicated, I will discover further implications of the definition" (1998, 24). Since Gandhi himself could not claim to be a perfect *brahmachari* (one who practices brahmacharya), he refused a full definition of the term. Brahmacharya was something aspirational and radically uncertain; it could produce infinite possibilities, yet he could not foreclose its definition. As I argued in the introduction of this book, where I sketched some qualities of mastery, definitional foreclosure can itself become a practice of masterful exclusion. Gandhi's refusal to offer a definition of something he is still (and will always be) learning points toward an embodied, material practice that exceeds what conceptual thought can contain. When turned inward, mastery for Gandhi refuses to be transparent and definable, even while for him it holds out limitless possibilities. Unlike foreign mastery, which functions through a logic of domination that is concrete in its aims (even while its effects may be intangible or diffuse), brahmacharya as self-mastery aims toward the uncertainty of its own practice and the experimental quality of its aims, with a will to the experimental subjection of the *self* as opposed to the domination of others in the pursuit of truth.

The Violence of Swaraj

Meditating on the wars of Europe, Gandhi questioned why one nation's cause should be considered right and another wrong, why brute force repeatedly governed instead of the pursuit of truth. The commitment to satyagraha as a governing practice refused outright this dynamic and insisted that the force involved in the pursuit of truth was a force imposed by but also toward the truth-seeker. The political pressure of the *satyagrahi* (one who practices satyagraha) in action, which was always driven by a principle of love, revealed to others their wrongdoings and urged them to correct their own actions. It also rendered powerless those in power, because for the satyagrahi no one external to him could make him act in ways that did not accord to his own will (1976, 16:64). The satyagrahi was one ready to submit himself to the punitive power of the state, willfully disobeying it when he found it to be unjust. He did penance for social injustices, and through this form of civil disobedience he could be violently penalized but never fundamentally governed by the state. The "complete independence" of the satyagrahi was born therefore through this unrelenting willingness to suffer for and in turn transform the disorders of society. Crucially, if the satyagrahi found that he had been misled in his pursuit of truth, only he (and his fellow satyagrahis) would have suffered through the enactment of satyagraha (1976, 16:63).

Gandhi's popular legacy as a renowned advocate of peace becomes quickly complicated, however, through a careful reading of his work. Claude Markovitz suggests that the critical contrast between Gandhi as icon and Gandhi as "blood-and-flesh individual" is the result of "selective memory" (2004, 163–64). Such memory is crafted both by Gandhi's own practices of historical self-representation and through political discourses in South Africa, India, and beyond that have employed his legacy selectively toward mobilizations for peace.[11] What this selective memory relies on is a popular conception of an unfailingly nonviolent humanity, in effect forgetting the ways that Gandhi himself was at times a proponent of violence, and that his trajectory toward swaraj was replete with violent practices. He understood that violence was not only inescapable in human life but also that at times taking violent action would be the best course toward avoiding greater violence. Violence was not only necessary but highly contextual and at times ethically imperative. Roy points us to "the complexity of Gandhian nonviolence, and his awareness not only of the proximity of violence and nonviolence but also of the coimplication of the nominally nonviolent in structures of violence" (2010, 105). Violence and nonviolence for Gandhi were intimate, collaborative, and far from antithetical. Because in Gandhian philosophy love was often "obliged" to fight (1976, 16:63), Gandhi did not eschew it completely, framing life as itself dependent on requisite forms of violence. He cited, for example, the necessary act of drawing breath that required the ingestion of microorganisms, and the need for the human use of disinfectants that would kill harmful germs (1976, 31:488).

Beyond these requisite forms, he also framed violence as something that was at times ethically imperative. To kill someone who sought to do extensive harm to others, for instance, could be deemed a necessary act of violence. In this respect, violence emerged as something contingent and contextual, something that could work in the service of nonviolence. While Gandhi insisted that "non-violence is the supreme dharma" (1976, 14:299), violence was so often at stake in his own pursuit of ahimsa (nonviolence). Indeed, the practice of satyagraha was for him "India's distinctive weapon" (1976, 16:64), a vehicle that was driven by a politics of love and nonviolence but was also bound to violence through the language of weaponry. Reading

Gandhi from the vantage point of a literary scholar, one cannot ignore the implications of this metaphor, how the metaphor itself reveals something vital about Gandhian politics. Satyagraha is a weapon used against the (colonial) master, a weapon necessary to undoing the hold of the master over Indian subjects. Gandhi did not see a tension between the language of weaponry and his politics of nonviolence because for him love could not be altogether extricated from violence. In Faisal Devji's provocative reading of Gandhi and violence, he argues that Gandhi's movement in fact "had nothing to do with avoiding violence" (2012, 7). Far from shunning violence, Devji argues, Gandhi appropriated and sublimated violence "by inviting and directing it through a series of political experiments, both theoretical and practical" (8). If Gandhi in effect courted violence in order to convert it within the colonial context, he did so in ways that were often contradictory. One struggles to account for a particular logic or pattern in Gandhi's engagements with violence, which are united, Devji argues, by a set of principles but are often difficult to reconcile.

In their recent work on Gandhi in South Africa, Ashwin Desai and Goolam Vahed argue against the dominant narrative of Gandhi as "a great inventor of the new tactic and philosophy of nonviolent popular politics and as a pioneer of anti-colonial nationalism" (2016, 25). Rather, Desai and Vahed argue that Gandhi's political imagination remained bound by a desire for equality within empire. They read Gandhian tactics as shaped by "a conservative defence of class, race and caste privilege" (25). Given Gandhi's popular legacy, it is almost unfathomable to think that in 1906, during the Zulu rebellion against debilitating taxes in Natal, he went to war as a stretcher-bearer on behalf of empire. This war produced very few British casualties, while "three thousand five hundred Zulu were killed, seven thousand huts were burnt, and thirty thousand people were left homeless" (20).[12] Desai and Vahed ask us to remember Gandhi before India, a Gandhi that does not square easily with his legacy. What was at stake for Gandhi in participating actively in the violence of war? Desai and Vahed argue that Gandhian politics in South Africa remained locked within a desire for Indian recognition from Britain at the expense of other disempowered groups: "Gandhi sought to ingratiate himself with Empire and its mission during his years in South Africa. In doing so, he not only rendered African exploitation and oppression invisible, but was, on occasion, a willing part of their subjugation and racist stereotyping" (22). This picture of Gandhi in South Africa, participating in the subjugation of non-Indian marginal communities, is one that confronts with great unease the legacies of Gandhi that dominate in popular and political discourse. If it has become almost an intellectual fashion of late to rehistoricize Gandhi and to draw out some of the most deeply unsettling aspects of his history, politics, and practice, this fashion signals a felt urgency to think critically about our legacies of nonviolence—ones that relied on the violent extermination of certain populations toward the recuperation of others. Such "inconvenient truths" (24) about Gandhi include his engagements in the war against the Zulus in South Africa when he was a mere three years away from the writing of *Hind Swaraj*, the doctrine of Indian self-rule that he would famously craft over a period of days on a return journey from England to South Africa on board the *Kildonan Castle* in 1909.[13] He was very close, in other words, to launching an explicit treatise on Indian independence, on the necessity of swaraj and nonviolent resistance to the British control of India as he participated in the violence against indigenous peoples in South Africa.[14]

Across Gandhi's political career, there would continue to be communities, groups, and bodies whose conquest became crucial to the achievement of the mahatma's "greater" political aims. In the section of *Hind Swaraj* titled "The Condition of India," the Editor overturns Gandhi's early political thinking about the strength of Indian bodies as the gateways to Indian independence. The Editor asserts of the pursuit of swaraj: "Strength lies in the absence of fear, not in the quantity of flesh and muscle we may have on our bodies. Moreover, I must remind you who desire Home Rule that, after all, the Bhils, the Pindaris, the Assamese and the Thugs are our own countrymen. To conquer them is your and my work. So long as we fear our own brethren, we are unfit to reach the goal" (1997, 45). Referencing here a host of groups perceived as "uncivilized" and thus expressly perilous to the mobilization of the nation-state, Gandhi insists that it is the job of those seeking swaraj through practices of self-restraint and self-sufficiency "to conquer them." In the English translation of the text, the phrase is supplemented with a clarifying footnote: " 'To conquer them': in the Gujarati text this reads 'To win them over' " (1997, 45n71). This translation is remarkable in its discursive shift from the Gujarati sense of persuasion to the overt subjugation at work in the English translation. The fact that such a slip happens within English—the language of the colonizer—is a problematic I will return to in the next chapter. Critical here is how the valence between "winning over"—a kind of seduction of self-rule that would entice these "uncivilized" groups—becomes expressly a conquest in which they are dominated by the "civilized" body politic who conquer in order to become independently ruled at the level of the nation-state.

Because Gandhi himself was actively involved in the translation of *Hind Swaraj*, this distinction deserves significant attention. Persuaded by English friends that he must translate the text, Gandhi states that it is not a "literal translation" but that it "is a faithful rendering of the original" even while it was written in some degree of haste (1997, 5). In his preface to the English translation, he writes, "It is not without hesitation that the translation of 'Hind Swaraj' is submitted to the public" (5). Of the Gujarati text, Gandhi declares that there are "many imperfections" in the original: "The English rendering, besides sharing these, must naturally exaggerate them, owing to my inability to convey the exact meaning of the original" (6). That his inability to convey exactly the meaning of his Gujarati text lends itself to natural exaggeration in translation is fascinating in itself, but here my interest lies in how this particular "exaggeration" betrays the slippery relation between persuasion and mastery across moments of Gandhian thought. To "win over" in the original Gujarati text designates some degree of agency to these marginal groups, indicating that the persuasion enacted by Gandhi's followers is a form of pressure that is placed on the wayward subjects of the state in order to usher them into the "proper" fold. This is a pressure that works on but not against such subjects, welcoming them into the fold of the proper through an engagement that they may or may not choose to pursue. The English translation betrays this aim by issuing "conquest" as the targeted act of seekers of swaraj. Within the translation, seekers of swaraj take up both of the early modern definitions of "mastery"—seeking to "best" these marginal groups as opponents and to educate them through the more knowledgeable frame of the swaraj-seeker. To bring these marginal groups into the proper fold of an independent, self-ruled nation-state requires in the English translation their masterful domination. If we follow Gandhi's insistence in the preface to the English translation, we might read this movement from winning over to conquest as merely one of the "natural" exaggerations that occur in the act of translation. I want to suggest that while this may well be so, the slip toward conquest reveals the ways in which the mastery turned inward in Gandhian thought cannot help but to seep outward—onto and against other bodies.

Yet another footnote contextualizing this passage informs readers that "in 1921 Gandhi apologised to the Assamese for listing them among the 'uncivilised' tribes of India" (44n71). In his apology, Gandhi calls his error "a grave injustice done to the great Assamese people, who are every whit as civilised as any other part of India" (44n71). He proceeds to explain that his "stupidity" in characterizing the Assamese as uncivilized was informed by his reading of an English account of the Manipur expedition by Sir John Gorst. Because Gandhi admits that he was "an indifferent reader of history," he suggests that he retained this historical account of the Assamese as *jungli* (wild/uncivilized) as historical fact, and subsequently "committed it to writing." This is a fascinating moment in which conquest is explicitly informed and delegated by a specifically Western history, a moment that reveals how Gandhian philosophy could not be dissociated from the colonial frame against which it positioned itself. It also illustrates how, through reading and writing practices, particular subjects become enfolded in or excluded from the realm of civility and thus subjected to masterful forms of action against them.

Gandhi's Animals

Mastery in Gandhian discourse slips between the internal and the external, between the colonizer and the colonized, between the individual body and the body politic, and, critically for Gandhian ethics, also between the human and the animal. Gandhi explained that the life of the satyagrahi is one governed by the discipline of the body and the soul (1976, 16:63). This form of discipline required both a pacification of the human's "animal passions" and an overcoming of the "enemy within" (Gandhi [1932] 2004, 5). It was by turning away from "the imagined enemy without" and turning toward the "enemy within" that Gandhi understood the social enactment of love. Such love required an overcoming of aspects and qualities of the human that signaled for him its unenlightened status. Sexual drives, among other yearnings, would need to be unremittingly tamed for the enlightened subject to emerge. Specific aspects of oneself as an uncontrolled animal being, therefore, would have to be mastered in order to pave the way toward a decolonized society. The effect of the satyagrahi was a politics of the unmasterful persuasion of the other, a practice that embodied forms of masterful violence against the self in order to do penance for individual and state injustices. The force of satyagraha was therefore to be found ex-plicitly in its determined refusal to enact violence against others by aiming toward complete mastery over oneself. For Gandhi, satyagraha was fun-damentally an act of love aimed toward the "so-called enemy," to illustrate the error of the adversary's ways. This was the critical method Gandhi em-ployed to show the British colonizers the error of their ways, but Gandhi also did penance for the acts of Indian political leaders and fellow ashram inmates who had, to his mind, strayed from the proper path. To love one's perceived adversaries it was essential to show them kinship and to persuade them that their ways were misleading or unjust. Violence directed at an-other betrayed this aim, and so the satyagrahi embodied the violence he refused in the political realm.

If other human groups become complex sites for understanding Gand-hian philosophy, so too does the nonhuman world leave open questions about Gandhian ethico-politics. Gandhi's key concepts—swaraj, ahimsa, brahmacharya—fundamentally implicated the animal.[15] Gandhi signals this repeatedly across his writings, for instance when he queried the seem-ingly arbitrary limits we attach to our spiritual and political imperatives. He called on Indians to query when they would know they had reached the limit of swaraj, urging them to consider whether treating the untouchable castes of India as "blood brothers" was enough. He asked them to consider extending this limit to include their animal brethren, positing that humans and animals share the same soul (1976, 19:518). Humans and animals were bestowed with the same life force, and true swaraj could not therefore be confined by a commitment to humanity. Swaraj properly achieved would produce a limitless openness toward all other beings—beings that were vitally linked to humans. Yet even while he insisted on the animal's place within ethics, he repeatedly returned to the exceptional status of the human by situating it at the top of a species hierarchy. Gandhi insisted on our need to avoid a life that was "animal-like," insipid, and improper (1993, 317). In this sense, while he advocated for a radical openness toward animals, he did so through a deeply anthropocentric and paternalistic frame that could not reconceive of human/animal relations beyond a hierarchical formula-tion. Humans should "serve" animals that were intimately tied to them, a service that was required because of the animal's "lower" status.

While humans held an ethical commitment to animals, the animal as-pects of human life needed paradoxically to be tamed in order to effectively perform this ethical commitment. Parama Roy points to this shifting status of the animal in Gandhian thought when she argues, "In his more mundane communications with correspondents from all over India and the globe, he was possessed by the question of the relative importance of human and animal life, arguing sometimes against an anthropocentric bias and sometimes in favor of the greater moral worth of human beings" (2010, 105). Animals were among Gandhi's most unreconciled, inconsistent, and indeed for him haunting aspects of his ethico-politics. The specific instance of a "mercy-killing" of an injured calf at Gandhi's Sabarmati Ashram and Gandhi's provocative gesture of serving meat at the otherwise all-vegetarian Ashram to his carnivorous allies, Louis Fischer, Jawaharlal Nehru, and Maulana Azad, are instances of public controversies around Gandhi's animal politics (Roy 2010, 106).[16] His ethico-political stance on stray dogs likewise shocked many of his readers and followers, which appeared to them to fall problematically short of ahimsa.[17] Often undernourished and carriers of disease, stray dogs in India were at times dangerous to human communities and had become a serious concern for the nation. To Gandhi's mind, stray dogs were a direct reflection of the "ignorance and lethargy" of human society. If the state was to blame for failing to control the epidemic of stray dogs, so too were seemingly benevolent citizens in the wrong for perpetuating the problem by feeding them. Gandhi insisted that to feed stray dogs was a "misplaced kindness" that left intact the structural problem that produced them (1976, 28:5). True kindness, he declared, would necessitate housing and caring for the dogs in all respects. He also argued that in certain circumstances, euthanizing stray dogs was necessary to the eradication of suffering and the welfare of human communities. This position outraged many, who saw Gandhi as abandoning ahimsa outright. His was not an easy position to reconcile, but it reflected the path of ahimsa as necessitating contextual decisions that would produce ahimsa even while pursuing nonviolence.

One of Gandhi's most revealing discourses on the limits of his spiritual capacity emerges through his failure to protect sheep, a failure on which he dwells during a recollection of a visit to the Kali temple in Calcutta. With great anticipation, Gandhi set off to see the famous temple but along the way witnessed a "stream of sheep" being led to sacrifice in the name of Kali (Gandhi 1993, 234). Gandhi stopped to converse with a *sadhu* (wandering ascetic), and both men agreed that animal sacrifice was by no means or in any circumstance properly religious. When Gandhi questioned why the sadhu did not preach against the killing of animals, the sadhu replied: "That's not my business. Our business is to worship God" (235). Dismayed by the distinction the sadhu makes between the worship of God and responsible religious practice, he proceeded toward the temple and was horrified to witness copious amounts of animal blood: "I could not bear to stand there. I was exasperated and restless. I have never forgotten that sight" (235). Later that evening, still haunted by the sight of the sheep blood, Gandhi found himself in conversation with a Bengali friend with whom he spoke about the cruelty inherent in this form of uncritical worship. The friend attempted to convince Gandhi that the sheep felt no sensations of pain during their death, since their senses became dull by the ceremonial drumming. Gandhi refused this logic outright, insisting that if the animals could speak they would undoubtedly attest to their suffering. Although he felt adamantly that the custom should be abandoned, Gandhi stopped short of acting on this feeling because he believed that the task of preventing the practice was "beyond" him. Despite his failure to act, he felt nevertheless compelled to elaborate the responsibility that the human has toward the animal. He declared: "He who has not qualified himself for such service is unable to afford it any protection" (235). He believed that he would "die pining for this self-purification and sacrifice," and this declared inability to fight against the sanctioned violence inflicted on sheep in the name of organized religion led him to long for another more exalted being to serve the animal as he wished but failed to do.

There is perhaps no clearer sign of the contingent, contextual, and at times irreconcilable aspects of Gandhian ethics than in his desire to protect and his will to eliminate animal forms of suffering. His reputation for a politics that hinged exclusively on peace becomes complicated through attention to his writing on women, his actions in relation to indigenous peoples of South Africa (which cannot be extricated from his willingness toward war in the service of Empire), his writings and translations of the "uncivilised" groups of India, and the various moments in which violence toward animals is enfolded into his pursuit of ahimsa as a path toward truth. What Gandhi shows us is the experimental necessity of contextual action, and while we may well disagree with some of the historical decisions he made, he leaves us with the promise and necessity of confronting inescapable violence. His is a politics in which violence not only exists but cannot be avoided. Gandhi's own confessed failings to act in purely non-violent ways, and the irreconcilability of his ethico-politics, is precisely the messiness we have to risk if we are to act differently in and toward the world. In this regard, what Gandhi saw as the limits of his spiritual capacity, and what I have identified as some of the tensions and contradictions within his thinking about how to live ethically, are essential resources that his thought continues to offer us today.

The Entanglements of Love and Violence

Fanon's oeuvre likewise reveals that his popular legacy is founded on striking elisions of the critical nuances of his anticolonial writings. Fanon's reputation is largely built on readings that emphasize his advocacy of violence while disregarding the many moments in which his thinking is inflected by love, and in which he articulates his vision for an almost romantic, thoroughly deracialized and declassed future of man. Situating Fanon within a squarely humanist frame, Nigel C. Gibson reminds us that far from a simplistic desire for violence, Fanon's project was "to understand as well as to abolish the divisive and hierarchical zones that divide, fragment, and destroy human beings" (2003, 6). Gibson writes that although Fanon is popularly remembered "for his powerful descriptions of, and prescriptions for, a violent engagement with colonialism and its logic, his project and goal is to get beyond Manicheanism both in its colonial form and as an anticolonial reaction" (6). Fanon was in fact explicitly geared toward new world dynamics that fundamentally relied on mutual love in the formation of emergent subjectivities. In an idealist gesture toward the end of *Black Skin, White Masks*, for example, Fanon asks: "Why not the quite simple attempt to touch the other, to feel the other, to explain the other to myself?" (1967b, 231). It is in such moments that we see crystalized a postcolonial vision in Fanonian thought that is no longer bound by the racial politics of colonization. Like Gibson, Homi Bhabha sees in Fanon the powerful potential to begin to live with/in difference. Bhabha declares: "The time has come to return to Fanon; as always, I believe, with a question: how can the human world live its difference; how can a human being live Other-wise?" (1994, 64). While Fanon points us toward a politics of love-in-difference, difference in his thinking is chartered through the terrain of racialized masculinity. He envisions a deracinated future of "man" that emerges through the rejection of alliances with other nonconforming bodies.

In Sara Ahmed's phenomenological work, she emphasizes how bodies are oriented toward different objects in space. Such orientations teach us—often unconsciously—about who we are, leading us toward certain socially sanctioned objects and away from others in the formation of "proper" subjectivities. Engaging with Fanon, Ahmed argues that "colonialism makes the world 'white,' which is of course a world 'ready' for certain kinds of bodies, as a world that puts certain objects within their reach. Bodies remember such histories, even when we forget them" (2006, 111). The colonized body *embodies* the histories of its oppression by recognizing in material ways that it is not free in relation to the world that surrounds it. The dehumanization of the colonized subject inhabits space in particular ways that signal its own subject/object status: "The black man in becoming an object no longer acts or extends himself; instead, he is amputated and loses his body" (139). Ahmed reminds us that the orientation of the black body in Fanon is one that is "lost" in a world that disavows it through forms of material restriction, restrictions that shape and echo his psychic existence.

Taking account of Fanon's reach toward others, and the limits of that reach under colonialism, we must also attend to how "otherness" and alliance with alterity come to matter selectively in Fanonian discourse. Renowned for its advocacy of violence, *The Wretched of the Earth* begins with the declaration that "decolonization is always a violent phenomenon" (1963, 35). In *Black Skin, White Masks*, however, Fanon specifically turns toward love as he relays the profoundly destructive bodily and psychic conditions that comprise the colonial relation. Aggression and love for Fanon were constitutive components of every consciousness, and the task was thus to navigate one's own capacity for each: "Man is motion toward the world and toward his like. A movement of aggression, which leads to enslavement or to conquest; a movement of love, a gift of self, the ultimate stage of what by common accord is called ethical orientation. Every consciousness seems to have the capacity to demonstrate these two components, simultaneously or alternatively" (1967h, 41). The entanglements of love and violence required a careful and relentless negotiation of constitutive parts whose relation overlaps and interchanges. Real love—which intends to oppose the will toward mastery—entails the "mobilization of psychic drives" by enabling one to become free of one's own "unconscious conflicts" (41). A love of this kind—love in its most "authentic" form—reaches between oneself and others. But to reach this authentic state of love, one has first to violently wrench away the material and psychological shackles of colonization; only having done so for oneself could this new man emerge, a man finally capable of authentic love. The violence necessary to decolonization was therefore intimately connected to, even inextricable from, the trajectories and aims of love.

While for Gandhi violence was deeply contextual, for Fanon decolonization was a specifically temporal practice. It was violence that had confirmed these "two forces" as master and slave, and it was also violence that would finally undo this dynamic. Seizing mastery over his master, the slave would insist on his recognition as man by refusing his own mastery. Violence against the master was therefore a productive act that would fundamentally transform the slave by ushering him into being as a "new type of man" (Fanon 1967f, 36). In so doing, through the act of violence he reinstated his own humanity in an act that would fundamentally alter the world (37). Fanon did not envision this temporal enactment of violence as remaining bound within a Hegelian structure of revenge and ongoing usurpation. Rather, the moment of anticolonial violence would fundamentally transform colonial subjectivity and reconstitute world relations beyond a politics of racial subjugation.

Sociogeny and Narrative

In "The Fact of Blackness," Fanon's famous narrative account of colonial embodiment, other subjugated bodies surface as prospective allies but are refused alliance with the black male body readying itself for decolonization. Fanon engages literary texts throughout the chapter as he tells the story of his own corporeal experience in relation to whiteness. He includes poetic and narrative accounts of other black thinkers such as Leopold Senghor, Jacques Roumain, David Diop, and Richard Wright, emphasizing the vitality of the literary in the thinking and articulation of anticolonial revolutionary politics. As I have already illustrated in his caustic approach to Mayotte Capécia's autobiography, here too Fanon posits a theoretical account of race in deliberately narrative terms. He calls this "sociogeny," which stands "beside phylogeny and ontogeny" (1967d, 11). Sociogeny is

Fanon's term for how social fictions like race come to shape bodies and subjectivities at particular historical moments. Sylvia Wynter uses the title of *Black Skin, White Masks* to explain the function of sociogeny, referring to "Fanon's redefinition of being human as that of skins (phylogeny/ontogeny) *and* masks (sociogeny)" (Wynter and McKittrick 2015, 23). Wynter explains that "we can *experience ourselves as human* only through the mediation of the processes of socialization effected by the invented *tekhne* or cultural technology to which we give the name *culture*" (2001, 53). Developing Fanon's concept of sociogeny, Wynter argues that in any given historical moment the dominant conception of "Man" shapes the "subjective experience" of being human, including how we *feel* about our own humanity and the humanity of others (46). What is vital here is that "feeling" human—as an embodied, affective state—becomes central to realms such as ethics and politics, which are most often understood to be removed from affective life. Both Fanon and Wynter emphasize how the dominant conceptions of Man at any political moment are shaped and carried over through cultural narratives. Fanon's narrative emphasis shows how the political and corporeal are always in fact tied to narrative—to elaborate not only politics *as* narrative with concrete material effects but also the transformative power of narrative in resistance to dominant politics. If the white man had woven the black man "out of a thousand details, anecdotes, stories" (Fanon 1967c, 111), Fanon responds with a black, intertextual, anticolonial narrative that details the tangible, embodied effects of colonial politics.

Early in "The Fact of Blackness," Fanon declares that "the black man among his own in the twentieth century does not know at what moment his inferiority comes into being through the other" (1967c, 110). He proceeds to describe how he discussed at length "the black problem" with black male friends and asserted through protest "the equality of all men in the world." Being satisfied with his "intellectual understanding of these differences," Fanon suggests that his experience of race was "not really dramatic." He ends the paragraph with a sentence fragment followed by ellipses: "And then . . ." (110). At the start of the following paragraph, Fanon picks up and completes this fragment: "And then the occasion arose when I had to meet the white man's eyes." Initially satisfied by his intellectual engagement with racial inequality, he then confronts the gaze of the white man— "and then"—comes to understand that his psychic and bodily experience of the world exists in a dehumanized relation to the white, fully human subject. "In the white world," Fanon writes, "the man of color encounters difficulties in the development of his bodily schema. Consciousness of the body is a solely negating activity. It is a third-person consciousness. The body is surrounded by an atmosphere of certain uncertainty" (110–11). It is through Fanon's experience with the colonial gaze, then, that he becomes acutely aware that "below the corporeal schema" exists "a historico-racial schema" (111).

"The Fact of Blackness" centers on Fanon's famous train scene, where he recounts his experience of disembodiment in relation to whiteness in the confined but peripatetic space of the locomotive. Having experienced the radical alienation of being "other" in relation to the fully human white man, Fanon writes: "On that day, completely dislocated, unable to be abroad with the other, the white man, who unmercifully imprisoned me, I took myself far off from my own presence, far indeed, and made myself an object. What else could it be for me but an amputation, an excision, a hemorrhage that spattered my whole body with black blood? But I did not want this revision, this thematization. All I wanted was to be a man among other men. I wanted to come lithe and young into a world that was ours and to help to build it together" (1967c, 112–13). Fanon's desire toward the end of this passage to be "a man among other men" in a collectively constructed world is perhaps the best illustration of both his commitment to humanism and his utopic desire for forms of human solidarity across difference. Rather than to have the opportunity to live this utopic desire, Fanon declares: "My body was given back to me sprawled out, distorted, recolored, clad in mourning in that white winter day. The Negro is an animal, the Negro is bad, the Negro is mean, the Negro is ugly" (113). Across the rest of the chapter, Fanon details the processes and effects of masterful erasure produced by and through the colonial relation. In doing so, he turns toward other figures whose own subjection to masterful distortion he evokes but refuses to mobilize alongside black male revolutionary politics.

Recalling his own Antillean education, Fanon describes a pedagogical moment in which he is taught to consider the oppression of the Jew in relation to that of the Negro: "At first thought it may seem strange that the anti-Semite's outlook should be related to that of the Negrophobe. It was my philosophy professor, a native of the Antilles, who recalled the fact to me one day: 'Whenever you hear anyone abuse the Jews, pay attention, because he is talking about you.' And I found that he was universally right—by which I meant that I was answerable in my body and in my heart for what was done to my brother. Later I realized that he meant, quite simply, an anti-Semite is inevitably anti-Negro" (1967c, 122). The logical progression in this passage is fascinating, as Fanon moves from the "strange" association between anti-Semitism and Negrophobia, to his reading of his teacher's declaration as a universal ethics in which Fanon becomes "answerable" in his body and heart to his Jewish "brother," and finally to a concession that forms of oppression are always linked. Here Fanon summons a universal, ethical bond, both bodily and psychic (registered via the metaphor of the "heart"), that links him intimately to the Jew. Yet later in the chapter, when Fanon critiques Jean-Paul Sartre for having "destroyed black zeal" (135) and for forgetting "that the Negro suffers in his body quite differently from the white man" (138), he moves away from the alliance between the two marginalized figures. Fanon declares in a footnote that although Sartre may well be correct in his reading of "alienated consciousness," the white man remains "the master, whether real or imaginary," and therefore Sartre's attempts to apply his formulation to "a black consciousness proves fallacious" (138n24). The Jew becomes proximate to the black man but fails to be mobilized as an effective ally in decolonization because he (dis)embodies oppression differently.

Detailing the risk of "the closure of difference instead of the expansion of political possibilities" (1997, 93), Ann Pellegrini illustrates how while Fanon expresses a commitment to heterogeneity, he repeatedly "replicates a hom(m)ologics of the same." If, as we have seen, black women mark what Pellegrini calls Fanon's "extended blind spot," the figure of the Jewish man in Fanon's writing extends the horizons of this blindness. Pellegrini argues that "the ambivalence of Fanon's own identifications with Jewishness and Jewish men holds out, as it turns its back on, the spare promise of speaking across difference" (93). Reading alongside his European interlocutor Sartre in *Anti-Semite and Jew* (1995), Fanon aims to cast the "sympathetic analogies" between anti-Semitism and Negrophobia without conflating them, signaling how in the European imperialist frame the Negro is characterized as body, as sexual predator, while the Jew is figured as cerebral, dangerously prosperous, but removed from the realm of body. In thinking the Negro in relation to the Jew—both historically racialized figures that pose "opposite" dangers to white Europeans—Fanon forges an alliance through difference. But Pellegrini illustrates that he does so by ultimately "assimilating Jewish men to the feminine" (1997, 121). The Jew becomes an almost impotent cerebral figure in relation to the overly sexualized bodily Negro, and the Jewish male body become more closely identifiable as "feminine" than as an allied masculinity in the rhetoric of decolonization. As black women disappear as entities about which Fanon "knows nothing," functioning as constituents of the colonized body politic who become disposable in the psychodynamic frame of Fanon's anticolonial struggle, other (racialized) masculine bodies in turn become feminized, emerging as allies only to be ushered back toward the negligible realm of the (racialized) feminine.[18]

The critical differences between the white man and the black man in Fanon are articulated through the language of mastery in ways that register the slave in a complex relation to masterful being. Fanon declares that "the white man wants the world; he wants it for himself alone. He finds himself predestined master of this world. He enslaves it. An acquisitive relation is established between the world and him" (1967c, 128). There is a form of passivity here in which the white man "finding" himself as "predestined master" is almost incidental—his mastery is a relational mode that has befallen him as inheritance. Fanon is, of course, expressly critical of this masterful mode in which the world—a term that implicates here other humans as much as it signals other "natural" beings and spaces—becomes the desired possession of the white man. Later, however, decrying his affective dehumanization produced by this masterful subject, Fanon states: "I feel in myself a soul as immense as the world, truly a soul as deep as the deepest rivers, my chest has the power to expand without limit. I am a master and I am advised to adopt the humility of the cripple" (140). Fanon passionately characterizes himself, like the white man, as master—but one disabled from embodying and performing himself as such. This soul, "as immense as the world" and "as deep as the deepest rivers," ties Fanon to nature even while his unrecognized status as master would, if recognized, situate him over and against it. Fanon's humanism makes little room for an African animism that would see natural elements as imbued with life, with subjectivities that (like the figure of the Jew) he could conceivably call his "brother." Instead, he "feels" himself as nature, as an expansive space that is being subjected by another master whose authorized mastery he paradoxically wishes to possess. To return to Bhabha (1994), we must ask: What forms of living "Other-wise" can emerge when mastery remains the horizon of Fanon's desired decolonization? What futures can be born from this attachment to mastery? To grapple with Fanon's self-conception through explicitly natural imagery—his "soul" and body living as "cripple" when in fact a master is "felt" therein—is to confront a desire for decolonization in which a "new type of man" will always emerge through the rightful subjugation of otherness. While Fanon employs nature metaphorically in his formulation of colonial racism, his humanism trails away from an ecological worldview, one that holds out the possibility of angling away from the dialectic of mastery.

Fanon's Cripple

Fanon's masterful self, "crippled" by colonial racism, is oriented in very particular ways toward and against other bodies. Beyond the prohibitions of the black male body's orientation in colonial space, the figure of the cripple also signals a disavowal that "cripples" the universal reach of Fanon's own anticolonial desire. His reliance on the cripple in "The Fact of Blackness" is among the least explored and most perplexing of his narrative disablings. Earlier in the chapter, when Fanon writes of his experience of alienation on the train, he asks: "What else could it be for me but an amputation, an excision, a hemorrhage that spattered my whole body with black blood? But I did not want this revision, this thematization. All I wanted was to be a man among other men. I wanted to come lithe and young into a world that was ours and to help to build it together" (1967c, 112). Here we witness Fanon's utopian spirit, his embodied desire to be "lithe and young" and to build collectively an inclusive world of men "among other men." Fanon explains the break of his utopian spirit via a "historico-racial schema" that produces an affective feeling of corporeal amputation, of excision, of hemorrhage. He employs the figure of the cripple—of amputation—to symbolize a racially embodied subject whose existence is one of bodily erasure, lack, and depletion. Set against the properly masterful white embodied subject, Fanon is crippled by the force and play of colonization. The cripple becomes, in effect, the *mastered* body, the one subjected to mastery, the one whose embodiment always performs and reveals externally its subjugation, the one who is, in effect, not fully man, and thus the one with whom Fanon cannot ally himself.

At the end of "The Fact of Blackness," Fanon turns again to the cripple, pronouncing: "I am a master and I am advised to adopt the humility of the cripple." Citing the final scene of the 1949 psychoanalytic film *Home of the Brave*, directed by Mark Robson, Fanon writes: "The crippled war veteran of the Pacific war says to my brother, 'Resign yourself to your color the way I got used to my stump; we're both victims'" (1967c, 140). Fanon responds to his own citation of the film by declaring that "with all my strength I refuse to accept that amputation." (And interestingly here, the racially unmarked body of the cripple produces an understanding for the reader that the body of the cripple is a white body.)

Fanon's gloss on this film is not incidental, since *Home of the Brave* is among Hollywood's inaugural engagements with race and war, and since the film revolves around the psychoanalytic treatment of a black patient, Private Peter Moss (played by James Edwards). Moss is a topography specialist in the army undergoing psychoanalysis (not coincidentally, by a Jewish analyst played by Jeff Corey) for a psychosomatic condition that has paralyzed him from the waist down in the aftermath of a secret mission on a Japanese-invaded island on the Pacific Ocean (fig. 1.1). We come to learn through flashbacks that Moss has witnessed the death of Finch, his only white friend and ally. As viewers we believe that Moss's paralysis is the result of guilt born from Moss's repudiation of his interracial friendship when, just before his friend is shot, Finch (despite his antiracist desires) calls Moss a "yellow-bellied nigger." The killing of his ally at the hands of the Japanese enemy (an enemy that remains a dangerous though altogether invisible presence in the film) becomes a convenient offing at the moment that the white friend betrays his own racism. Through the doctor's narco-synthetic treatment (injections that prompt the patient to relive his traumatic experiences), we come to believe that Moss is paralyzed by the guilt of disavowing his friend at the moment before death.

What the analyst finally reveals, however, is that Moss's paralysis is not a result of guilt born from racism but about the guilt of feeling relief when it is his best friend and not he who is killed in war. The analyst therefore reorients the orientation specialist, curing Moss's paralysis by pointing him toward a universal response to war that is detached from racial politics. At the end of the film, Moss is sent home with Sergeant Mingo (Frank Lovejoy). Mingo is a new amputee who has lost his right arm, having been shot on the island with Moss. Throughout the film, Mingo has been rather apathetic to the problem of racism on which the film hinges. In the final scene, however, as the two men wait to be escorted back to the United

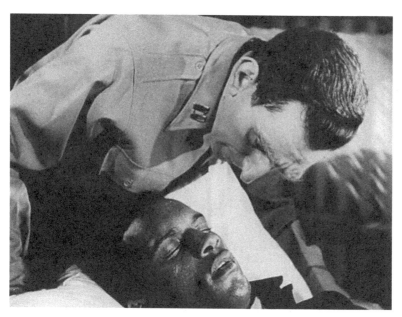

1.1 Private Peter Moss undergoes analysis for psychosomatic paralysis. James Edwards as Moss and Jeff Corey as army psychiatrist in *Home of the Brave* (1949), directed by Mark Robson.

States, Mingo becomes a "crippled" substitute for the dead Finch. While in this final scene Mingo initially scolds Moss and insists that he "get over" the paralyzing effects of racism, the amputee quickly turns toward an offering of radical friendship: Mingo confesses that despite a confident, quick-witted demeanor, he is undone by his newly configured body, and offers to fulfill Moss and Finch's dream of opening up a restaurant and bar together. The one-armed Mingo—newly amputated and struggling with his disability—articulates promise in his alliance with Moss, as both men recognize that they will struggle against systems of oppression that refuse their full subjectivities. Mingo offers himself up as both business partner and "one-armed bartender," forging an economic and sociopolitical alliance with Moss that not only refuses either as "resigned" but collectively and collaboratively reenters the social world through an unlikely but newly empowered body-politic. In the final moments of the film, Moss helps to hoist Mingo's duffle bag over his armless shoulder as they prepare to leave the war behind them. Awaiting their transportation "home," they gaze out

1.2 Private Moss and Sergeant Mingo look together out the window and toward a collective future. James Edwards as Moss and Frank Lovejoy as Mingo in *Home of the Brave* (1949), directed by Mark Robson.

the window together—beyond the war and toward a futurity marked by new forms of collective embodiment (fig. 1.2).

Fanon thus misrepresents this final scene in *Home of the Brave* in order to conclude "The Fact of Blackness." His peculiar glossing of the film avoids the profound political, economic, and social alliances boldly forged at the end of the film, where promise is based on the recognition that the notion of "lack" itself is socially produced. What Fanon reveals through his gloss— through the assertion that the crippled war veteran wants a shared victim status with the black man and wants him to "resign" himself to his color the way that the cripple has become accustomed to his stump—illustrates a resistance in Fanonian thought to claim the power of prospective alliances between differently "othered" subjects. Fanon's rendering of the cripple betrays in this sense his own conception of "man" as one that is conceived not merely through a specifically masterful masculine body but through a body that is "whole" by those very standards that maintain the hierarchies Fanon's own politics aim to renounce.

Dehumanism against Mastery

If I am appearing at moments harsh in my readings of Fanon and Gandhi, mine is a critique born of real indebtedness and driven by the profound potentialities still embedded in their political writings. There is a beautiful moment in "The Fact of Blackness" in which Fanon pauses to consider his own character. He writes: "If I were asked for a definition of myself, I would say that I am one who waits; I investigate my surroundings, I interpret everything in terms of what I discover, I become sensitive" (1967c, 120). I am entirely taken by Fanon's "becoming sensitive" as a self-defining quality, and I am interested in how sensitivity itself—especially within the discourses of liberation that are grounded in love and the pursuit of less violent human futures—can continue to refuse alliances with other discrepant bodies that are cast as excessive to particular political aims.

While so much of my own attention to both Gandhi and Fanon emphasizes moments in which they appear quite insensitive to their own rehearsals of mastery, my aim has been to consider carefully how even the most impassioned thinkers of liberation—thinkers driven by love and less violent human futures—continuously refused alliances with certain bodies that did not conform to the political aims of their movements. It is by returning to these figures of decolonization, and by politicizing their knotty contradictions, that we can begin to register those that are currently excised from our own political moment—those others we continue to produce in our ongoing practices of mastery and, paradoxically, through our struggles for justice.

Fanon's "becoming sensitive" as a quality of the self is instrumental to vulnerable reading, to becoming porous to texts in ways that might reshape our subjectivities and our political aspirations. Pairing Fanon's sensitivity with Gandhi's always shifting experimental practices in search of truth, we can begin to see the possibility for a dehumanist praxis in which the remainders of anticolonial political thought—women, indigenous peoples, animals, the disabled, and nature writ large—become sites that can cultivate our own sensitivities to those we are currently (and often despite ourselves) producing as remainders to our purportedly inclusive politics. The decolonizing politics of our present moment might reach for sensitivities we ourselves cannot yet anticipate through experimental practices that can lead us into radically other forms of feeling and acting. Such practices include vulnerable reading, which I take up in the last three chapters of the book as I turn toward a dehumanist ethico-politics. The decolonizing potential of dehumanism against mastery must reach beyond the historically contingent figure of the human toward other forms of living and being. Dehumanism's promise is in becoming sensitive to those human and inhuman beings that we currently conceive as proximate to us, and most urgently to those which we still imagine as radically distinct.

CHAPTER 2

The Language of Mastery

Mastery of language affords remarkable power.

—FRANTZ FANON, *Black Skin, White Masks* (1967)

The choice of language and the use to which language is put is central to a people's definition of themselves in relation to their natural and social environment, indeed in relation to the entire universe.

—NGŨGĨ WA THIONG'O, *Decolonising the Mind* (1986)

Man acts as though he were the shaper and master of language, while in fact language remains the master of man.

—MARTIN HEIDEGGER, *Poetry, Language, Thought* (1975)

Yes, I have only one language, yet it is not mine.

—JACQUES DERRIDA, *Monolingualism of the Other, Or, The Prosthesis of Origin* (1998)

In the spring of 2015, after weeks of campus protests, a statue of the British colonial magnate Cecil John Rhodes that symbolically lorded over the community was removed from the University of Cape Town's campus. The protests were initiated by an activist who threw human feces on the statue, an act that repudiated the enduring legacies of racism at UCT. The subsequent public debates around the removal of the Rhodes statue brought to public attention the extraordinary racial inequality of UCT's campus environment. Across South Africa and beyond, the removal of the Rhodes statue came to signal the necessity of refusing the legacies of colonization, emphasizing the critical relation between symbolic spaces and material realities. As Rhodes continued to reign symbolically on the campus decades after the formal end of apartheid, it made a certain disturbing sense that UCT should have a scant five South African–born black professors on its faculty.

A few months later, in the fall and winter of 2015, the legacies of colonial mastery on college campuses in the United States likewise came to public consciousness through mainstream media attention. At the University of Missouri, the football team protested the administration's lack of attention to incidents of racism on campus, resulting in the resignation of its president, Timothy Wolfe. At Yale University, the spouse of a "college master" (known elsewhere in the United States as a "resident dean") publicly disparaged a student-led request that the campus community be considerate in choosing their Halloween costumes. The college master, Nicholas Christakis, and his spouse, Erika Christakis, both faculty at Yale, insisted that no one should be allowed to "control the forms of costumes" that students elect to wear, and in so doing advocated for freedom of self-representation—even if that representation may be racist. Around the same time at Princeton University, student protests over Woodrow Wilson's legacy on their campus prompted their own college "masters" to be renamed "heads of college."

Across these various and ongoing instances of student protest, the legacies and language of mastery have been challenged and transformed by mobilizing student bodies. Through these various protests, the haunting questions of race, domination, silencing, and abjection have been brought to the fore of campus politics. At Yale and Princeton, the language of mastery reflects a particular political practice: the "master" is not merely a title but a relation that signals a very specific history of colonization and slavery. This relation has continued to linger and to be confirmed through everyday speech acts across even the most elite college campuses. What the language of mastery does is to enforce legacies of violence, erasure, and dehumanization on which the nation—and indeed our educational institutions—have been erected. The language and practices of mastery that underscore these debates are critically instructive. For so-called racial minority students, mastery names a global political relation on and well beyond the site of the college campus. Indeed, watching the viral videos of black and brown student protesters, it is virtually impossible not to see the palpable traces of slavery and colonialism playing out. By no means am I arguing that students of color in privileged college institutions are *in fact* slaves—but the dynamics of power in which they are enfolded and the legacies (linguistic and material) that they are aiming to confront are *at least* inseparable from the exploitation, torture, and deaths of people who gave rise to the very institutions in which many thrive today.

In U.S. mainstream media, these student organizers have been cast as overly sensitive "cry-bullies" demanding "safe spaces" in place of a real brass tacks education. This radically insufficient notion of education as a practice that holds no room for "sensitivity" is at its root a colonizing gesture that casts education as a practice of *subjecting* others to the exclusive force of a firmly established hierarchy. Both the student protests and their critiques draw attention to the linguistic and symbolic force of colonial mastery that continues to resound in the ostensibly postcolonial present. Like anticolonial discourse, student protests and the media attention that has followed them have underscored mastery—most often implicitly—as an enduring ethico-political problem. In support of student organizers internationally, and against the deeply problematic registers of education in mainstream media, we might think toward a decolonized education that would engage education as praxis, as a process of critical becoming that entails various (and at times totally unanticipatable) forms of care and practices of unlearning that which we already "know." Education in this sense is a transformative act of becoming profoundly vulnerable to other lives, other life forms, and other "things" that we have not yet accounted for or that appear only marginally related to us. Nathan Snaza calls this a practice of "bewildering education" (2013, 48), one that insists on our vital entanglements with other forms of life and matter. Following Snaza, I would call for a *dehumanist education* through which "subject matter" comes not merely to describe a topic of study but to signal the physical matter that makes study possible. Coming to "know" ourselves through education must also be a radical renarration and reorientation of what it is that we are aspiring to know. A dehumanist higher education would insist that knowledge production itself become unpredictable, unanticipatable, unmasterful. Recalling my discussion of Frantz Fanon and Sylvia Wynter in the preceding chapter, coming to know ourselves in this way will require taking account of "sociogeny," and engaging new narrative inventions that bring into being alternative modes of subjectivity. As Snaza proposes: "We must learn to think of ourselves as something other than 'human,' and we have to imagine and experiment with pedagogies that do not presuppose this 'human' as their *telos*" (2013, 50). This education would have to take language seriously, to interrogate how we name and what histories of conquest, erasure, and profit are embedded in the words through which we come to "know": Education *as* ethics; education as a radically unmasterful act that requires that our ethical grounds are always aspiring, shifting, experimenting, failing—but striving nevertheless toward more ethical orientations.

Possessing Language

In *Monolingualism of the Other*, Derrida writes of his own intimate estrangement with the French language, declaring, "I have only one language, yet it is not mine" (1998, 2). Derrida reminds us, as an Algerian writing in France, of the historical force rooted in the very use of language. To elaborate the fantasmatic notion of language as "possession," he turns to the colonial politics of language: "Because the master does not possess exclusively, and *naturally*, what he calls his language . . . because language is not his natural possession, he can, thanks to that very fact, pretend historically, through the rape of a cultural usurpation, which means always essentially colonial, to appropriate it in order to impose it as 'his own'" (23). This "always essentially colonial" relation between the master and his language reveals the fraudulency of the master who by *performing* language possession conquers and usurps foreign cultures. Gauri Viswanathan's account of British language and literature education in India emphasizes this foundational element of colonial "masking" in her argument about how "English literary study had its beginnings as a strategy of containment" (1989, 19). Aiming to "teach" colonial subjects how to mimic British civility, this strategy of containment was, Viswanathan argues, a mask for "the vulnerability of the British, the sense of beleaguerment and dread" felt by British colonial administrators who anticipated an almost certain rebellion by natives against their authority (10). English language and literature education was a "humanistic" method of civilizing natives by teaching them how to approximate their colonial masters. Yet, as Viswanathan elucidates, "the view that a humanistic education holds the same meaning and purpose for both colonizer and colonized quickly crumbles under the weight of even the most casual scrutiny" (7). When we read Viswanathan and Derrida together, colonial language and its masterful framing emerge as a fantastic defense against the vulnerability of the master who fears his own lack, and who responds to that fear through instituting and enforcing his "own" masterful language.

Derrida's declaration of French as his sole language *and* as that which is not his own is not only a historico-political problem but also an ontological one in which language both shapes and refuses to become the property of the subject. The language Derrida speaks is neither historically nor ontologically his own; it belongs to another as Other. The intimate political nexus of language, mastery, and colonization always summons the problem of what language *is*. I engage in this chapter evocations of language and mastery across anticolonial and postcolonial discourses, thinking alongside those whose language relation has been overtly caught up in the political and dehumanizing stakes of colonization. I illustrate how mastery surfaces repeatedly in colonial and postcolonial language debates around the force of the colonial language over colonized subjects, the desire to reclaim mastery over native languages in decolonization efforts, and the advocacy of language mastery as the aim of literary studies in the purportedly postcolonial world. Across the complex and widely divergent formulations of decolonization, language and mastery return us to the figures of women, animals, adversaries, and weaponry that were at play in the preceding chapter. Querying the figurative evocations of language in relation to colonial mastery and decolonization, I turn at the end of the chapter to the contemporary discourse of "world" literature in an effort to reconsider the current aims of literary practices. Current discourses that detail the aims of ambitions of literary study, I argue, speak to a much wider tendency in academic thinking and aspiration today. Calling into question intellectual production from the vantage point most intimate to me as a literary scholar, I urge scholars away from intellectual mastery and toward the horizon of a dehumanist education.

Decolonizing Languages: Fanon and Memmi

Across twentieth-century anticolonial discourses, language repeatedly emerged as one of the most vital problems in the production and articulation of decolonized subjectivities. If in Western thought language has been understood as key in the shaping of human subjects, anticolonial thinkers pressured and elaborated the crucial place of language for those dehumanized by political formations of the proper human subject. Thinkers like Frantz Fanon, Mohandas Gandhi, and the Tunisian writer Albert Memmi charted the political function of humanization *and dehumanization* through language use and acquisition. Because these thinkers insisted on thinking the politics of language from the position of those excluded from the status of the fully imbued human, they were already pointing us toward a dehumanist politics even if they also remained caught up with a masterful thinking of the human.

The gender politics of decolonization and mastery that I charted in chapter 1 echo across debates of colonialism and language, in which a male speaking subject is often cast in relation to a feminized language that he is either in pursuit of or at war against. Rife with metaphors of antagonism, emasculation, and patriarchal force, the predominant discourses of decolonization in the last century characterized language relation through gendered violence. Whether through struggles with colonial language and its enforcement in the colonies, through the colonial subject's torturous embodiments of colonial language, or through the reclamation of "native" languages, gendered force repeats across discussions of language and colonial power. Language and the speaking subject are repeatedly caught up in colonial and anticolonial force exerted (literally and metaphorically) against "other" bodies.

Both Fanon and Memmi dwell on the corporeal force of colonial language for the educated colonized subject. In "The Negro and Language," Fanon writes that "to speak means to be in a position to use a certain syntax, to grasp the morphology of this or that language, but it means above all to assume a culture, to support the weight of a civilization" (1967f, 17–18). *Locution* for Fanon is directly tied to *location*, to the arduous labor of the speaker who endures a civilization's "weight." The act of speaking is locational, "to be in a position" to "grasp" the forms of language, and to carry the historical pressure encompassed by language. The speaker, cast as a capable and laboring subject in a particular time and place, is also locked into a relation of power with language. Within the relay of power between the speaker and the world, Fanon declares that "it is implicit that to speak is to exist absolutely for the other" (18). The existential quality of this statement seems to imply an ethical relation to another; yet in the colonial context where language is imposed on the colony, this absolute existence that language entails becomes a confirmation of the mastery at stake in the colonial enterprise. The colonized subject who speaks a language he has inherited by force comes to "exist absolutely" for his master.

As I illustrated in the previous chapter, Fanon was not one to decry mastery outright but rather insisted on the emergent master-status of the masculine, colonial subject. He situates himself as a "master" who has been "crippled" by the force of the colonial relation (1967c, 140). In so doing, Fanon claims mastery as the proper status of all men, regardless of race. Beyond the exclusions that this masculinist frame of mastery produces, what Fanon does not attend to is how his declaration "I am a master" relies on a relation to language that is fundamentally dependent. Fanon must articulate himself as master through language, revealing a dependency on language that threatens his own self-conception as master. In order to identify himself in the first place, through the written utterance "I am," Fanon troubles his own master-status by showing mastery as a fantasy. If one needs language to identify oneself as master, one cannot hold "true" mastery over language and the world it signals. Fanon attempts, then, to renounce colonial mastery while recuperating the masterful subject toward a deracinated global politics.

Fanon's relation to language mastery is as complex as it is at times confounding. He declares that the "mastery of language affords remarkable power" and that the speaking subject who masters a language "possesses the world expressed and implied by that language" (1967f, 18). By "mastering" language, the speaker comes not only to "possess" language but also to hold power over the "world" that language signals. Like Heidegger (1995), who frames language as "world forming," Fanon as psychoanalyst ascribes a fundamental significance to the phenomenon of language in the human's relation to the world. At the end of *Identification Papers*, Diana Fuss turns to Fanon's own "complete reliance upon translators to converse with his Muslim patients" (1995, 162) to remind us of the intimate bind between politics and language. As both Fuss and Fanon's biographer Irene Gendzier (1985) note, as a French-speaking analyst treating Arabic- and Kabyle-speaking patients in Algeria, Fanon's analytic practice hinged on local Algerian hospital staff who translated for him throughout his analytic sessions. These vital intermediary figures—Algerian men working as nurses who were not permitted to become doctors under the colonial administration—appear only incidentally in Fanon's analytic notes. Fuss dwells on how the use of translators not only reveals Fanon's own inability to "master" Arabic and Kabyle but how the question of language so crucial to psychoanalytic practice—the word choices and slips—are "lost in translation" through Fanon's own linguistic lack and his reliance on others to make his analysis possible (1995, 162). What Fanon is interpreting, Fuss argues, is the language of the translator as opposed to the patient. What I find so fascinating about Fanon's Algerian translators is how they come to illuminate his own complex relation to language mastery. Fanon-as-analyst does not give sustained attention to his fundamental reliance on the language of his Algerian translators as third parties in the room. By not critically engaging with these third parties and *their* language as translators, he produces a theory of the colonial psychopathology through the erasure of these vital "third" linguistic figures. In reading his patients, he is invariably also always reading the translator, whose translations necessarily alter, build on, adjust, and elide the language of the patient. Foreign language in this analytic context necessitates a palimpsestic reading of language as an impossible plurality, as that which is always mediated and dispersed, as always in translation—in other words, as thoroughly unmasterable. His own practice reveals already the impossibility of language mastery, just as the presence of a literal third body in the room signals the always present social body therein, even in the more traditional frame of two—patient and analyst—engaging through a "common" language.

While Fanon props up the idea of language mastery as that which affords remarkable power, in the colonial context he dwells on the impossibility of language mastery for the educated colonial subject. He binds linguistics to racism, emphasizing how the European holds a "fixed concept" of the Negro that irrevocably confirms his inferiority. The result is that the mastery of the French language for the colonized subject is strictly and finally impossible, regardless of the fluency of the colonized speaker. Yet the colonial subject is driven by this impossible pursuit of language mastery, which produces in him "paranoia" and physically deforms his body. For this subject, colonial language is both a mobilizing and subjugating force. On the one hand, "the Antilles Negro who wants to be white will be the whiter as he gains greater mastery of the cultural tool that language is" (Fanon 1967f, 38). French is the "key that can open doors" historically barred from the colonial subject (38), but it is a power that is contingent and comes at a vital cost. In his characterization of this quest for mastery over the colonizer's tongue, Fanon turns to its absolutely bodily aspects, to how the pursuit of language mastery produces both psychic and physical alterations to the colonized subject: "The Negro arriving in France will react against the *R*-eating man from Martinique. He will become aware of it, and he will really go to war against it. He will practice not only rolling his *R* but embroidering it. Furtively observing the slightest reactions of others, listening to his own speech, suspicious of his own tongue—a wretchedly lazy organ—he will lock himself into his room and read aloud for hours—desperately determined to learn *diction*" (21). Going to "war" against his historico-political location (Martinique) and his racialized body (that "eats" the consonant *R*), this split colonial subject violently cultivates himself as a new man. In Fanon's "verbal performance" (Pellegrini 1997, 97), speech becomes a site of self-embattlement because the colonial subject must prove his likeness to his colonizer through fluency. Going to war against his "lazy organ," Fanon ties the tongue to the phallic virility of the colonized black body. While the black man is cast as a hypersexual and dangerous force whose active "organ" is threatening to the colonial regime,[1] here Fanon's "lazy organ" reveals a bodily paradigm in which the black man cannot train his body into proper civility and is thus symbolically emasculated by its ineptitude. If he is seen as a body that poses a phallic threat to his colonizer, this other lazy organ betrays a cultural impotence because of which he can never come to pass himself off as properly civilized. The colonized subject thus becomes attentive to his speech to the point of paranoia, hyperaware of how his own sounds register to/through his colonial masters. Seeking relentlessly to master French, his education in the colonial language becomes a process of locutionary exile in which his body—through its particular relation to colonial force—becomes impotent, paralyzing, imprisoning.

The speaking subject in Fanon is saddled with the burden of a civilization that language beholds, and in the colonial context this requires taking on the weight of an alien civilization. For the colonized speaker, his power over the colonial language will remain insufficient: he will be perpetually bound as slave to his colonizer's language. While Fanon provides a fascinating psychoanalytic account of the kinds of psycho-dynamics and what Ann Pellegrini (1997) calls "performance anxieties" produced through the colonial language relation, his argument hinges on an actual potential of language mastery, one that refuses the colonized as a language master. Abiding by Derrida's (1998) formulation that language is never a human possession, we see a tension arise in Fanon's thinking: he claims language mastery as factual as opposed to fantasmatic before turning to the colonial context. In framing the problem of language in the colonial context, he upholds the possibility of language mastery beyond the colonial context in order to emphasize how racism disables certain subjects from becoming themselves (language) masters.

In *The Colonizer and the Colonized* (1991), Memmi anticipates Derrida's formulation by insisting that the colonizer must always understand himself as a "complete master" and must in turn enact mastery over others. Responding to his master, the colonial subject's first ambition is "to become equal to that splendid model and to resemble him to the point of disappearing in him" (1991, 120). For Memmi as for Fanon, colonization and the acquisition of the colonial language in particular forms and deforms colonial bodies, resulting in the devaluation and "disappearance" of the self. Like Fanon too, Memmi argues that regardless of how well the native speaks the colonizer's language, his linguistic skills are always marked as deficient because of his racial difference. Memmi places critical emphasis on race and education in the deformation of colonial subjectivities; in order to succeed, the educated colonized subject must participate actively in this devaluation by succumbing to the colonizer's tongue: "If he wants to obtain a job, make a place for himself, exist in the community and the world, he must first bow to the language of his masters" (107). By "bowing," he sets out to discard his own "infirm language," concealing his native tongue while he diligently pursues that of the colonizer. Here again, as in the preceding chapter, we find the language of disability in discourses of decolonization, positing in this instance an abject native tongue against a robust colonial language. Rather than being a "polyglot's richness" or a form of coexistence between native and foreign, colonial bilingualism for Memmi is a "linguistic drama" that creates in the colonial subject a "permanent duality" (108). Within the play of this drama, the colonized speaker engages in a "wholesale subjugation" of his native language and erodes its vitality. In essence, his attachment to pursuing the master's tongue leads (perversely) to the complete subjugation of his own.

Memmi argues that language must be the primary site of decolonization, and that native language reclamation and revitalization are key to cultural "self-rediscovery": "To this self-rediscovery movement of an entire peoples must be returned the most appropriate tool; that which finds the shortest path to its soul, because it comes directly from it" (1991, 134). Embracing the limited vocabulary and "bastardized syntax" of the native tongue is an act of accepting the linguistic debasement that the bilingual colonial subject has himself helped to produce. While this language cannot yet reflect "higher mathematics or philosophy," it cuts directly to the "souls" of the people, and by articulating those subjectivities it can lead toward other forms of critical discourse. As we shall see imminently, Gandhi shares this conception of a debased language that can be mobilized and revitalized.

Memmi concludes his meditation on the role and necessity of language reclamation by turning to the construction of a "whole and free man" who at last speaks his own revitalized language: "Having reconquered all his dimensions, the former colonized will have become a man like any other. There will be the ups and downs of all men to be sure, but at least he will be a whole and free man" (1991, 153). If native language reclamation is an act that Memmi insists will redirect the colonized subject away from the "permanent duality" created by his bilingualism, he does not pose this act of reclamation outside colonial discourse. Rather than to embrace his lost dimensions and to enable the emergence of other forms of (human) being, the colonial subject must instead "reconquer" them. Here, the language Memmi uses to think about the primordial dimension of language reclamation and revitalization gives way to a colonial mindset in which particular (male) subjects continuously engage in a linguistic practice of conquest. This language reveals the abiding structure of mastery at work in the formal colonial relation and in the act of decolonization. Becoming "a whole and free man" remains in Memmi's thought bound to conquest, and through acts of self-conquest (as we saw in the previous chapter through my discussion of Gandhi), mastery is reoriented against a colonized subject that has already experienced the force of mastery by another. His fantasy is that conquest—which I have argued necessitates splitting—can lead to wholeness. As such, he imagines that colonial language's mastery over the colonized subject can give way to another form of conquest in which the colonized man becomes "whole and free" through the masterful reclamation of those "dimensions" taken from him through colonial violence.

Gandhi's (Inter)National Languages

The urgent need to restore native languages to colonized subjects is likewise prominent in Gandhian thought. While he would insist that the question of language was not as critical as that of truth and nonviolence—in other words, that *swaraj* (self-rule) could be attained even if the English language prevailed (as it has) in India—it is clear that Gandhi could not think liberation without repeatedly returning to the problems that language posed for Indian independence.[2] Like Fanon and Memmi, Gandhi attends to language as a crucial aspect of India's decolonization movement. He argued repeatedly that Indians had impoverished their "mother tongues" as a direct result of colonial India's love of the English language (1965, 1997). What was needed in order to achieve an independence worth its name was twofold: the mobilization of a *rashtrabhasha*—a national language of the masses that would unite the Indian nation—and the restoration of mother tongues that had been sacrificed through the colonial encounter. Gandhi would ultimately envision "Hindustani" as India's national language, one that would combine Hindi and Urdu to create a language aimed at uniting the otherwise divided Hindu and Muslim parties by reflecting the linguistic intimacies of both in the quest for national liberation.[3] Yet, as Sumathi Ramaswamy reminds us, it was finally Hindi that rose to national prominence and displaced other regional languages: "Hindi, the putative 'official' language of India, is but the tongue of one region masquerading as the language of the nation" (1997, xx). If Hindi finally emerged as India's "official language," it did so through the subjugation of other languages made marginal through its rise to national prominence.

Gandhi wrote often about language, repeatedly issuing the figure of the mother in relation to language politics. His formulations of language as feminine and maternal reflect a broader political discourse characterizing the relation between the speaking subject and language. In her study of Tamil language devotion, Ramaswamy "opens up for critical scrutiny the feminization of languages in modernity, a feminization that has been so naturalized as to have sealed off the 'mother tongue' from history" (1997, 17). Ramaswamy asks us to consider the political implications of a "naturalized" formulation of language-as-female through her attention to Tamil. Teasing out the ways that Tamil devotees evoke the language using "mother's milk," "mother," and "mother tongue" as synonyms (17), she illustrates how language devotion is "multiply manifested, as religious, filial, and erotic, and struggling for prominence and domination" (21). In the case of Tamil, while the language was posed as female, its speaker was invariably a masculine devotional subject. Gandhi participates in this discourse, insisting that "language is like our mother. But we do not have that love for it, as we have for our mother" (1965, 12). Here language as mother is suffering and impoverished under colonial rule because the Indian body politic does not love her as its subjects love their mothers. To bring language back to health, to resurrect the mother as the nurturing figure she is expected to be, Indians (cast as male children) must love her appropriately.

Following the simile between language and the mother, Gandhi claims the milk one receives from one's native tongue as "pure" in opposition to the watered-down and poisoned milk ingested by Indians who spoke the colonial language. From this historical vantage point, we would do well to take pause at Gandhi's claims of purity, given how often the politics of purity in the South Asian context has continued to lead to the violent control of bodies marked as "impure." But here, rather than to take aim against an "impurity" marked by gender, caste, or sexuality, Gandhi critiques Indian elites for refusing their own "pure" languages. He argues that the educated classes had developed a profound "distaste" for the milk of their mother tongues, spellbound by the insidious lure of the English language. In his refusal of the power of English language over India, Gandhi declares, "This slavery to an alien language has kept our millions deprived of a great deal of necessary knowledge for many long years" (1965, 131). Undoing the mastery that English holds over the colony and liberating its "slaves" therefore requires the restoration of the primary bond between the mother (as language) and the child (as both educated elite and as local native subjects). Such a return to the linguistic bond characterized as properly maternal and wholly nourishing would lead directly to the achievement of swaraj (self-rule) and would give rise to relations not predicated on the politics of domination.[4]

For Gandhi, there was nothing intrinsic about a particular language that made it powerful. If English was a language of power, this was so only because the British had committed completely to their mother tongue: "No language is intrinsically all that the correspondent says. A language becomes what its speakers and writers make it. English had no merit apart from what Englishmen made it. In other words, a language is a human creation and takes the colour of its creators. Every language is capable of infinite expansion" (1965, 64). English had therefore failed as the lingua franca of India because, like French for Memmi, it did not reflect the cultural spirit of the people. What's more, the English spoken in the cities was a "broken English," a substandard version of the language that was incapable of producing a liberated subject (23). In the postcolonial moment, it is precisely these forms of "broken English" that come to be politicized by writers like Evelyn Nien-Ming Ch'ien (2005), who engages "weird English," and Ken Saro-Wiwa (1994), who mobilized "rotten English." But for Gandhi at this historical moment, there was no recuperative potential in speaking "cast-off" forms of the colonial language. The only path to freedom was to give English its proper place, to abandon its use as the language of Indian politics and social engagement, and to turn back toward the local Indian languages as mothers who had been abandoned by their children.

Reflecting on the eager adoption of English by India's colonial elite in their desires to mimic their masters, Gandhi turns to English-language use as a practice of dehumanization: "In slavery, the slave has to ape the manners and ways of the master, e.g., dress, language, etc. Gradually, he develops a liking for it to the exclusion of everything else" (1965, 101). Aspiring to become like the master, the slave works alongside his master in order to dehumanize himself. Not merely does the slave desire to become *like* the master; the slave *apes* his master and in so doing is rendered animal.[5] Until the educated elite consciously returned to their native languages, freedom was not possible. Since for Gandhi all language is "capable of infinite expansion," he also insisted that languages—even those that have deteriorated because of the fetishism of the colonial language—could become evocative, powerful systems of expression if only we bound ourselves to them. In this respect, the resurrection of native language is a process both of becoming human, of restoring one's humanity through the refusal to "ape" the master, and of returning to the primary site of the mother-as-language in order to grow toward individual and political freedom.

In Gandhi's thinking on language, the nuanced dynamics of mastery appear in his own relation to language acquisition, in the relation of the Indian masses to language, and in the relation of the language teachers to the new rashtrabhasha (national language). As David Lelyveld (2001) has illustrated, Gandhi was not someone for whom languages came easily even though he was well versed in several. A native Gujarati speaker, his broader experience with Indian languages came during his tenure in South Africa, where much of his critical philosophy about the achievement of swaraj was likewise developed. There he studied Hindi, Urdu, and some Tamil while in and out of prison for his activism, insisting on the importance of uniting Indians through the medium of language acquisition and developing a rashtrabhasha that would mobilize the nation (Lelyveld 2001, 69). What is key is that for Gandhi knowing languages gave one access to others and opened the possibility of dialogue, but it was not his personal aim to become a language master. While he apologized repeatedly for his flawed spelling and grammar, even in his native Gujarati, he himself did not aim for complete control over language.

Of his own verbal style, Gandhi declared, "My language is aphoristic, it lacks precision. It is therefore open to several interpretations" (qtd. in Chatterjee 1986, 85). Asserting the malleability of his language, the importance of being able to make it speak by others within and across multiple contexts, Gandhi's rendering of his own use of language posits it as fundamentally open-ended. That he aims to speak "openly" suggests his refusal of a master discourse, one that declares the right and the proper and in so doing subjugates other interpretations. Yet for him, language was not merely an open-ended form, and the language one used to articulate one's thoughts had critical political consequences: "When I find myself able to express my thought with more facility in English than in Gujarati, I tremble" (1965, 2). If for Gandhi English most readily expresses his thoughts, it is a sign that he has internalized his subjection by the colonial master. English in this sense speaks *for* him, rehearsing its mastery over him as it reveals his enslavement. Yet his relation to English is certainly not one of mere animosity: "It is necessary to say that I do not hate the English language. I myself have benefited from many of the precious gems of the great treasury of English literature. We have also to acquire a knowledge of science and such like through the English language. Knowledge of English is, therefore, very necessary for us. But it is one thing to give it its due place, and quite another to make a fetish of it" (16). Here Gandhi reveals that English was a benefit to him, something that contained the "precious gems" of the English literary tradition—or what Matthew Arnold (1993) called its "sweetness and light"—and that therefore enriched him with artistic beauty. English for Gandhi was not merely the language of conquest but also vitally of art and knowledge.

As such, Gandhi refused to "drive out the English language" from his other languages (1965, 130). While at times he admitted his great love of the English language, at others he revealed his intense struggles with it. Of his various languages, English was the most frustrating for him to learn. Gandhi claimed for this reason that it is "a huge waste" to spend years studying English, a notoriously difficult language, when native languages were more easily and swiftly learned. Excising English as a prospective language of the Indian masses was not therefore merely a political and philosophical position but an entirely practical one toward mobilizing the country: "If we spend only half the effort we do in learning English in the learning of Indian languages, there will be born a new atmosphere in the country and a good measure of progress will be achieved" (1). Gandhi cites his own experience with English, having spent seven years "mastering" English in order to pass the matriculation examination. In his native language, he insists, he could have passed the exam in a year. This, to Gandhi's mind, was a great "misfortune," a squandering of precious time that could have been used toward other ethico-political efforts (94).

Just as English was the language of India's enslavement for Gandhi, it was also because of British imperialism an essential world language, indeed the language of global commerce, and could not merely be discarded. It holds in this respect an ambivalent position in Gandhian thought. Within the pages of *Hind Swaraj* (1997), his manifesto on Indian self-rule, Gandhi advances his most vital declarations about the achievement of Indian independence. What he insists repeatedly therein is that Indians have been complicit in their own subjugation. The key to independence, then, is not to overthrow the colonizer but to change radically the colonized self and its relation to society at large. If, as he declared in an earlier work, "the character of a people is evident in its language" (1965, 2), their use of English at the expense of their native tongues signals their own self-devaluation and reveals how at the most intimate level of thought and speech they have enabled themselves to be subsumed by an outside force. To refuse English as the language of the educated classes and to mobilize the native tongue to speak of politics and liberation were necessary steps toward the psychic transformation of the colony into a liberated nation-state. English held a wealth of information that Indians needed, and scientific and commercial discourses needed to be "translated" or infused into the rashtrabhasha that did not yet contain it. Like Memmi, Gandhi figured the native language as that which had been debased by colonization yet also needed the colonial language to infuse it with those forms of knowledge it lacked.

For artistic and practical reasons, then, Gandhi desired to preserve his own knowledge of English and encouraged other Indians likewise not to "give up or abandon" their English. While he defended his right to communicate in the colonial language, he also insisted that English must not be allowed "to transgress its rightful place" (1965, 131). English should never emerge as India's national language nor should it become, as Thomas Babington Macaulay advocated, the language of Indian education.[6] Macaulay's call to enforce English-language education in the colony aimed famously to produce hybrid subjects—Indian in appearance but English in every other way—whose familiarity with English language and culture would enable them in turn to "enrich" vernacular dialects with Western thought. This new class of Indian subjects would infuse local dialects with Western ideology, rendering them "by degrees fit vehicles for conveying knowledge to the great mass of the population" (1835, 8). For the native, learning English was the best way toward civilization: "Whoever knows that language has ready access to all the vast intellectual wealth, which all the wisest nations of the earth have created and hoarded in the course of ninety generations" (3).

Gandhi explicitly refuted Macaulay's claims about English and argued that Indians had enabled the impoverishment of their own languages and in so doing enslaved themselves (1997, 103). While he agreed with Macaulay's insistence on the central importance of bolstering India with "modern" knowledge, he understood that Macaulay's vision would confirm the subjugation of Indians well beyond the achievement of national independence. Instead, Gandhi advanced and worked toward the idea of an India that employed the new Hindustani to serve intra-Indian political exchange while bolstering native dialects with the language of modernity. Both Hindustani and the native dialects would then shift and advance through proper use and increasing education.

Gandhi became the leader of the Hindustani Prachar Sabha, an organization aimed at mobilizing and spreading Hindustani across the country. In order to accomplish this task, he set out to create a fleet of rashtrabhasha workers across the nation whose advanced language training would then enable them to educate the masses in Hindustani. These rashtrabhasha workers, Gandhi insisted, should have "perfect mastery over both Hindi and Urdu." Only once they had mastered these two languages could they hope to be "true *Rashtrabhasha* workers" (1997, 55). Yet for those students who would be taught Hindustani, mastery was not the aim. They simply needed an "All-India heart" or an "All-India will" and Hindustani would come to them, not as a language that they would aim to hold dominion over but as a language that would unite them with others through a mutual and noncoercive devotion to the nation. The teachers of Hindustani would thus be Hindi and Urdu language masters, but their mastery would serve to establish an abiding unity among Indian communities through the ability to speak a common national language. The mastery practiced by some would lead, then, to the decolonization of others.

Across diverse geopolitical contexts, Fanon, Memmi, and Gandhi share a conception of colonial languages as holding mastery over the colonized. They also each, in very different though intimately connected ways, advance forms of linguistic "countermastery" as gateways to undoing the psychodynamics of colonization. Perhaps the fact that Gandhi, the world's most renowned practitioner of *self*-mastery, never considered himself a master of languages can serve as a valuable touchstone. Recalling the discussion in chapter 1 of Gandhi's inability to define the practice of *brahmacharya*, I suggest that here too Gandhi's practice exceeds his political conceptualizations. Mastery recurs in Gandhi's writings on language, but his own language practices present an unmasterful approach that might well be more radical than his stated politics.

Language and Literature in the Postcolony

As we have seen so far, language was a central problematic in the political discourses of anticolonialism. It was likewise a contentious debate in colonial and postcolonial literary production where writers theorized the vital work of literature in the realm of decolonization. The Francophone theorist and poet Aimé Césaire (who was, importantly here, Fanon's teacher) describes his use of French as innovative: "Whether I want to or not, as a poet I express myself in French, and clearly French literature has influenced me. But I want to emphasize very strongly that—while using as a point of departure the elements that French literature gave me—I have always striven to create a new language, one capable of communicating the African heritage. In other words, for me French was a tool that I wanted to use in developing a new means of expression. I wanted to create an Antillean French, a black French that, while still being French, had a black character" (2001, 83). Césaire begins with a sense of removal, a lack of agency—"whether I want to or not"—that is part of the subjectivization of any linguistic subject, and which marks his relationship to French as the language of his poetry. Like French literature, French language is also a "point of departure" for Césaire, who envisions his poetic use of language as a means of developing new forms of expression through surrealism. The fact that they are rooted in the colonial language reflects the historicity of French colonization in the Antilles, but surrealism works to undo the character of the language in order to shape it anew. Poetry breaks the "stranglehold" that the standard French form held over him, and surrealism offers a mode of summoning unconscious forces within the postcolonial subject and finding within the French language a fundamentally black character (82). Far from holding mastery over him, he envisions this new "black character" of French as a "weapon"—like Gandhi's practice of *satyagraha* discussed in chapter 1—that can be wielded to express colonial and postcolonial black subjectivities. Here we see the force of language, articulated through the metaphor of weaponry, yielded against itself: the French once used to colonize will now return through the colonized pen with a vengeful, recuperative force aimed toward decolonization.

The Martinican writer and poet Edouard Glissant draws on Césaire to contend that language itself cannot limit human expression even when it is an imposed or inherited tongue. To those who insist that the colonizer's language cannot reflect the colonial experience, Glissant retorts: "To say that is to dignify a language beyond its due. In our present world, the equivalence between self and language is an aberration that disguises the reality of dominance. Let us challenge the latter with the weapon of self-expression: our relationship with language, or languages, that we use" (1989, 171). What Glissant proposes is that power is more fundamental than both "self" and "language." These two latter categories "disguise" the reality of dominance that underlies them. The self and language come into existence because of already existing power relations, which following Glissant's thought means that unmasterful politics will enable the formation of new kinds of selves and new forms of language. I will turn to these new forms of language and subjectivity in the second half of this book, but for now what I want to emphasize is the "equivalence" between the self and language as an equation that for Glissant mischaracterizes the relation between them. Language for him is a "weapon" that can be wielded by the self regardless of the historical stakes that have led to its utterance by the speaking subject. The writer, then, who uses language as a mobilizing force need not be unduly hindered by the historicity of language. Extending Audre Lorde's (1984) famous assertion that you cannot dismantle the master's house with the master's tools, Glissant suggests that it is not the tools that pose the problem but the relations that precede and give rise to the tools as such.

In the postcolonial moment, we have witnessed a continuation of colonial language debates in literary production that hinge on metaphors of violence and weaponry. Chinua Achebe and Ngũgĩ wa Thiong'o, both participants at the 1962 Conference of African writers of English Expression at Makerere University College in Uganda, illustrate the oppositional positions of this debate. In tracing their positions, however, we can see a fascinating affinity across both writers for seeking unmasterful relations to language at the same time as they continuously rely on violent metaphors to seek them out. With the publication of *Things Fall Apart* ([1958] 1994) and its rise to global popularity, Achebe's aim was to speak of "African experience in a world-wide language" (1965, 29). For him, the fact that this worldwide language is English is almost incidental: realizing that a "world language" is critical for cross-cultural exchange, Achebe concedes to English as the language of his literary production even while he acknowledges that there is both "good" and "evil" that accompany this inheritance (28). Speaking of the flourishing body of literature being produced by African writers in the midsixties, Achebe identifies a "new voice" emerging from Africa that articulates a particularly African experience through English prose (29). For him, the English language must accept its "submission to many different kinds of use," and in this sense English offers itself to a practice of antimastery in which new forms of English emerge from within it (29).

For the serious postcolonial writer, argues Achebe, the task is to use English pragmatically. As a world language, writers must carve it in ways that make it speak to their own postcolonial cultural experiences. Here I employ the metaphor of carving intentionally, since Achebe goes on to suggest that "a serious writer must look for an animal whose blood can match the power of his offering" (1965, 29). For Achebe, this "animal" is the English language, and a skilled writer can sacrifice it through the manipulation of its grammar, its syntax, and its style and in so doing render the postcolonial literary text as global offering. (I return explicitly to the complex relations between language use and animal sacrifice in chapter 4 through my reading of J. M. Coetzee's lecture-narrative *The Lives of Animals*.) The metaphors of sacrifice and offering here return the violence of the English language back unto itself: If English was first a violent imposition on the colonized tongue, its sacrifice by the (formerly) colonized writer is redemptive in the Fanonian sense, giving voice through violence to new forms of expression and being. Achebe declares that English is a "world language which history has forced down our throats," but rather than banishing English he envisions a counterassault on language that will reflect other forms of being (29). On African writing in English, Achebe declares: "My answer to the question, Can an African ever learn English well enough to be able to use it effectively in creative writing? is certainly yes. If on the other hand you ask: Can he ever learn to use it like a native speaker? I should say, I hope not. It is neither necessary nor desirable for him to be able to do so. The price a world language must be prepared to pay is submission to many different kinds of use" (29). Using English as a nonnative speaker, then, should not be an act aimed at language mastery. Rather, the use of the colonial language in postcolonial literature should aim to produce new forms of English that reflect the colonial and postcolonial experience and the cultural traditions from which they emerge. What is critical for Achebe is that in creating these new forms of English, in subjecting them to "sacrifice" and "submission," the writer always maintains the capacity of English as a "medium of international exchange" (29). The sacrifice of the colonizer's tongue is therefore only ever partial, because it insists on a sustained relation to Standard English that while potentially destabilizing to a global readership remains accessible to them. What emerges through Achebe's prose is a narrative in which the colonized writer must sacrifice, carve up, and consume the colonial tongue in order to digest it, and in so doing produce (or excrete) a new living language that would nourish a postcolonial body politic.

Implicitly evoking Shakespeare's wayward "savage" Caliban, Achebe declares of English that "for me there is no other choice. I have been given this language and I intend to use it" (1965, 30). Like Caliban, to whom I turn again in the coda, Achebe can decry colonization and its ongoing effects precisely through the language that has been thrust on him. Through language, he can curse his masters. Yet Achebe continues to express his great hope that there will be those who continue to carry on their ethnic traditions by writing in their native tongues, even while he himself reaches toward the global through his use of English prose. These ethnic literary traditions, he hopes, will "flourish" alongside the national ones that are being reflected through the colonizing language.

For the Kenyan writer Ngũgĩ wa Thiong'o, Achebe's hope for a thriving ethnic literature appears willfully to forget that the language of the colonizer is inextricable from the colonizer's ongoing economic and political power. In his chapter "The Language of African Literature," Ngũgĩ recalls his experience at the Makerere meeting of African writers. There, he recalls, "the only question which preoccupied us was how best to make the borrowed tongues carry the weight of our African experience by, for instance, making them 'prey' on African proverbs and other peculiarities of African speech and folklore" (1986, 7). Against this ideological tendency in African writing, Ngũgĩ famously abandons his "Afro-English" writing in 1977 in order to write in his native Gikuyu. By this time, of course, Ngũgĩ had established himself as a significant name in postcolonial African writing, and his notoriety as such ensured that his writing would be translated to circulate globally. For Ngũgĩ, writing in one's native language enriches the language and reflects the experience of one's own community, one's own history, by refusing the physical and mental shackles of colonization. Implicating Achebe, he provocatively asks: "What is the difference between a politician who says Africa cannot do without imperialism and the writer who says Africa cannot do without European languages?" (26). Since the fact of English as a "global language" cannot for Ngũgĩ be extricated from the fact of its colonial mission, he refuses Achebe's logic of writing in a language that is decipherable by a world audience, since that world is a direct reflection of colonial mastery. Ngũgĩ concludes "The Language of African Literature," however, with this declaration: "We African writers are bound by our calling to do for our languages what Spencer, Milton and Shakespeare did for English; what Pushkin and Tolstoy did for Russian; indeed what all writers in world history have done for their languages by meeting the challenge of creating literature in them, which process later opens the languages for philosophy, science, technology and all the other areas of human creative endeavors" (1986, 29). While Ngũgĩ rehearses colonial discussions about language recuperation and revitalization, he does so in an interesting twist that situates European literary "masters" as models for what African writers are "bound" to replicate. If the European literary giants of the last centuries are models for African writers through what they have done for English and Russian languages, Ngũgĩ runs the risk of remaining bound to a logic of literary mastery that may well efface some of the critically unmasterful potentialities of African languages, literature, and imaginative capacities. What would it mean to turn away from European writers designated as "literary masters" toward African artists and storytellers whose own worldviews and cultural deployments could alternately become antimasterful models of imbuing native languages with new potentialities?

If brute European force confirmed the physical subjugation of the colony, language for Ngũgĩ marked its "spiritual subjugation" (1986, 9). To redress this subjugation, to reclaim African identity and to refuse the subsuming nature of colonial languages, in 1968 Ngũgĩ famously called for the abolition of the English department at his then home institution at the University of Nairobi. Responding to proposed developments of the English department and its ties to other departments, the justification for the necessity of English is articulated by way of a need to study "the historic continuity of a single culture" (1973, 145). If this is so, Ngũgĩ asks, "Why can't African literature be at the center so that we can view other cultures in relationship to it?" (146). To answer this question we must recall Macaulay's stance on Sanskrit literature and the vernacular languages of India: they are simply too unrefined, too void of elegance and too inept at expressing the more profound and philosophical subtleties of human existence. Ngũgĩ insists that the continued centrality of English language and culture in Africa is neocolonial, a pedagogical device to ensure the ongoing supremacy of the Western world and its traditions. Instead, he summons a course of literary study that would move from the local toward the global regardless of whether the local includes works that have been subjectively bestowed with titles of literary excellence. For him, it is urgent to study oneself from the point of view of one's culture first and to expand from this point toward other linguistic and literary traditions.

While Achebe and Ngũgĩ appear as opposing figures in the postcolonial language debates, their own uses of language similarly rehearse the violence at stake in claiming or recrafting language in the postcolony. Employing animal metaphors of "sacrifice" and "prey" to think the relation between humans and their languages, both writers take for granted human mastery over the nonhuman world. Language is repeatedly figured as something to hunt, to kill, to subject. Yet this metaphorical attachment to human practices of mastery is also challenged through their mutual insistence on thinking postcolonial language *beyond* mastery, as a relation of human reconfiguration and entanglement that does not necessitate mastery. Achebe does not long for African writers to master the languages of his colonizers; he envisions instead an African literary landscape that implicitly engages newfangled forms of the colonial language that redraft rather than master the colonial linguistic tradition. Even while he wants English to "submit" itself to various uses, this submission does not for him entail wholesale domination. In turn, Ngũgĩ articulates a desire for writing in African languages that reflects specific historical, cultural, and spiritual realities, even while he looks back to European literary masters as inspiration for African language revival and literary production. Postcolonial literary debates are, like the discourses of decolonization, fundamentally concerned with language politics. Yet quite unlike the colonial-era debates that continuously returned in more and less explicit ways to the need for language mastery, these writers take up a relation to language that is ambivalently situated between masterful and unmasterful forms. While there is much disagreement in these debates, the will toward language mastery begins to dissipate and is replaced by the possibilities that languages embody—or can be crafted to embody—through the pens of colonized writers. Anticolonial thinkers tended to insist (even sometimes despite themselves) on language mastery as a crucial practice aimed at undoing the force of colonial rule in the colonies without theorizing the inextricable relations among forms of mastery. Postcolonial writers like Achebe and Ngũgĩ, while positioning themselves in opposition to each other, share a desire for unmasterful ways of formulating the relation between language and the postcolonial imagination.

World (Literature) Mastery

In *Thou Shalt Not Speak My Language* (2008), the Moroccan writer Abdelfattah Kilito asks: "Can one possess two languages? Can one master them equally?" Although Kilito's central concerns are with translation and with the problems that mastering multiple languages poses for translation, he steps back to ask:

> Can one possess any language? I remember hearing something, the source of which I have not yet been able to find, about one of the ancients who described his relationship to language in this way: "I defeated her then she defeated me, then I defeated her and she defeated

me again." His relationship with language is tense, and the war between them has its ups and downs, but language, this ferocious creature that refuses to be tamed, always has the last word. The battle always ends with her victory, leaving one no choice but to make truce and to surrender, however reluctantly. (21)

If today the discourses of world literature remain preoccupied with the problems and politics of translation—as Emily Apter (2005) signals by beginning her "manifesto" with the declaration that "everything is translatable" and ending with the assertion that "nothing is translatable"—Kilito reminds us that an engagement with translation must first and foremost attend to the power relations between the speaker and language itself. Here the unidentified "ancient" characterizes his relation to a notably feminine language as an unending battle with a "ferocious creature" who continues to win. Although Kilito does not answer his own query, he foregrounds that language has a long history of being framed as the enemy. Indeed, the problem of translation often misses a step that inhibits the inquiry. The ancient's formulation of language rhymes with Heidegger's assertion that "man acts as though *he* were the shaper and master of language, while in fact *language* remains the master of man" (1975, 146). Despite this, contemporary language discourses continue to think language as that which must be mastered or subjugated, as something that we chase after in order to conquer, to own, to use at our own wills.

To be in a position to study language, as Edward Said (1994) insisted, means to be in a position in which one must contend with the power of the act and its relations to the nonlinguistic power relations that the pursuit entails. To vie for mastery is to ignore these relations and to isolate oneself in the "ivory tower" without recourse to the real world effects that intellectual engagement produces. To believe that mastery (of texts or of languages) is possible, and to desire such mastery, solidifies our complicity with the very sources of imperialism that so many intellectuals and activists are wont to resist. For serious students of language, for those who continue to struggle toward a nuanced understanding of multiple languages, or even one's own native tongue, and who believe that language learning is always inevitably a lifelong pursuit, the concept of linguistic mastery should seem perverse. When you study language, any language, you learn quickly that you do not possess it. To the contrary, the study of language and literature is precisely the study of how language escapes, evades, and crystallizes differently at different times and through different speakers.

In the history of my own language learning, Hindi is one at which I have remained woefully (even shamefully) novice. After years of graduate school struggle to possess it, like Kilito, I found myself defeated. Almost as if in reverse of Gandhi—who as we have seen claimed to have failed to master his colonial tongue—I was a child of the Indian diaspora raised and educated as a speaker of colonial languages (English and French). As an emergent postcolonialist—and a comparative literature student no less—I found myself vying to become "fluent" in a language that symbolized (albeit perversely) my heritage. Hindi was so heavily loaded with historical significance and a personal desire to become "properly" Indian (identity politics haunts even those of us who eschew it) that I could not in any sense relax in relation to its learning. It pained me deeply that the white peers with whom I studied soared so quickly and so far beyond me in their language skill, while I punished myself unrelentingly for not having *already known* what felt to be "rightfully" mine.

In Hindi, one commonly expresses one's ability to speak the language as follows: *Hindi mujhe aati hain*, or "Hindi comes to me." I do not possess the language. Rather, the language brings itself to me. Somewhere between my summoning, my calling it forth, and its own mobility and malleability, it arrives—almost agentially—and I speak it. It is as though when we speak to another *through* language, we are always also in conversation *with* language itself. What I could not concede during those years of torturous language training was that language moves the speaking subject; it is not the speaker who controls it. I could not let language come to me precisely because I was too busy trying to claim Hindi as my own, which was also an act of covering up my historical losses and my inadequacies as a hybrid subject. Mastery here turns out to be a fantasy, and its rhetoric is used to justify ever more mastery—of language itself, but also of my own body (like Fanon's tongue), of perceived enemies, of whole and diverse collectives. What would it mean to refuse the rhetoric and pursuit of mastery? Could such a gesture dramatically alter the ways that we conceive of ourselves as scholars? I am suggesting that it is false to imagine ourselves as masters of languages, authors, bodies of texts, areas. We must abandon mastery in order to give ourselves up to wider and less hostile horizons. It should be clear that I am not insisting that we all avoid a skilled relationship to our intellectual fields. Rather, I am advancing a practice of vulnerable engagement, a practice of opening ourselves up to our dependence on other discourses, peoples, beings, languages (that we know and do not yet know), and things that give rise to the ways that we think and the claims that we make.

The current popularity of world literature sweeping literary studies has often abandoned the more vulnerable approaches to language and literature that began to emerge through the postcolonial language debates. *Weltliteratur*, a resurrection of an old concept with newly defined aims, emerged initially in the early nineteenth century in the work of Johann Wolfgang von Goethe (1973) to describe a universal conception of literatures around the world that together form a whole. Later, Marx and Engels (2002) recycled the term to describe the global circulation of literatures as part of a capitalist network. These early evocations of world literature characterize the "universal" in a thoroughly Eurocentric sense, understanding Western Europe—with perhaps a smattering of Asian languages and literatures— as the true heart and value of literary studies. After the decolonization struggles of the mid-twentieth century and the upsurge of multiculturalism in the later part of the century, world literature has resurfaced with an aim toward a self-consciously non-Eurocentric focus. Today, studying Kikuyu should be no less relevant than studying French, and rather than to approach literary studies through a politics of linguistic supremacy, many scholars aim to redress the damages done by linguistic dominion and to read the intricacies of all linguistic and literary traditions as uniquely valuable and contributing to a global literary landscape.

The central problem facing world literature is therefore how to conceive of world literature scholars, since they cannot possibly attain linguistic fluency in every world language. David Damrosch correctly refuses a construction of the world literary scholar as one who strives in vain to master the whole breadth of world literary traditions. In *What Is World Literature?*, Damrosch urges us away from "a possessive mastery of the world's cultural productions" (2003, 303). Instead, he envisions "collaborative work" among "broad-minded specialists" that will lead us toward a more fully global practice of literary study (286). This vision of collectivity attempts to turn a prospective disciplinary crisis—the impossibility of truly being a scholar of all world literatures—into a communal intellectual enterprise. Across keynote addresses in the last decade, however, Damrosch has at times articulated this as a collectivity among specialized "language masters." This irresistible return to mastery from one of its outspoken opponents signals the pervasive logic of mastery that underscores the fields of world and comparative literature.[7]

Of course, comparatists such as Damrosch employ the term "mastery" to signal not straightforward domination but rather great skill. Yet, as I argued in my introduction to this book, such skill can never be detached from the relations of power that make it possible. Skill and power are both rhetorically and economically linked to the mastery of other peoples and places, and to forget this fact is to abandon the foundations of the practice of world literature itself as a movement to bring all languages and literary traditions together in a dialogue that is not contingent on domination and subjugation. The demonstration of our skill and power, our "mastery" of texts and languages, should not be thought outside its referential connection to the "dominion," "superiority," and "control" that both the term and the practice also entail. A renaming of our pursuits as literary scholars would miss the point altogether: This is not a problem of semantics, of substituting one noun for another. What we must critically consider is our own discourse as language scholars in order to examine the contradictions and slippages that define our work. (This would be true of all scholarship, which relies in every way on language.) The radical gesture of giving up mastery is imperative because, whether implicitly or explicitly, our work bears on a world of power relations that exceeds our attention to language. The postcolonial language debates encapsulated by Achebe and Ngũgĩ took the question of language in the postcolony seriously by attempting to engage language in unmasterful ways. This movement toward the unmasterful approach to literature is what is lost in the discourse of world literature today.

Damrosch's notion of collective intellectual engagement is certainly compelling—even necessary—at a moment in which every aspect of intimate and intellectual life is being increasingly privatized and corporatized. Yet his vision of a scholarly commune of masters forgets the complexity of language and literature as entities that, as poststructuralist and postcolonial discourses have encouraged us to recognize, themselves refuse mastery. The study of world literature in this sense signals the problem of mastery that is at stake in literary studies and, critically, for intellectual thought more broadly. As I will illustrate in chapter 4, literary studies is governed by its will toward mastery and despite itself continuously returns to this aim.

If what distinguishes world literature today from its early iterations is its particular drive to undo the ideological supremacy of a Western European literary tradition—what Dipesh Chakrabarty (2007) refers to as the gesture of "provincializing Europe"—the rhetoric of mastery that grounds the field reveals its own misleading aims. The notion of mastery therefore needs urgently to be reconsidered as the driving force and the aim of the field. At a moment in which the language of mastery sounds so harmoniously with the discourse of U.S. imperialism and the global reach of neocolonialism, it is essential that we redress the aim of literary and linguistic mastery even of the smallest bodies of authors or texts.

Edward Said echoes the necessity of this gesture by summoning Friedrich Nietzsche's formulation of the truth of history as "a mobile army of metaphors and metonyms" whose meaning is to be ceaselessly interpreted without the drive to solve the riddles of the past (2004, 58). Indeed, Said gives rise to a postcolonial thinking that is driven by the intersections between language and colonization, and that is concerned with how the hybridization of languages speaks to or against neocolonial forms of domination. Aligned with the anticolonial thinkers who came before him, Said makes frequent claims about intellectual mastery without giving pause. He famously argued in *Orientalism* that the "unremitting ambition [of Orientalism] was to master *all* of a world, not some easily delimited part of it such as an author or a collection of texts" (1979, 109). Here he points to the *limitless* scope of Orientalism, the absurdity of imagining that the Orient could be mastered as such. Yet to Said's mind, the absurdity of this ambition was less in the drive toward mastery itself than in the notion that knowledge of some far-flung and nebulous place called "the Orient" *could* be mastered. The central problem of Orientalism as both intellectual practice and ideology is that in order to gain so-called mastery over the orient, it had to conflate and regurgitate common narratives about vastly different cultures and histories. If Said proved this body of knowledge to be both racist and absurd, we must in turn consider the role that mastery itself plays in this intellectual practice. As scholars, what we learn from Orientalism (the text and the scholarly practice) should not be that we must limit our reach as masters over our fields. Selecting "easily delimited parts" for mastery, or knowing how to "limit or to enlarge realistically the scope of [our] discipline's claims," binds us to more limited, precise forms of mastery. Rethinking what we do as something other than mastery—whether over vast or miniscule, human or inhuman terrains—pushes us toward different forms of scholarship and different relations to our practices—indeed, toward different relations to the worlds we engage.

The writings of activists, political theorists, and literary scholars that I have engaged in the first half of this book form an archive of resistance to and engagements with mastery in anticolonial contexts. These thinkers passionately sought to resist colonial mastery while remaining entangled with other iterations of masterful practice and thought. While a majority of my attention has been centered on the ways in which "alternate" forms of mastery are unthinkingly reproduced in efforts to disengage colonial mastery, I have also gleaned from their writings the crucial seeds of a dehumanist practice. For the remainder of this book, I am going to be illustrating how postcolonial literature opens us toward dehumanist subjectivities, practices, and politics. My aim will be to approach literature with an unmasterful method of engagement, reading vulnerably the ensnarements of mastery in figures who, like me, desire and fail to resist it. My abiding interest in the postcolonial literary archive rhymes with Wynter's assertion that we, as humans, are products of narrative (1984, 50). For Wynter, literature produces the humans we understand and feel ourselves to be, and it may well be that through literature, through the narratives it casts and questions, we can begin to produce ourselves otherwise. What kinds of subjects—and what kinds of objects—can we be for ourselves and for others if we loosen the hold of mastery?

CHAPTER 3

Posthumanitarian Fictions

Despite the popular mantra of multiculturalism in the 1980s, I grew up in central Canada at a moment when interracial marriages were frowned upon, a moment when old women responded to the childish misbehaviors of our brood by whispering *It's the mixed blood!,* a moment when the word "shit" circulated with schoolyard titillation to describe the color of my skin. My father was a child of Partition, born in India in a region of rural Punjab that would, in 1947 when he was six years old, become Pakistan. In the mass upheavals and extraordinary violence of that political moment, he migrated with his family to Amritsar, just on the edge of the Indian border hedging against a newly carved Pakistan. He would later immigrate to Canada to study at McGill University in Montreal, where he would meet my mother. She was herself a child of the diaspora, born in Ireland to a German Jewish mother who had been sent away from Berlin with the rise of Hitler, and to an Irish intellectual father who would accept a position at McGill and shift his family to Canada in the 1950s. My parents were drawn to each other's differences and beauty, filled with the enchantments of the 1960s, the glamor and possibility of unions across divides. But theirs was an uneasy marriage, fraught with cultural differences and the legacies of personal and political violence that persisted and proliferated through them. By the time I was born—the fourth and last of a motley hybrid crew—the utopian spirit of the '60s had quite dispersed.

When I was young, my father completed medical school and we moved from a two-bedroom unit in a duplex to a huge, bedraggled blond-brick home in an area menacingly known as "the Gates." Couched in a small bend of the Assiniboine River, it was an estuary of Winnipeg's old money, the homes of the nation's early bankers and their ilk. It was made clear to us that *our kind* was not uniformly welcome in this neighborhood. But my mother had a special fancy for historical homes, and for trees whose lives and legacies far exceeded our own. Despite my father's protests, we moved into what would become my mother's decades-long preoccupation: restoring, improving, and preserving a small space of the earth and its minor histories.

The lore of my family casts me as a difficult child, signaled unabashedly by the nickname "the little tornado"—a name bestowed on me during the one and only visit from my Babu Uncle, my father's brother from whom he was mostly estranged. My mother sketches the scene of a preverbal me tearing out my hair in frustration (from where this frustration emerges is conspicuously absent from the narrative) and offering it to her in menacing handfuls. I was a no-less-difficult teen—suspended regularly from school, remiss in class participation and attendance, and impatient with the confines of my world.

But there is a singular story couched within this family lore, and it is a story that I have always quietly cherished whenever my mother feels compelled to share it. It is the story of my inaugural act as a "humanitarian": I was perhaps five years old (in the narrative, I am always younger) when, wandering home alone after visiting a friend, I saw a white man in tattered clothing eating out of a neighbor's garbage can. I was shocked at the sight and understood that I had a responsibility to act. I ran home in tears and pleaded with my mother to help, which she did readily. We brought him home and sat together in the backyard eating homemade pizza, learning the details of how he had come to be scavenging for discarded food in our affluent neighborhood. As it turned out, he was a ward of the province living in a group home for people with "mental deficiencies" in a neighborhood adjacent to ours. My mother would come to discover that his overseers had left their wards alone for a long holiday weekend without anyone present to distribute food and medications.

For all the ways in which I would or could not conform, for all of my bad behavior within the narrative remembering of our shared family history, this was my narrative of redemption. It is perhaps unsurprising, then, that it became profoundly influential to my own self-formation, to how I learned to read myself in relation to the more negative (and indeed more frequent) narratives that circulated within the family. This redemptive narrative was one that propped me up against an errant past; humanitarianism became for me a kind of refuge from the tornado that had otherwise defined me.

Through my readings of the recurring humanitarian figures of postcolonial literature, I began to return again and again to this redemptive scene of my own self-formation. We do not always understand why we attach ourselves to certain things and ideas in the world, yet as I reread these literary figures, I began to think critically about my own formative narratives—narratives that, in ways both clear and less accessible, have shaped my self-understanding as a particular kind of subject. There was, indeed, a critical continuity between this scene of redemptive self-formation and the fact that I would pursue a doctoral degree in the critical humanities. One seemed to lead directly into the other, as though the work of the humanitarian and the work of the humanities were sutured. Yet through a vulnerable engagement with posthumanitarian fictions, I began to recognize mastery at play in what is commonly understood as a height of ethical action in the service of others. Becoming vulnerable to the self-narrations of other subjects, I also saw how the more and less overtly humanitarian aspects of my own self-constitution were in fact intimately interlaced with those less redemptive qualities that had also formed me. Rather than to rely on a dialectical ethics in which we are either "good" or "bad" subjects, an antimasterful approach to reading our own histories—and the histories of others—opens us to the messiness of our pasts, to the entanglements of our lives, and to the unsolvable riddles that shape us.

Moving in this chapter between readings of J. M. Coetzee's novel *Life & Times of Michael K* (1983) and Mahasweta Devi's Bengali short story "Little Ones" (1998), I engage postcolonial literary texts that pressure the ways humanitarian work has been imagined, represented, and enforced in the neocolonial present.[1] These texts, which are exemplary illustrations of what I call posthumanitarian fictions, hinge on the narratives that humanitarian characters tell themselves to confirm their work, narratives that position them as inherently nonmasterful actors committed to the labor of advancing humanity. I am interested in the figure of the humanitarian precisely because of its attachment to narratives of humanitarian benevolence that are revealed to have concrete, material effects in the production of human inequalities. That these narratives are postcolonial is crucial to my reading of posthumanitarian fictions, because I employ the term "postcolonial" not merely to signal particular geopolitical spaces but rather to name a constitutive modality of global political economy today. In this sense, my movement between the terms "postcolonial" and "neocolonial" insists on the ongoing entanglements and critical forms of mastery that carry over an imagined temporal divide between formal colonial rule and its afterlives.

The figure of the humanitarian and its narrative attachments illustrate how our conceptions of the "best" human practices in the globalized world today remain committed to—indeed founded on—forms of violence and erasure that continue to be framed uncritically across popular and academic discourses. In these texts, humanitarians, who desire to work in the service of others less fortunate, finally cannot be extricated from the unequal power relations they seek to redress.[2] They emerge as figures that stand in opposition to the colonial mastery of others but also unwittingly work alongside its modern-day iterations. In this way, they represent the complex entanglements of politics and ethics through forms of humanitarian aid, and they offer an urgently needed perspective on the neocolonial valences of humanitarianism as ideology and practice. Despite the fact that humanitarian characters *desire* deeply to act in ethical ways, these narratives emphasize the complicity of humanitarian actors with the systems they oppose. I engage complicity through Mark Sanders, who argues that "when opposition takes the form of a demarcation *from* something . . . it cannot, it follows, be untouched by that to which it opposes itself. Opposition takes its first steps from a footing of complicity" (2002, 9).[3] Etymologically signaling a "folded-together-ness," complicity becomes for Sanders "the very basis for responsibly entering into, maintaining, or breaking off a given affiliation or attachment" (x). In this chapter, I turn to the humanitarian as a crucial figure through which to begin to reframe and renarrate the complicities of liberal subjectivity broadly, and to pressure us to loosen the attachments to which, as individual readers, we cling in order to frame ourselves as particular kinds of subjects.

Set amid an unnamed South African civil war during apartheid, Coetzee's novel charts the path of the harelipped protagonist, Michael K. Having spent his life outcast and institutionalized, K is driven by ecological attachments and by acts of cultivation. After the untimely death of his mother, he desires to extricate himself entirely from his war-torn environment, investing himself in the landscape as a refugee of war. Toward the novel's end, K is captured by the state and, after his collapse, is sent to a camp hospital where the medical staff aims to restore his health in order to release him once again into a prisoner work camp. At this moment, the novel abandons the otherwise omniscient narrative voice, shifting instead to the first-person narration of an unnamed pharmacist hired as a wartime medical officer. Through the narration of the officer, a self-characterized humanitarian actor, the reader is delivered into liberal desire squarely within and alongside the frustrations of the humanitarian worker. At this juncture, the novel recounts the medical officer's bewildering encounter with K, whose emaciated body by all medical accounts should no longer be living. Against his patient's own desires to be left alone, the officer is driven to restore his patient to proper health. Ultimately, this drive to heal his patient is revealed to be fundamentally entangled with the medical officer's need to enforce his self-understanding as an agent of goodness.

In "Little Ones," Devi emphasizes the longing of the humanitarian actor to extricate himself from a relation of mastery. Mr. Singh, the story's protagonist, is a government employee hired for a short-term position to establish a relief camp in an impoverished region of Bengal. Singh's mission is to oversee the rationing of annual supplies for the starving *adivasi* (tribals)—the indigenous peoples of India who are excluded from state-afforded rights. He finds himself thrust into his role as a relief officer, and while initially repelled by the human bodies of those in need, he quickly comes to embrace his exalted status as a humanitarian. But Singh's humanitarianism reaches its limits when, at the end of the story, he is confronted by fugitives of the state who, having been deprived of basic nutrition, have become (in)human pygmies. Even more horrifying than the starved and emaciated bodies of those Singh has been serving, these unbelievable "inhuman" bodies force him to concede to his own complicity within a postcolonial system that produces healthy human subjects at the expense of others. Assailed by these unbelievable bodies, Singh's alibi as a good humanitarian subject collapses in on itself.

Posthumanitarian fictions such as these are a subgenre of postcolonial literature that create and then problematize alliances between the reader and humanitarian characters, functioning through the psychodynamics of identification at play in reading.[4] Situated in relation to the humanitarian, the reader becomes aligned with humanitarian ideology. As humanitarian protagonists confront their complicities within systems that produce their objects of aid, the reader dwells intimately within the narrative frames and sutures of other "good" subjects. Posthumanitarian fictions represent characters whose work is revealed to harmonize with the more overt force of colonial mastery, and readers are led through the structural form of the texts into a double identification with humanitarian figures *and* the aid recipients against whom they come to struggle. By doing so, these fictions ultimately urge readers beyond a politics of compassion for the other, directing the reader back to its own complicit relations.[5]

Posthumanitarian fictions urge us toward a radical revision of the discourses of human rights and humanitarian action and of the notion of the properly "human" that gives rise to them. They summon the erasures and exclusions that make these efforts possible, implicating the reader through narrative devices that highlight, and in turn upset, our alliances. Novels, Lynn Hunt (2007) has argued, were instrumental forces in giving rise to human rights through their capacity to represent and create empathy from bourgeois readers toward "common" people. She illustrates how eighteenth-century upper-class readers (not unremarkably, mostly bourgeois women) began to imagine the interiority of lower-class people through narrative representation, creating a frame of empathy that made possible a thinking of (other white, Western) humans as beings with a critical likeness that were deserving of "universal" rights. For Hunt, whose work is invested in a politics of empathy, reading novels allowed privileged readers to imagine that all other humans (delineated via the shared whiteness of English and French peoples) had an interiority much like their own.

In his analysis of what he calls the "Third World *Bildungsromane*," Joseph Slaughter (2007) traces how empathetic reading takes on a much less idyllic political function. This increasingly popular genre represents despotism abroad through characters that are able to escape or challenge the barbarity of their native lands. Through these texts, readers identify with characters that have suffered and survived the atrocities of elsewhere. They are able to feel that they themselves have, through the act of reading and thus "knowing," staged a "humanitarian intervention." However much I may want to recuperate a sense of the reader as one engaged in the cultivation of critical capacities, Slaughter's formulation warns how readily reading can reaffirm rather than challenge global politics. Indeed, as Freud argued in *Civilization and Its Discontents*, reading practices based on empathy have a disturbing habit of allowing the reader to insert themselves universally: "We shall always tend to consider people's distress objectively—that is, to place ourselves, with our own wants and sensibilities, in *their* conditions, and then to examine what occasions we should find in them for experiencing happiness or unhappiness. This method of looking at things, which seems objective because it ignores the variations in subjective sensibility, is, of course, the most subjective possible, since it puts one's own mental states in the place of any others, unknown though they may be" (2010, 62). Because empathetic reading does not challenge the reader's own subjectivity but instead allows them unthinkingly to impose their own "wants and sensibilities" on others, it becomes a masterful gesture in which the self is always authorized above and beyond its others. Empathetic reading might allow readers to extend their sense of who is human, but without calling into question the presupposed humanity of the reader and the politics that gave rise to it as such.

This is precisely why vulnerable reading is so crucial to the exchange between reader and text. In contrast to the work of the novel in the eighteenth century and to empathetic readings of contemporary representations of Third World despotism, posthumanitarian fictions unsettle the narrative sutures of the empathetic reader—to open the fissures that join the reader to its textual allies, to pressure the racial politics of the humanitarian/recipient relation, and in so doing to query the reader's particular claims to and performances of humanity. Posthumanitarian fictions anticipate—but crucially, do not announce—ways of being that exceed or depart from the hegemonic "human" of modernity: the bounded, Western, white, heteromasculine, able-bodied subject. This work of the text on the psychic and bodily life of the reader is crucial to the double-pronged project of dehumanism: on the one hand, a critique of Western humanism through attention to narrative and its fissures, to how exclusions are revealed through close attention to narratives that seem otherwise seamless; and on the other, an opening toward alternative, creative, and as yet unimagined forms of political action and relation. Critically, this opening toward the unknown is radically different from the psychic splitting of the subject. The latter defensively closes down the possibilities by moving too quickly to cordon off the good from the bad, the pure from the persecutory. By bringing readers into this defensive disavowal of the split subject, posthumanitarian fictions invite us into the splits and crevices of our own subjectivities, inviting us to inhabit ourselves differently.

Humanitarian Fetishism

Posthumanitarian fictions enable us not only to see the interrelations among structural, material, and ideological forms of oppression but also to begin to envision alternate forms of alliance that exceed those that currently define global relations. In posthumanitarian fictions, narrative form and fissure reveal humanitarianism to be part of an ideological imaginary—a way of relating to the structural and material facts of the neocolonial enterprise through what I call "humanitarian fetishism." Coupling Marx's (1992) formulation of the commodity with Freud's ([1962] 2000) conception of the fetish, humanitarian fetishism is a process that negates one's own complicity in the mastery of the state over its disenfranchised subjects by obscuring the material, social, and psychic aspects of humanitarian practice. In Marxist theory, "commodity fetishism" names the process of disavowing the "definite social relation between men" in the production of material objects (1992, 165). This disavowal leads to the fantasy that in capitalism one simply exchanges money for an object. Marx compels us to recognize that material objects do not magically appear but are produced by and through material labor, which is in fact the source of an object's value. Fetishism in Freud takes a decidedly psychic turn, naming the overvaluation of an inappropriate sexual object. What is important here is that for Freud the choice of the fetish object has a very determinate psychological etiology. A fetish is a fantasmatic way of covering over a traumatic realization; in response to trauma, which must be disavowed, the subject immediately rescripts the original trauma with an object-ideal that governs the subject's fantasy life.

Despite a long-standing difficulty in reconciling the Marxist and Freudian accounts of fetishism within critical theory, Christopher Breu concatenates the two versions in his analysis of what he calls "avatar fetishism." Drawing on Slavoj Žižek, Breu is interested in how materialities and bodies are disavowed by postmodern culture's production of identities. For Breu, "avatar fetishism" names the disavowal of "the material processes, objects, and embodiments that structure and enable everyday life in our ostensibly post-industrial era" (2014, 22). In psychoanalytic terms, avatar fetishism is "akin to the construction of an ideal self or an ideal ego" (22). Breu's merging of the valences of Marxist and psychoanalytic fetishisms helps us to see how the inability to register and attend to the materialities and material agencies that make particular kinds of life possible is intimately tied to processes of subject formation and of psychosocial life.

While humanitarian action hinges on relations of power (since the humanitarian is one who is in a position of relative power and thus able to offer aid to those in need), posthumanitarian fictions illustrate how this power becomes masterful through humanitarian fetishism. By obscuring and enforcing one's own power in the humanitarian effort, by upholding the narrative of humanitarian benevolence and disavowing material complicities, humanitarian characters come to reproduce the very structures of power they desire to dismantle. The humanitarian ego becomes the benevolent master of someone else's house. Singh's and the medical officer's work turns out to humanize themselves but does little to uphold the humanity of those they seek to uplift. Critically, this process of humanization that looks to the other but ultimately turns back toward oneself echoes the historical justification for the humanities, which has sought expressly to humanize its students. Humanitarian fetishism allows these characters, like those engaged in the humanities, to fantasize about becoming more fully human precisely by repressing their participation in the constitutive dehumanization of aid recipients. Put simply, humanitarians can only come to understand themselves as the kinds of subjects that do good in the world by ignoring the masterful material relations that enable their work. Humanitarian fetishism applies not strictly to those who work in explicit spaces of aid but is also a critical compulsion of liberal subjectivity itself. Focusing on the figure of the humanitarian throws humanitarian fetishism into relief by turning readers toward our own relations to mastery, whether we pretend to be unmasterful in order to prop up the ideal of our benevolent subjectivities or we believe in "good" forms of mastery as necessary to the elevation of all humans.

In her work on the politics of humanitarian aid, Lisa Smirl argues that "the practices involved in post-crisis reconstruction by the international humanitarian aid community are inseparable from the production and reconstruction of global relations and identities" (2008, 237). Smirl illustrates how humanitarian aid practices, and in particular the spatio-material politics that enable such practices, ultimately confirm and "reconstruct" the disparities between aid workers and those they seek to assist. The aim of Smirl's work is to intervene in what she calls the "humanitarian imaginary," a mode of intervention that is based on "idealized assumptions regarding social organization and community" (2015, 2). The practices of humanitarianism reproduce, often devastatingly, the divides between the Global North and South. Indeed, as Costas Douzinas (2007) and Elizabeth Bernstein (2010) have argued from quite different vantage points, humanitarianism can easily couple with the military objectives of imperial power.

Both *Life & Times of Michael K* and "Little Ones" pressure the "humanitarian imaginary," emphasizing how humanitarian subjectivities are foundationally shaped by forms of mastery they persistently disavow. In these stories, the impulse toward mastery over other human bodily and psychic lives cannot be extricated from the aims of humanitarian characters, and the power to disavow one's own complicity becomes folded into mastery's particular function in the neocolonial crisis zone. As fictions, these texts reveal the always fantasmatic nature of mastery, positioning disavowal as that which paradoxically makes mastery flourish. The qualities of mastery that I elaborated in the introduction to this book emerge subtly but powerfully across these stories: despite their own profound desires, humanitarian characters work to distinguish themselves from their objects of aid, to form hierarchical relations between themselves and their aid targets, and to extend this relation across time.

What we see through representations of humanitarian action in the postcolony is a humanitarian subject that is split. On the one hand, the humanitarian sustains a self-narration as a benevolent political subject working to amend the damages of oppressive regimes. On the other hand, this subject disavows its material and ideological entanglements with neocolonial power. Repeatedly, the humanitarian protagonists of these fictions cannot bear to confront their complicities and they cling to a need to neatly demarcate the good from the bad. By inviting readers to identify with humanitarian protagonists, posthumanitarian fictions urge readers to attend to their own fictions, to the ways their conceptions of themselves as fundamentally benevolent often require a forgetting of the negative valences of their entanglements. Posthumanitarian fictions can in this sense be read as narratives *about* narratives and are fictions that beckon readers to engage literature as an ethical terrain from which intimate forms of self-reflection become critical potentialities.

The spatio-material politics of humanitarianism resounds with what Fanon in the colonial context called the ever-present "lines of force" that structured the colonies (1963, 38). For Fanon, the spatial politics of the colony revealed overtly the force of the colonial relation; the colonies were divided into "compartments"—different zones of restriction and access that reinforced the power of the master while ensuring the subjugation of the slave. Emphasizing the spatial politics of queer life, Sara Ahmed builds on Fanon to argue that "colonialism makes the world 'white,' which is of course a world 'ready' for certain kinds of bodies, as a world that puts certain objects within their reach" (2006, 111). Ahmed's argument builds on the ways the world becomes oriented toward certain bodies well beyond those colonial contexts in which the "lines of force" are directly demarcated. Fanon and Ahmed resonate in posthumanitarian fictions as they represent the psychic and material lives of humanitarians whose presence in the crisis zone continuously confirms and situates their superiority over those they have come to serve. The critical continuities across colonial regimes and humanitarian practices are crystalized through postcolonial representations of the crisis zone as the ground on which the human is revealed to be not only a historically contingent subject but one that continues to be ideologically and structurally enforced. Through their representations of humanitarian actors, Coetzee and Devi emphasize those "best practices" of liberal action by attending to the narratives issued by these characters about their own benevolent functions. These texts insist that dehumanization is a structural problem that not only implicates but *sustains* the humanitarian as a figure of liberal excellence.

When *Life & Times of Michael K* turns abruptly two-thirds of the way through the novel to the narration of the medical officer, much attention is given over to K's body as a site of bewildering emaciation. Although K refuses treatment, his body continues to be subjected by the state via its workers. The bodily enforcements and discomforts to which our protagonist is subjected are narrated and queried by the new narrative voice of the humanitarian. It is as though within the narrative only those who are deemed downcast are embodied, while those more normative and able bodies that give aid come under a privileged bodily erasure. It is not simply that K falls victim to this system and suffers as a result; it is that those well-fed bodies thrive within the systems they seek to amend. This thriving is perversely represented through a critical narrative absence, the novel's casual erasure of the bodily conditions of the medical officer's modes of sustenance in the hospital. Here we might recall the critical function of the mundane in Gandhi's writings that I signaled in chapter 1. For Gandhi, the details of everyday bodily habits and processes were vital to the subject in search of truth. Scrupulous attention to the mundane for Gandhi was crucial to the pursuit of an ethical life. Yet while so much narrative attention is given to K's body—and to how this body is (mis)read in the hospital/camp—the medical officer's bodily habits, spatial relations, and alimentary practices are made powerfully invisible in the text.

While the medical officer imagines himself to be a caregiver in pursuit of healing, he confronts the fact that his work within the militarized space of the hospital is absolutely complicit with the penal system that will in turn take his patient's healthy body and put it to service in a war his patient wishes to avoid. This aligns with the novel's provocative skirting of race and its particular force in the South African context; while race is virtually imperceptible across the novel, the style and form of the medical officer's narration forcefully insinuates racial difference and its attending dehumanizations. What the novel "forgets" to include emerges poignantly, asking readers to re-member the material and psychic structures that prop up our own intimate and political lives.

"Little Ones" plays more directly with the contrast between the bodies of those in need of aid and the bodily comforts to which Singh as humanitarian is privy. As a political activist, Devi insists that the "sole purpose" of her fiction is to "expose the many faces of the exploiting agencies" and to write fiction that is a documentation of reality (1998, ix). Based on nutritional and anthropological research, Devi depicts the "stunted" body of tribal peoples not as a metaphor for dehumanization but as a fact of deprivation. While Devi's insistence on the factual does not account for the instrumental work of narrative itself in the making and shaping of particular bodies, her overtly political fiction does point us to the tangible failures of the postcolonial nation-state and to the liberal bourgeoisie's complicity with the creation of abject postindependence tribal life.

At the start of the story, Singh is characterized as "extremely honest and sympathetic" and is set against the region's impoverished inhabitants who have "no *honest way of living*" (Devi 1998, 1). Taking up a short-term position away from his comfortable city office in the food department, Singh is shocked by the desolation of the geographic region and its people. The narrator reveals that Singh has been educated about tribal life exclusively through commercial Hindi films, in which the adivasi are represented in perpetual states of ecstatic song and dance. As such, Singh "had the impression that adivasi men played the flute and adivasi women danced with flowers in their hair, singing, as they pranced from hillock to hillock" (2). His filmic illusion of tribal life is shattered by his contact with the "near-naked, shriveled, worm-ridden, swollen-bellied" bodies of the adivasi, and the encounter initially "repels" him (2).

Set against this scene of absolute dehumanization are details of the comforts afforded to Singh as aid-giver: "A bath in cool well water. His aunt's husband—a Minister. Hence, top quality rice served at table. Peas pulao. Meat, gulabjamun, pickle. At night, beds out in the open. The earth dampened with water, so slightly cool" (Devi 1998, 9). While Singh remains psychically unsettled by the sight of the adivasi people and by narratives that circulate among the government workers of terrifying ghost children that live in the forest and steal food rations, the story offsets Singh's own bodily entitlements against those he serves. Unlike the conspicuously absent bodily comforts of the medical officer in Coetzee's novel, Singh's comforts are embedded in the narrative as spatial objects that physically and psychically orient Singh as distinct from those he serves and that waylay the haunting facts and fantasies of life in the region.

While Singh accepts these comforts, he continues to be haunted by stories—not only of inhuman thieving children but also of government officials who themselves steal food and other rations to sell on the black market. The logic of his informant suggests that since the "savage," "irresponsible," and "animalistic" tribal populations cannot care for themselves despite government charity, there is little use in ensuring that the rations properly reach them. Ration theft turns out to be not only the work of little inhuman bodies that emerge from and disappear back into the forest but also the work of those who represent and serve the state. The story in this sense collapses the division between the state and its adversaries.

The acuity of the story is in how it characterizes Singh's desire to break from the system he represents. Making a decision to set himself off from other corrupt government officials, Singh engages the humanitarian imaginary by believing that his politics can be parsed from his privilege. He is by all accounts a successful humanitarian actor: he runs a "disciplined camp" that appears to be free of government corruption and supersedes protocol by insisting on an increase of medical and nutritional supplies (Devi 1998, 14–15). But humanitarian fetishism seeps into the narrative through Singh's increasing comfort with his status as a successful humanitarian. Despite the fact that the narrative from its outset has emphasized that "the entire area is a burnt-out desert" on which nothing can grow (1), he fantasizes that he can persuade the tribals to engage in agricultural life: "He also wonders whether it will be possible to change their future. Honest and compassionate officers are needed. Such officers will be able to *convert* these people to agriculture. He decides to submit a *note* the moment he gets to Ranchi. It's not possible for so many people to survive only on relief year after year" (15). The language of "conversion" in this passage emphasizes the split between Singh's desire to help those in need and the simultaneous desire to bring them into the fold of his own ideology. This profound desire to help becomes folded into an ideology of conquest in which Singh—imbued with rights as a humanitarian citizen and with a degree of state authority—is the exceptional figure who can enact radical change simply by persuading the tribals to act differently and by submitting a simple note to the authorities informing them of his solution. Singh cannot see that couched within his own purported claims to goodness is a desire for conquest. Precisely because he refuses to see his own complicity at work, he is able to set aside the haunting legacies of both state-employed and ghostly thieves and to fall calmly into "untroubled sleep" (15). What "Little Ones" illustrates is how Singh's desire, through its fetishistic play, refuses the ecological and political realities that not only give rise to the abject lives of the tribals but also, perversely, enable his own humanitarian ego-ideal to flourish.

Sociogeny and Narrative Force

Literature, I am arguing, is a crucial site through which to explore how narratives instantiate subjectivities. For Fanon, as we saw in chapter 1, narrative has a sociogenetic function, producing and sustaining humans in ways both material and ideological. Although Fanon's attention is toward black male embodiment in the colonies, his formulation of sociogenesis extends to all modern embodied subjectivities. Reading literature can be a crucial vantage point from which to rethink the human as a product shaped and enforced through narratives that are historically, socially, politically, and filially produced. Shaped through narrative, subjects are always also (and often unthinkingly) engaged in the ongoing narrative productions and enforcements of themselves—and of others. Posthumanitarian fictions emphasize how even those of us deeply invested in the labor and ethics of human care remain active in the creation of "human" subjectivity and in the enforcements of its abject alterities. Put concisely, these fictions show us how claims to goodness (signaled through humanitarian action) are ensnared in the production and enforcement of dehumanization.

Approaching these constitutive narratives with vulnerability—with a willingness to engage that which we have wished to avoid, and in so doing be crafted anew—can be a world-making practice through which we become other to ourselves. Posthumanitarian fictions draw readers toward their own critical complicities with structures of dehumanization, emphasizing how complicity becomes obscured through narrative practices that continuously obfuscate responsibility toward others. In the effort to approach a dehumanist ethics—which is itself an enduring and irreducible commitment—we must read deconstructively and approach texts, as Gayatri Chakravorty Spivak reminds us, not as anthropologists but as imaginative readers prepared for forms of self-othering as "an end in itself" (2003, 13). Through vulnerable reading, and through an avowal of complicity to which I turn in the next chapter, we might begin to revise, rewrite, and elaborate ourselves by untangling and demystifying the narratives that have crafted us to date.

Life & Times of Michael K underscores the medical officer's failure to become vulnerable to the narrative force that has produced both himself and his patient as particular kinds of subjects. The novel maps an intricate connection between the medical officer's claim to goodness and his unrelenting need to hold control over his dehumanized patient. Through a psychodynamics of narrative identification, which sutures readers to the narrative voice(s) of the text, the reader becomes textually and ethically implicated in this paradigm. Structurally, the novel begins and ends with an omniscient narrative voice, but three-quarters of the way through it shifts to the first-person voice of the nameless humanitarian medical officer before returning to the omniscient narrator to conclude the novel. These two narrative voices, critically distinct in tone but linked through their repeated dehumanization of K, likewise reveal the sociogenetic force that unrelentingly bears down on the "disabled" protagonist.

In the first sentences of the novel, a sympathetic midwife obscures K's newborn body from his mother before assuring her that a child with a harelip is a sign of good luck. Despite this assurance, his mother "did not like the mouth that would not close and the living pink flesh it bared to her" (Coetzee 1983, 3). Relaying the mother's dislike for the physical body of her child, the narrator takes on through free indirect discourse the mother's alienation from her child, repeatedly describing the baby K as "it." Unwanted and dehumanized from the outset of the novel, K's body reveals an openness (a mouth that would not close) and externalization (the baring of living pink flesh) that is unpalatable to the social world embodied through the mother. As the novel progresses, K is repeatedly evoked in animalistic terms, likened, for example, to "a dumb dog" (28). Unabatedly harsh in the portrayal of K, the narrator presents the reader with an unsettling and un-restrained "factual" account of K's bodily, psychic, and social life.

After following the exhaustive details of K's journey through dispos-session, the death of his mother, his search for her ancestral home, his re-treat from a social world at war, and his increasingly conflicted relation to eating as a necessary act of violence against that which one consumes (a fascinatingly Gandhian crisis), he is misrecognized as an accomplice to war deserters and captured by the state. The novel then turns abruptly to the narrative voice of the nameless wartime medical officer, a voice that ap-pears initially sympathetic toward K and comes as a form of readerly relief. Yet these two narrators are in crucial ways aligned, not only through their persistent dehumanization of K but through their roles as "social" voices: the first, omniscient, and the second, a poignantly nameless liberal subject.

The medical officer's narration begins with a fundamental misrecogni-tion of K and with a concern for his patient's well-being: "There is a new patient in the ward, a little old man who collapsed during physical training and was brought in with very low respiration and heartbeat. . . . I asked the guards who brought him why they made someone is his condition do physical exercise" (Coetzee 1983, 129). The novel establishes an initial identification between the reader and the humanitarian narrative voice, on the one hand distinguishing them by virtue of the reader knowing the details of K's backstory (which situates the reader, interestingly, in a posi-tion of narrative authority over the medical officer), while on the other hand aligning them through a shared desire to preserve K's body and to bestow him with full humanity. This alliance is distressed, however, as the narrator becomes increasingly ambivalent and forceful toward the object of its humanitarian desire. Initially characterizing himself as "soft" within a hard system and a healer amid systemic degradation, the medical officer is finally disabled through his relation to K from remaining within his own well-crafted narrative about his exceptional status as humanitarian. Under-standing that his patient's story has been radically misrepresented by the state, the medical officer struggles to recraft K's history through his medical assessments and through the insufficient details of a patient who refuses to abide by the strictures of self-accounting that the state demands of him. In the geopolitical space of the camp hospital where prisoners, inmates, and patients become interchangeable categories, K's anomalous body comes to haunt the medical officer as he realizes that it signals not only its medical exception but the pervasive exclusions of the nation-state in and beyond times of war. While K's shocking emaciation may at one level be read as self-induced, it also betrays for the medical officer the systemic injustices that produce it and that sustain his own fully imbued humanity (132).

Benita Parry argues that in Coetzee's oeuvre, various "figures of silence" are "muted by those who have the power to name and depict them" (1998, 151). Following this logic, K stands in contradistinction to the medical officer, who attempts through his own narrative projections to account for his patient's silence. Parry's concern that such figures of silence may well reinforce the supremacy of Europe—of Europe's historical claim to the word and the world—is crucial to a consideration of the medical officer's function in the novel. Although his encounter with his patient begins with compassion and with a desire to revise the state's narrative about K to protect him from criminal punishment, his language and logic continuously reveal his masterful drives. His narration begins with repeated pronouncements of uncertainty about his patient: "Though he looks like an old man, he claims to be only thirty-two. Perhaps it is the truth" (Coetzee 1983, 130). Signaled by the "perhaps" that throws the truth into question, the narrator shows a willingness to suspend his authority and to engage other narrative possibilities. Yet his claim to authority comes quickly into conflict with his commitment to being "soft." Having successfully stalled the authorities from an undoubtedly torturous interrogation of his patient, the medical officer declares: "the long and the short of it is that by my eloquence I saved you. . . . I hope you will be grateful one day" (142). Insisting that his "eloquence" is K's saving grace, the medical officer's work as a medical practitioner becomes bound to his desire to wield discursive power; he cannot help but to wish for the gratitude of his patient, and in so doing reveals the congruencies of discourse, enforcement, and aid in humanitarian action.

K's unwillingness to comply with his enforced medical treatment becomes for the narrator a rejection of his own self-designated identity as a humanitarian amid the war. What the medical officer cannot see is how K's refusal to comply with the treatment is part of a much larger resistance to institutional force. Noting K's lack of desire for "status, authority, community, and property," Anthony Vital suggests that while K fosters no resentment for his own lack and is "imposed upon utterly, yet without complicity," the medical officer by contrast "finds his own complicity simultaneously distasteful and inescapable" (2008, 91). K's recalcitrance becomes for the narrator a paralyzing force: "You have never asked for anything, yet you have become an albatross around my neck. Your bony arms are knotted behind my head, I walk bowed under the weight of you" (Coetzee 1983, 146). Crippled by the symbolic weight of K's body, a body that is evoked now as a dehumanized albatross, the medical officer struggles to rationalize his position in relation to his (inhuman) patient. He claims control by renarrating their relation and filtering it through the canon of Western Romanticism as he leans on Samuel Taylor Coleridge's "Rime of the Ancient Mariner" ([1798] 1951), and he shores up his own human subjectivity by dehumanizing his patient. Through this double movement, Coetzee signals that the subject of Western Man cannot be separated from the literary production of its inhuman and dehumanized others. Establishing K as the albatross, the medical officer becomes the mariner who is stifled by a creaturely imposition. The point is not that Coleridge's poem necessarily restores the medical officer's humanitarian power over K but that this renarration allows him to continue to be the subject who narrates, who spins the narrative structure within which the present takes on its meaning.

Not long after reconfiguring his narrative in relation to Coleridge's "Rime," the medical officer appears to undergo a radical transformation and wishes to "surrender" from his position of authority, a position that insists on the refusal of his complicity in the dehumanizing effects of war (Coetzee 1983, 149). Couched within the middle section of the novel is an epistolary plea from the medical officer to his patient. Therein the medical officer writes: "You are going to die, and your story is going to die too, forever and ever, unless you come to your senses and listen to me. Listen to me, Michaels. I am the only one who can save you. I am the only one who sees you for the original soul you are. I am the only one who cares for you" (151). The use of "care" here works as a euphemism for the medical officer's ability to preserve K's story by making it legible to state bureaucracy. The persistently declarative stance of the letter reveals how the medical officer repeatedly fails to persuade K to behave according to his will, and in consequence the language he employs to frame K becomes increasingly commanding. This is because K's silence threatens the medical officer's power to *make* the patient speak, or what Michel Foucault calls "the incitement to discourse": "an institutional incitement to speak . . . , and to do so more and more; a determination on the part of the agencies of power to have it spoken about" (1990, 18). While the medical officer's repeated refrain that he is "the only one" who cares about or can save K registers his self-appointed exceptional status, Foucault reminds us that this does not in any way make him exceptional: the power to make speak is precisely what allows the operations of bureaucratic power. All at once, his insistence that "Michaels" *must* listen to him and obey his commands stands in stark contrast to the more ambiguous and open "perhaps" that earlier characterized his relation to K. He ends his letter in command form: "I appeal to you, Michaels: *yield!*" (Coetzee 1983, 151). Preserving his anonymity to readers, this "appeal" issued as a command to "yield" is signed by "A friend." This marks the fantasy of the medical officer's perspective and his willful blindness to his own coercive and corrective desires. Because friendship is characterized by reciprocity,[6] the medical officer's declaration of friendship is not only a delusion but another moment of asserting his coercive will.

The force of narrative comes into its sharpest focus when the medical officer pronounces K's life not worth living: "In fact his life was a mistake from beginning to end. It's a cruel thing to say, but I will say it: he is someone who should never have been born into a world like this. It would have been better if his mother had quietly suffocated him when she saw what he was, and put him in the trash can" (Coetzee 1983, 155). Here, the medical officer hits on one of the greatest obstacles of humanitarian ideology today: How does the humanitarian avoid enforcing judgments about a worthy or valuable life? What standards apart from one's own can one seek to provide for those one wants profoundly to assist? Recalling Dipesh Chakrabarty's (2007) emphasis on the coercive work of bringing all humans into the fold of modernity, here the medical officer's discursive power is one that aligns entirely with modernity's unrelenting quest for increasingly uniform and consumptive ways of living.

Finally, when K disappears from the camp hospital, the medical officer confronts the folly of his thinking and, with a "great force," realizes that it is in fact his own life and not K's that is wasting. Reversing his narrative logic to envision himself as the "prisoner to this war" (Coetzee 1983, 157), the medical officer desires suddenly and urgently to become K's disciple. Yet he yearns to become his wayward patient's disciple, to give up on a certain form of forceful human being, only after his patient has vanished. The sudden wish to become K's "foot follower" (which I will return to in more detail in the next section) turns out to be yet another narrative fantasy. While the medical officer can entirely change his narrative, what he cannot surrender is the compulsion to *construct* the narrative, to hold mastery over its production and his particular position within it.

Ultimately, the medical officer of *Michael K* butts up against the borders of his own narrative but cannot breach them. Although he fantasizes about becoming K's disciple, his final words in the text betray the medical officer's ongoing attachment to mastery. Conceding that K will not speak to him, the medical officer poses a question followed by an imperative: "'Have I understood you? If I am right, hold up your right hand; if I am wrong, hold up your left!'" (Coetzee 1983, 167). Like the "yield!" that closes his letter to K, the medical officer finally cannot relinquish his imperative mode, still desiring to govern over the movement of K's body. His inability to avoid command, to depart from the logic of the master that underscores his humanitarianism, exposes the contradiction at the heart of his desires. Coetzee's novel brings humanitarian fetishism to crisis while he illustrates through the language of the humanitarian that this fetishism cannot simply be overturned by a desire for noncoercive human relations. The medical officer's failure to move out of a paradigm of mastery reveals the unremitting force of humanitarian fetishism. His status as master appears constitutional at the end of his narrative: the desire to undo his own mastery, to relinquish his mastery and emerge as disciple, becomes perversely folded into the activity of the master as such.

Singh's Specters

"Little Ones" likewise plays on a tension between the well-intended liberal notions of the relief officer and the necessity of his coming to terms with his complicity in a system that creates the need for relief. Yet the narrative closure suggested by "coming to terms" is precisely what does not and cannot happen: Singh reveals that complicity can be felt, can be registered, but it cannot be *admitted* within the masterful narrative of humanitarianism. He is an intermediary figure explicitly situated between institutional initiatives that it is his job to carry out and the experience of poverty that proves his efforts ineffective. Across the story, the narrative grammar reveals the acute ambivalence Singh feels toward both ends of this spectrum, and finally, toward himself.

The story dramatizes and exceeds Coetzee's humanitarian actor by emphasizing and confronting the force of narrative through the psychic undoing of its protagonist. Parama Roy acutely locates "Little Ones" as "the bureaucratic gothic" (2010, 127), a haunted narrative that requires its administrative protagonist to accept as fact that which is firmly held as fictional in the rational mode. Devi exposes the vital link between fiction and fact by historically situating her story within scientific research that confirms that starvation can lead humans to become pygmies. She employs haunting throughout the story to reveal that Singh's fear is generated not by otherworldly bodies but by subaltern human bodies that are deformed as byproducts of liberal democratic life.

Singh's own narrative unfolds in relation to two other crucial narratives that circulate within the story. The first is that of the troubled political history of the region, a narrative about tribal protests and retaliation over a government resource excavation of sacred lands. Having killed the government officials who desecrated their sacred space, these tribals disappeared into the forest and were never seen again. The other narrative alongside which Singh's story develops is a ghost story that circulates within the camp about "inhuman," animalistic, thieving children who come from the forest and steal food rations from the government base. These two narratives, the historical and the haunted, weave through the story and implicate Singh as a government employee. Singh's own narrative of humanitarian benevolence, and the adjacent narratives of historical violence and ghostly haunting, are revealed to be inextricable: the tribal enemies of the state turn out to be the terrifying "little ones" who steal the rations that Singh is paid to distribute. The story pressures us to consider how the separation of these narratives is necessary to preserving the functioning of the welfare state and to Singh's subjectivity as a humanitarian therein. Humanitarian fetishism, which structures Singh's subjectivity and shields him from the material realities of his work, is sustained precisely through this narrative splitting.

This discourse of conquest heightens and becomes more overt when two bags of rations are stolen and Singh discovers that his child disciples are accomplices to the crime. As a result, his disciples emerge for Singh as false worshippers and are transformed into strangers: "Befuddled and wounded with the realization of trust betrayed, he looks at them. Unfamiliar, unknown faces. Those same boys. But in their faces there is no echo of the despairing question that rends his heart. Smiling the cruel smiles of the victorious, they disappear into the darkness of the forest in the wink of an eye" (Devi 1998, 16). At this moment of betrayal, the roles are reversed and it is the child thieves who emerge victorious and not the humanitarian worker who "saves" them. Unlike Singh, whose victory confirms his status as the humanitarian imbued with full humanity, the boys are relegated to strangers and animals as a result of their small victory over him. Standing "befuddled and wounded," Singh's dedication to his "disciples" is contingent on their reverence for him; without this devotion, Singh's narrative quickly recasts them as enemies. This moment in which Singh envisions the boys as strange and animalistic marks a significant shift in the story from a view of the Other as that which is to be pitied (and therefore helped) to the Other as something precisely threatening and inhuman. These two formulations are closely bound, of course; in each case the other remains something to be *overcome*. As a result of their betrayal, the boys swiftly cease to be appropriate subjects of pity; they are no longer seen with compassion but rather are defined by an animal savagery that encroaches on Singh's safety and sense of self.

Whereas Coetzee emphasizes the entrapments of narrative and its often subtle force through the humanitarian's own narrative tropes, Devi pushes beyond the borders of self-narration to stall the proliferation of masterful subjectivity. When Singh follows the ration thieves into the forest, he encounters not the little ghosts of local lore but the tribal renegades whose bodies have over years of starvation radically mutated. Unlike those other thronging adivasi bodies Singh has been helping to feed, these bodies have survived off so little that their statures have mutated from the status of starved but recognizably human (like Michael K) to starved and unrecognizably human. Singh becomes literally paralyzed by the incomprehensible sight of their bodies, and as he stands in disbelief, the adivasi renegades encircle and molest him with their shriveled, "grotesque" bodies (Devi 1998, 18). For Singh, his implication in this system of oppression is absolutely unfathomable. He has, after all, worked diligently to feed the starving populations of India despite his own privilege. But their deformed and diminutive bodies in contact with his own lead him to a crisis of his own subjectivity.

In her reading of this scene, Roy argues that "this touch of the other . . . makes his own body monstrous to himself. More than the ghost's body, it is the body of the definitively living human that is rendered grotesque through this spectral logic" (2010, 138). Roy points us to a powerful depiction of the postcolonial uncanny, in which the haunting spirits of the conscience press on Singh in ways he cannot comprehend. The narrative concedes that these unbelievable human bodies *must* finally be believed, that the lines between fact and fiction can no longer be upheld in his consciousness: "Because if this is true, then all else is false. The universe according to Copernicus, science, this century, this freedom, plan after plan. So the *relief officer* reiterates—*Na! Na! Na!*" (Devi 1998, 19). Singh's articulations of disbelief are quickly silenced by the terrifying spectacle and sexual confrontation of the renegade bodies. In the final moments of the story, he is rendered speechless as he struggles to locate himself within a scale of global oppression, wishing to extricate himself from the role of oppressor: "The logical arguments *motor-race* through the *relief officer*'s mind. He wants to say, why this revenge? I'm just an ordinary Indian. Not as well-developed or tall as the Russians-Canadians-Americans. I've never eaten the kind of calorie-rich food required for the development of a strong human body, the failure to consume which is construed as a crime by the World Health Organization" (20). Ultimately, Singh's attempt to position himself as an "ordinary Indian"—and as therefore somehow innocent or exempt—cannot be sustained. He can no longer deny that the crime of disallowing the human body the right to eat well is as much his own crime as it is the crime of public policies that ensure that he eats and that the adivasi cannot do so sufficiently.[7] In this instant of recognizing his own complicity, Singh struggles to characterize himself as likewise underfed.

The story ends with a scene of fascinating performativity between Singh and the "little ones." As Singh silently proclaims his own guilt, the tribals surround him with their abject bodies: "He can't say a word. Standing under the moon, looking at them, hearing their laughter, feeling their penises on his skin, the undernourished body and laughable height of the ordinary Indian male appear a heinous crime of civilization. He feels like a criminal sentenced to death. Pronouncing his own death-sentence for their stunted forms, he lifts his face up to the moon, his mouth gaping wide" (Devi 1998, 20). While the renegades force their abject bodies on his, Singh's self-proclaimed condemnation registers as a profound and penetrating recognition of his complicity—as a liberal democratic subject, as a humanitarian worker, and as a healthy human being—in the subjugation of other human lives. His silence is finally a pronouncement of metaphysical guilt, of what Karl Jaspers (2001) defined as the guilt of staying alive despite the other's suffering or death. By elaborating this form of guilt, Jaspers (notably a liberal himself) specifically attempted to make sense of the German situation by charting the registers of German guilt and responsibility in the aftermath of the Holocaust. Metaphysical guilt is a universal guilt shared by those who chose to live rather than to sacrifice themselves in protest of Nazi atrocities. For Singh, his own guilt is born from the realization of his largely unconscious decision to thrive despite the state sacrifice of the adivasi tribes. In this sense, the story represents the argument advanced by Hannah Arendt (1976) and Giorgio Agamben (1998) that we come to understand the human only when it is deprived of every other thing but bare life.[8]

Witnessing bare life, Singh registers the force and paradox of humanity only at the moment when the unthinkable body of the other reveals to him the forms of oppression that constitute his own suddenly estranging body. He relinquishes his claims to knowledge and truth, staging a radical act of antimastery by submitting himself both physically and psychically to the thoroughly dehumanized "objects" of his humanitarian aims. Singh's desperate desire at the end of the story is to utter "the howl of a demented dog," a howl that would signify his "liberation" by becoming animal and descending into madness. It is important here that this submission is also a desire for transspeciation; he does not submit himself to becoming other as a pygmy human but to becoming animal. His desire to howl is therefore a desire to escape altogether the psychic structures of dehumanization by leaving the human behind completely. But Singh's muteness disables this descent; he is left in the final moments of the story with an inability to claim (through the howl) an "inhuman" psychic life and an inability to continue verbally to sustain his own alibi. Surrendering himself to the sound and touch of his ghosts, Singh brings us to the threshold of other psychic and narrative possibilities.

After the Humanitarian

Posthumanitarian fictions uncover humanitarian fetishism by refusing to separate the ideological fantasies of "doing good" from the material supports and consequences of those actions. They compel readers to linger with dehumanization, not to repudiate it uncritically but to abide by it, activating the potentialities of dehumanism through which we might let ourselves be haunted by those we have (in more and less overt ways) aggressed. These fictions ask us to become haunted, to listen to our hauntings even when we cannot translate their ghostly messages.

Across posthumanitarian fictions, the ability to be a "good" human is afforded to humanitarians precisely through their material participation in dehumanization; the humanization of the humanitarian and the work of dehumanization turn out to be inseparable practices. While posthumanitarian fictions do not proscribe radically new forms of political being, their representations of humanitarian actors ask us whether it is possible to imagine a humanism that would not structurally and materially (re)produce mastery and dehumanization. My desire is to engage dehumanism as a recuperative practice that casts ourselves as vulnerable to the ways that other beings—"human" and otherwise—have been subjected to dehumanization. These ways of living in exile from the realm of "Man" can become, as Alexander Weheliye (2014) argues, critically instructive in the imagination of alternate forms of collective life and being. If we can learn how to recognize our own surprising complicities with dehumanization, we can also learn how to abide with others (human, inhuman, and dehumanized) that have enabled us to become particular kinds of masterful subjects. Precisely in this abiding, in consciously reading ourselves and attaching ourselves to that which we have subjected, we can begin to learn how to become differently relational with others. Perhaps more radically still, we might also learn how to become relational with ourselves as intimate others.

What comes after Singh's failure to howl? What forms of ethical action might circumvent the need to undo oneself completely in the face of one's own complicity? If we can stall the disavowal of our masterful complicities and stay with dehumanization as it presents to us other forms of human being, we might offer ourselves new ways of becoming human. What is vital to this becoming is to revise our own narrative formations, making our narratives infinitely more dynamic than we have yet let them become. Embracing Antonio Gramsci's (1971) summons to elaborate the infinity of traces that have been left on and through us as particular psychic and embodied subjects, we can begin to discover the limits of our own narrative formations and to layer and unfold them as we shape ourselves into new kinds of subjective beings.

Like the medical officer and like Singh, in my own inaugural moment as a humanitarian in a house of hybrid Singhs, I was caught up in a series of complex power relations that shaped my actions and reactions. Of course, as a child I could not have understood, as I would later begin to, the complex power relations and forms of mastery that were mapping the scene of this inauguration: I was a child privileged enough to intervene on behalf of a grown man; I was comparatively wealthy and he was undoubtedly poor; I was able-bodied and psychically sound, while he—at least by my childhood memory—was both physically and mentally ill; I was a mixed-race child staging an intervention in a neighborhood in which neither of us were wholly welcome, or welcome at all.

The absolutely formative (and at times for me instrumental) narrative of my emergent humanitarianism did not include these complexities, and, like the protagonists of posthumanitarian fictions, I have hit up against the limits of my own narrative. In place of sheer frustration or the howl of madness, instead of throwing up our hands, tearing out our hair, or succumbing to a dialectic between humanitarian fetishism and madness, I am proposing a praxis of dynamic narration that not only avows the inescapable complicities of the "good" subject but also refuses the ability to neatly separate my humanitarian impulses from those less redemptive and messier qualities that have shaped me through the power of narrative structures. Recalling Sanders's etymological formulation of complicity as "a foldedness in human being that stands as the condition of possibility for any opposition to a system that constantly denies it" (2002, x), complicity becomes not something negative to be resisted and disavowed but something to be affirmed in order to assume responsibility. By elaborating, upturning, and reshaping those narratives that have cast us as particular kinds of subjects, dynamic narration moves us beyond dialectical formulations toward a politics of entanglement from which other world relations can begin to flourish. Dynamic narration is therefore a gesture toward dehumanism—an act of narratively inhabiting the gaps and fissures of our own subjective constructions in an effort to refuse the violence of splitting ourselves off from the less agreeable aspects of our being.

CHAPTER 4

Humanimal Dispossessions

In the opening sentences of Indra Sinha's *Animal's People*, the teenaged protagonist Animal declares: "I used to be human once. So I'm told. I don't remember it myself, but people who knew me when I was small say I walked on two feet just like a human being" (2007, 1). The novel is a thinly veiled representation of the 1984 Bhopal disaster, broadly interpreted as the world's worst industrial disaster, in which the American-owned Union Carbide corporation exposed over half a million people to methyl isocyanate, among other chemicals. It represents the disaster and its long aftermath, politicizing the power of transnational corporations and their dehumanizing effects. Animal, whose spine is twisted, has been formed into a quadruped as a result of toxic exposure. The movement of Animal's inaugural sentences presents us with a fascinating formulation of the human, and of Animal's particular relation to its figuration. He begins by signaling that the human is not something that simply "is" but rather is something contingent that can be moved toward and away from. In the second fragmentary sentence, Animal signals the human as a narrative creation: "So I'm told." The human from the very outset of the story is thus positioned as provisional, as a product of narrative structure, and Animal distances himself from his humanity through his insistence on the past tense of it. More subtly, he complicates the narrative of his former humanity in his own telling, posing this "human" past as one in which he walked on two feet *just like* a human being. Even when he was a human, then, Animal's sly rhetoric signals that he was always only ever proximate to it.

In the previous chapter, I explored posthumanitarian fictions, in which humanitarian actors face their complicity with the dehumanization of those they wish to humanize. Here, I turn to figurations of the human *as* animal in postcolonial literature. This is not as sharp a turn as might first appear. The question of the animal emerges in the final section of the preceding chapter with Mr. Singh's simultaneous recognition of his own complicity and his desire to utter the "howl of a demented dog" (Devi 1998, 20). At the end of Mahasweta Devi's story, Singh straddles humanity and animality, unable to claim either as his proper topography. This is to my mind a most poignant promise at the end of a story that can so easily be read as hopeless. Singh finally does not, and cannot, locate himself within a fraudulent typology that rends the human from the animal. As I argued in chapters 1 and 2, anticolonial discourse has been caught up in a recuperation of the proper humanity of the colonized, one that remained in many respects bound to a masterful formulation of an emergent postcolonial subjectivity. In contrast to this tendency within anticolonial discourse, I am interested here in postcolonial writers who have affirmed the animality of humans as a hopeful politics of postcolonial becoming. To mobilize one's animality is to dispossess oneself from the sovereignty of man, to refuse the anticolonial reach of becoming masterful human subjects. This literature pressures a sovereign imperial worldview that both refuses the human's animality and insists on the mastery of "animal" others. Against the recurring tendencies that I emphasized in the first two chapters of this book to disavow animality in anticolonial movements that aimed to restore the colonized subject to full humanity, postcolonial literature offers us critical counternarratives of human becoming—ones that struggle with and in opposition to the sovereign subject's disavowal of its own and other animalities.

I build in this chapter on Judith Butler and Athena Athanasiou's work on dispossession, a "troubling concept" that signals both a hopeful dis- of the masterful sovereign subject and the systematic jettison- lations from "modes of collective belonging and justice" (2013, xi). Although the "double valence" of dispossession suggests distinct if not antithetical modalities (3), Butler and Athanasiou engage the fundamental relation between, on the one hand, the "dispossessed subject" that avows the "differentiated social bonds by which it is constituted and to which it is obligated," and, on the other hand, those communities that are and have been dispossessed by an external force (ix). We might say that in the first instance, the dispossession of the sovereign subject from its masterful reign is an act that aims toward unmasterful forms of being and relationality, while in the second instance, dispossession is made manifest through an external masterful force. Yet for Butler and Athanasiou, these dispossessions are crucially linked through an acute shared awareness of our fundamental dependencies on "those powers that alternately sustain or deprive us, and that hold a certain power over our very survival" (4).

Animal's Dehumanist Solidarities

Dehumanism—which articulates the brutalities of dehumanization at the same time as it names the open and antimasterful possibilities that can emerge from dehumanized forms of living in the world—shares with dispossession a "double valence." Although they do not dwell extensively on the animal, Butler and Athanasiou argue that we must struggle against the "versions of the human that assume the animal as its opposite" and that the formation of an unmasterful political subject requires a mobilization of the human's own animality (2013, 34). Through its dispossessed protagonist, *Animal's People* persistently collapses a neat distinction between humans and animals and politicizes forms of humanimality that refuse their demarcation.

The novel shows us the unity between the two valences of dispossession: Animal is, on the one hand, dispossessed through abject poverty and a dehumanizing physical disability produced by external forces; and, on the other hand, he refuses to be given back to the human by insisting on his own animality. Animal is thus doubly dispossessed through the force of neocolonial power that has disfigured him, and through self-cultivating practices that willfully reject "the world of humans" in an effort to cultivate other forms of solidarity (Sinha 2007, 2).

Animal engages in what I call *dehumanist solidarities*—social bonds that are mobilized and sustained through a refusal of the sovereign human subject and that enact agential forms of inhuman relationality. In this sense dehumanist solidarities are inherently queer ones. They are, to recall Donna Haraway, practices of "becoming worldly" through transformative acts of "becoming with" our own and other creaturely selves (2008, 3).

I clearly do not wish to elide the crucial fact that Animal comes to embrace his animality *because* he has been critically dehumanized; I do think, however, that through this dehumanization Animal comes to tell his readers—to whom he narrates and implicates directly as the "Eyes" interpreting his story (Sinha 2007, 12)—something vital about their own disavowed animalities. The title of the novel itself politicizes the possessions and dispossessions of the human, complicating from the outset the prescriptive divisions between humans and animals. On the one hand, "Animal's people" indicates the people "of" or "belonging to" Animal and thus appears as a simple possessive form. Within this apparently simple form, we are already asked to consider what form of possession the animal can have over people. This becomes more complex when we read "Animal's people" as a contraction of "Animal *is* people." In the most humanist formulation, we might read this as an insistence that Animal is "human" despite his abjection. But what if we read Animal as a "person" who *is also animal* in and through his belonging? The title wavers provocatively between the ontological mode (Animal *is* a person) and a relational one, in which Animal is caught up in an undecidable form of belonging with and to "people." This wavering, from the title onward, loosens the borders of the human and opens toward more expansive dehumanist forms of relational collectivity.

I have written elsewhere (Singh 2015b) about *Animal's People* as a post-humanitarian fiction through which readers are brought critically into the fold of Animal's dehumanization, but at this juncture I am interested in how Animal teaches us about the potentialities born from being dehumanized, from claiming one's own vital potentialities from outside the masterful reign of the human. Until the final page of the novel when he commits unwaveringly to his animality, Animal vacillates between an insistence on his inhuman status and an often "wild" desire to become human. But even before this final commitment to his animal subjectivity, he illustrates dehumanist solidarities through his relations with other nonhuman and dehumanized characters. Among the most poignant of these is his friendship with his canine companion, Jara. His narrative introduction of Jara refuses initially to name her species, and readers are confronted by their assumptions that she, like Animal, is "really" human: "Jara's my friend. She wasn't always. We used to be enemies. In the days of living on the street we were rivals for food" (Sinha 2007, 17). Jara's emergence in the novel posits her as a former "rival" and as a current "friend" who shares with Animal a struggle for basic bodily sustenance. While some of Animal's most overtly animal performances happen in relation to her—"I rushed at her snapping my jaws, growling louder than she, the warning of a desperate animal that will stick at nothing" (17)—Jara also becomes for Animal a reflection of himself: "She was as thin as me, her hide shrunken over her ribs. . . . A yellow dog, of no fixed abode and no traceable parents, just like me" (18). Here we witness a rhetorical repetition with a critical difference: The *just like* of the novel's inaugural sentences in which Animal becomes distanced from the properly human subject ("I walked on two feet *just like* a human being") resounds in this passage but works instead to bring Animal into transspecies alliance with the canine Jara. Both her physical abjection and her "untraceable" genealogy enable for Animal a compassionate alliance with another creature fighting for her survival. Jara thus becomes folded into the novel initially as a "friend," as one who has made the passage from "enemy" to ally, and as one whose species is registered as ancillary to a more expansive form of alliance.

Animal's vacillation across the novel between wanting to claim his animality and wanting to become human is repeatedly articulated along sexed and gendered lines: part of his animality resides in a stature that exposes his genitalia to public view; he desires (at times desperately) to have sexual intercourse with a human female and understands this as a possibility only if he can become human; and he is offered by the novel's white, Western, female humanitarian the opportunity to become "upright" (aka human) through the promises of Western medical intervention. The novel works through human/animal distinctions via sexuality, especially through its evocations of sexual violence and sexual liberation.[1] Animal imagines that "the whole world fucks away day and night" and thus bemoans his exclusion from this copulating human world (Sinha 2007, 231). His articulation of exclusion from the world of human heterosexuality produces both a compulsive desire to "master" his penis, to conquer it so as to make it cower "like a sulky dog" (245), and a deeply violent and disturbing fantasy of female penetration, in which Animal declares: "I'll pierce her and open her up until my cock is stroking her heart and she's crying my name, 'Animal! Animal! Animal!' and I will suck the sweetness of life from her lips" (231).

Teased for an inability to control his frequent erections, Animal becomes impotent at the moment he is given the opportunity to sexually penetrate the prostitute Anjali. Far from fulfilling his murderous sexual fantasy, Animal fails to enter into the economy of sexual intercourse and instead, in the aftermath of a drug-addled Holi celebration, finds himself curled up with Anjali, characterizing them as "two rainbow-coloured animals" (Sinha 2007, 242). From this position of shared "animality"—the prostitute who has been sold into prostitution and lives outside civil society and the once-human boy whose disfigurement marks his exclusion from the human world—Animal reconceives of sex and sexuality. Moving away from the violent desire to "pierce" a woman's body and to "suck the sweetness of life from her lips," Animal now desires not to penetrate but simply to witness sexual difference by looking at Anjali's genitals. What he finds in his desire to see sexual difference, however, is a "nothing" that "is" and makes everything possible: "She shows me how the rose cave leads to a tunnel whose mouth at first was hidden, this is the way that leads to the womb, where life begins, where I began, where we all began. I try to imagine the womb and realise that it's an empty space, which means there's nothingness at the very source of creation" (243–44). With the discovery of this "empty space"—the "very source of creation"—Animal moves away from the rhetoric of sexual difference toward an intensified desire for liberation. Saving the funds he has earned over the course of the novel through his work for a justice group seeking recompense from the company that has devastated the community, Animal tells his readers on the last page of the novel that rather than spend his money toward "corrective" surgery, he will embrace his animality unwaveringly and will use his funds to "buy Anjali free" (366). While Anjali's freedom will bring her to live with Animal, there is importantly no sexual contract between them (her freedom is crucially not premised on their marriage), and the novel ends with the promise of a dehumanist community—the newly freed prostitute, the newly avowed Animal, and the canine Jara—who will live in queer solidarity despite the systemic forces that have produced and will continue to produce and enforce dehumanized lives.

Humanimal Bonds

I am taken by the dehumanist possibilities of transspecies identification and cross-species solidarities and the queer collectivities that can form through active, unmasterful forms of self-dispossession. As I think my way through such possibilities, I am keenly aware of my longtime companion Cassie, whom I can hear downstairs navigating blindly toward her food. I first encountered Cassie in 2000, when I was an early undergraduate and she a feral stray living on a Canadian riverbank behind my mother's home. She was young and small in stature, though her age (as with all cats, especially strays) was difficult to pinpoint. She displayed bodily signs of having birthed offspring, though she had been spayed. I have no sense of how long she had been living as a stray, though her staunch refusal of human contact suggested that it had been some time. My mother, afraid that Cassie would not survive the brutalities of an oncoming Canadian winter, persuaded me to house her in my miniscule undergraduate apartment. It took four adults (with a couple of pairs of oven mitts) to capture her, and when I released her into her new home, she mauled my hand so badly I was sent to the hospital for shots and bandages. Because of my mother's certainty that Cassie would be beheaded by the government and her head shipped to Ottawa for testing (this still sounds absurd to me, but she was unwaveringly insistent), I pretended in the hospital that I had been randomly attacked by an unknown street cat.

Like Animal and Jara, then, we were initially adversaries: between the mauling and her repeated escapes from my apartment—after which, to rub salt in my psychic wounds, she would reappear at my mother's house!— I did not have any special love for this creature. There was, however, a critical moment of transformation that fundamentally changed our relationship. One fall afternoon, as I watched Cassie (yet again) hightail it out my back door, down the fire exit, and toward the river (where she would no doubt begin her journey back to my mother), I decided not to chase but to follow her. Conceding to her preference for another home, and her insistence on remaining a creature of the outdoors, I trailed after her with a calmness I had not yet experienced with her. She knew I was behind her but she also knew I was not giving chase, and very quickly the lines became blurred between which of us was following the other. Eventually, we wandered home together, back up the fire escape steps and into our apartment. We began to wander together every day, without fixed destination, sometimes exploring the river bank and at other times just meandering along the sidewalks of our neighborhood. We became, and would remain across three cities and two countries, a somewhat notorious neighborhood phenomenon (she was often hailed by neighbors who did not know us well as "the cat-dog," and I "the cat-girl"). I would frequently read novels as I walked, and Cassie would tear up and down trees, getting ahead and trailing behind as she so desired. For most of our lives together, I lived in places from which she could come and go at her leisure, and she made plain to me at every turn that she had *chosen* to stay with me but in no sense depended on me for her survival. Across seventeen years, ours has been a friendship founded on the refusal of mastery and on a vital resistance (despite the well-worn insistence of veterinarians and many cat lovers on the benefits of bounded feline domesticity) to the prescribed roles of animal "pet" and human "owner."

Cassie dispossessed me of a masterful desire to domesticate her "properly"—one that was for me built into a socially instantiated idea of what an urban relation between humans and felines *should* look like. While I never shared with Jacques Derrida (2008) his famous discomfort with being nude under the inscrutable gaze of his feline companion, I did share with him a relation to another creature that insisted on the profound recognition that my initial desire for mastery over her was predicated on positing Cassie as an "animal" against my own confirmed and practiced "humanity." Against this enforced division, we cultivated a *humanimal bond* in which neither of us could simply stand as conceptual unities. We were specific beings and shared as such a relationality founded on our individual and collective needs, and on what we could and were willing to sacrifice. We came increasingly toward each other and discovered a frame of alliance that remained—for most of her life and much of mine—vital and sustaining. While I would not say that we have ever been in any sense "equals" (I confess, against liberal discourse, that I have always been ill at ease with a politics of equality that seems relentlessly to produce its opposite), her *style* of being and her mode of *becoming with* me urged me toward an embrace of my own (often forgotten, elided, and disavowed) animality.

The endurance of our solidarity is marked by many things, including that our relation has spanned the entirety of my adult life. Some years ago when I was pregnant, Cassie began to climb insistently on my body and purr, as though conjuring the creature developing inside me. She seemed in communion with this forthcoming addition to our humanimal pack and lay committedly against the seam of my flesh, over the curious temporal mappings of zygote, embryo, and fetus (what strange ways to imagine becoming!). But she was also communing with *me* in a more intense, more persistent way throughout a period in which I simply could not ignore that I was an embodied and embodying creature. Pregnancy was an intensely pedagogical time, not because I was eager to take in the discourse of parenting that was suddenly inundating my daily life but because it was an unrelenting lesson in my own primate animality. Housing another creature within me, I could neither disavow the animality of my own being nor forget the daily bodily acts that we are otherwise trained to ignore (that is, to master) as we move through the world as humans. Insightful creature that

4.1 Cassie and infant child together, adjacent in repose. Photograph by Julietta Singh.

she is, Cassie responded to these dynamic forms of creaturely becoming with striking attentiveness. I had been warned through popular parenting discourse and pedagogy against the "dangers" of allowing animals to commune with newborns, but Cassie drew me away from such enforced distinctions when, in the first days with this newborn child, she enacted such keen sensitivities toward our new creature. Anyone who had known Cassie across time, or who knew the legend of her becoming, was amazed by how this "wild" cat had become friend, ally, and in some critical ways parent to other (human) beings. She has played no small part over the last years in the pedagogy of our human child, in the teaching of relational boundaries and care, and in the formation and flourishing of a queer family unit.

As I type bleary-eyed through increasingly achy fingers, I hear Cassie's howl and can so easily envision her own now blind and arthritic body navigating the well-charted paths toward food, litter, and rest. She is undeniably old and a very different creature from the ones she has been across the many stages of our lives. (We are aging together, but her body is stiffening much faster than mine and transforming in ways more readily apparent.)

I admit to being deeply pained by this stage, not only because it feels "final" but because I am haunted by a feeling that I am failing her in companionship. She is dependent on me now in ways that she was not before. And in biopolitical fashion, I have claimed the right to treat her kidney disease and high blood pressure medically, just as I will likely claim one day the right to end her life. I feel tugged away from the humanimal bond we shared across a decade and a half, a tug that is produced in part through the dependencies of creaturely disease and aging, and a preemptive mourning for what we once were.

This mourning for what feels like an increasingly distant humanimality is also located squarely within the specifically human productions and performances with which I am now more than ever acutely engaged in my roles as both mother and intellectual. As a mother, I find myself ceaselessly crafting my child—at times quite discomfortingly—as a material, ideological, and narrative being. While I urge her toward unconventional ways of thinking (I am told that this is a "plight" of children raised by intellectuals), which entail ways of conceiving our relations to others human and inhuman that are in excess of and sometimes in stark contradiction to empirical thinking, I also realize that I am raising her *as* a human subject. My responsibilities "as" a mother sometimes feel in tension both with my relation to Cassie and with my intellectual passions (which are more than "just" intellectual) for unthinking my own claims to humanity. I am in the odd position of having another human in my care who has from the outset depended on me for survival, and whose sense of the world is being shaped by particular performances of—and pedagogies in—family, community, and citizenship that are geared toward being and acting human.

As an intellectual situated within the humanities, and currently propelled by the encroaching temporality of the tenure-track, there is no doubt that I have become increasingly driven by certain modes of human mastery—especially over myself—even while my intellectual thought is compelling me to work against them. This became most palpable two years ago when, hard at work on a text about Gandhi's complex ethics toward the animal, Cassie suffered the detachment of her retinas and became suddenly blind. She howled and wandered aimlessly through the house, summoning me with an urgency I could not interpret. I moved back and forth over the course of hours between attempts to comfort her and the drive to meet a writing deadline. I thought initially that she was suffering from the dementia of old age, and I was, admittedly, annoyed at her "neediness" during my few sacred child-free writing hours. As the pitch of her howl intensified and her confusion became impossible to dismiss, I wondered if she had gone deaf. Finally, in our first emergency visit to an animal hospital, we learned that she had been blinded as a result of other as yet undetected medical conditions.

There could have been for me no more palpable contradiction between my intellectual ethics and my performance as a subject than this moment in which—working through Gandhi's own often confounding relation to animals he vied so earnestly to protect—I repeatedly turned my back on Cassie's call in her moment of creaturely crisis. Working toward my instantiation as a tenured professor of the humanities has necessitated certain forms and practices of mastery that starkly confront my own political hopes and aspirations. Recalling that painful moment in which I moved between Gandhi's writings on animals and my beloved old friend, I am keenly aware of how disciplinary knowledge production obscures—at times violently— other ways of reading, creating, and being. The discomfort of that moment and its recollection produces in me a wish to return myself to my own humanimal bonds, not in the sense of moving back in time but in the queer sense of moving forward toward forgotten possibilities. This is a wish made manifest in my own animal body, a wish that remembers our changing humanimal bodies and our still mutual and vital dependencies—even those we are not, through our blind and bleary eyes, yet able to see.

Feeling Undisciplined

At the 1997–98 Tanner Lectures, sponsored by Princeton's Center for Human Values, J. M. Coetzee stood before his academic audience and read stories, respectively titled "The Philosophers and the Animals" and "The Poets and the Animals."[2] These coextensive stories situated particular kinds of humans (philosophers and poets) in relation to animals (writ large). Coetzee has become renowned for reading stories in academic settings, which are notoriously better accustomed to academic prose. At his Princeton reading, he emphasized the potential of creative work to disrupt conventional disciplinary boundaries, delivering what Marjorie Garber calls a "lecture-narrative" (1999, 73). With the crucial exception of sexual difference, the protagonist Elizabeth Costello is, like the author himself, an aging, white postcolonial novelist invited to deliver lectures at a prestigious U.S. academic institution. The *genre* trouble Coetzee engages in this text is thus entangled with *gender* trouble (Butler 1990), implicating his readers/ audience in the policing of specious boundaries that produce authoritative knowledge. They (Coetzee and Costello) are expected to speak within their realm of expertise as novelists: that is to say, they are expected to elaborate some aspect of the human condition. Instead, they discomfort (a term I will return to in detail in the next chapter) their academic audiences with anti-intellectual "lectures" driven by counterlogical claims about human/ animal relations and the urgent need to rethink our relations with and re- sponsibilities toward animals.

Coetzee toys with the theme of the Tanner Lectures, "Disciplinarity and Its Discontents," reading aloud a fictional tale that advances a politics of feeling in place of the violence and erasures produced through Western reason. In so doing, he formally compromises the validity and value of the lecture as authentic knowledge production by articulating it through the imaginary terrain of fiction. The content—the unethical human rela- tion toward animals—is likewise disruptive, positing the animal as subject where listeners and readers expect to find the human. Thus, while his au- dience may anticipate that the South African writer will tell them some- thing illuminating about the function of racial violence, white supremacy, or postcolonial guilt—something that he "knows" by virtue of his race and nationality—Coetzee posits at the center of his text the "illogical," un- masterful claims of an aging female novelist. He tells us, in other words, about how an aging white woman *feels* about the human treatment of ani- mals. What, we might well ask, could seem less important to postcolonial thought?

Although *The Lives of Animals* has been interpreted as one of Coet- zee's least "postcolonial" narratives, the central preoccupations of these narratives are critically aligned with those of postcolonial studies. From the very earliest formulations of postcolonial studies—whether through Edward Said's (1979) attention to orientalist discourse and its own racist refrains about the non-West or through the Subaltern Studies Collective's insistence on the need to redress the exclusions of official historical narra- tives[3]—the postcolonial project has pressed on disciplinarity as a system of knowledge production that necessitates claims to authenticity as it sub- jugates other perspectives and peoples. In *The Lives of Animals*, Coetzee emphasizes this foundational postcolonial critique but extends its potential beyond the human. The boundaries that have historically differentiated properly human subjects from inhuman objects must today, his protagonist insists, be extended to a thinking of the limit that separates humans from animals. By proposing a critical turn toward the animal, the narrative unsettles what have now become conventions of postcolonial thought by insisting on a rethinking of the status of the animal therein. While there has been a recent scholarly turn in postcolonial studies toward the environment, most notably through the publication of Graham Huggan and Helen Tiffin's *Postcolonial Ecocriticism: Literature, Animals, Environment* (2010) and Elizabeth DeLoughrey and George B. Handley's *Postcolonial Ecologies: Literatures of the Environment* (2011), the question of the animal remains a vital hinge between the "postcolonial" and the "ecological" that still needs careful consideration and mobilization. In the language of anticolonial discourse and postcolonial studies, the animal continues to be put to work as a figure for injustices toward dehumanized human subjects—or as that which, because of its inhumanity, remains a largely unquestioned and thus "proper" sacrificial body. Among others, Fanon has insisted on the historical and material forces that produce some humans *as* animals. Coetzee's text does not displace that critique but pushes us to consider the animal not solely as a figure for racist logic. It folds Fanon's processes of producing particular bodies as animal (such as Animal's) into a wider thinking of the animal (like Cassie) as a being whose existence exceeds and is not predicated on its relation to the human. This excessive singularity is the ground for humanimal relations.

In his antidisciplinary mobilization of queer failure, Jack Halberstam argues that "disciplines actually get in the way of answers and theorems precisely because they offer maps of thought where intuition and blind fumbling might yield better results" (2011, 6). If we are accustomed to believing that disciplinarity makes intellectual inquiry possible, Coetzee shows us that it also necessarily obscures aspects of its own task and ignores what falls beyond its purview. The discipline follows in the footsteps of the masterful subject by being founded on the refusals of its own vulnerabilities. To make concrete its authority, a discipline must remain blind to what is beyond its limits, disavowing the ways that it remains affected and permeated by its outside. Coetzee breaks provocatively with discipline, productively confusing the lines between fact and fiction, between author and protagonist, and between human and animal. In a sense, Coetzee's lecture-narrative—perhaps especially through the genre and gender trouble it offers—is an act of dispossessing his own claim to authority by submitting himself (as woman, as animal, as fiction) to others trained to disavow vulnerability. Through his female double, he engages imaginative, even utopian performances of humanimality that radically extend the horizons of our ethics. Although the protagonist of his narrative is bound to fail in her anti-intellectual emotional plea to her intellectual audience, her failure against the force of discipline ultimately brings us toward "more creative, more cooperative, more surprising ways of being in the world" (Halberstam 2011, 2–3). Through what Halberstam calls "counterintuitive modes of knowing," Costello privileges *feeling* over the rational mode in order to dispossess us from the disciplined and disciplining subjectivities from which we have been crafted and to which we have remained bound.

Disciplining Anxieties

Underlying the academic response to *The Lives of Animals* has been an anxiety about how much of Coetzee's political and ethical beliefs are registered through his fictional female protagonist. Initially delivered orally, then published in 1999 as a Tanner Lecture, and finally included as two chapters in the novel *Elizabeth Costello* (2003), the text upsets the rigid boundary between truth and fiction, lecture and story, author and text, male and female, and human and animal. This interpretive anxiety tells us something vital about the relation between intellectual thought and fiction, about how ungrounded we become when "truth" is disrupted by less authorized ideas, genres, forms, and concepts. Perhaps just as importantly, it reveals how profoundly we—and by "we" I mean to include those situated squarely within Western culture, those working in relation to Western academia, and, perhaps most perversely, those of us who are literary scholars—distrust the word (and the *world*) of fiction. The novel *Elizabeth Costello* "helps" to ease both the genre and gender trouble caused by Coetzee's addressing his audience "as" an aging white woman writer.

Critics of *Elizabeth Costello*, Derek Attridge writes, "complain that Coetzee uses his fictional characters to advance arguments . . . without assuming responsibility for them, and is thus ethically at fault" (2004, 197). According to the logic of this complaint, by couching his arguments in fictional form, the genre becomes an alibi that absolves the author of responsibility. Attridge refuses this logic by returning to the relation between Coetzee and Costello through the event of the public readings of the lecture-narratives, proposing that "the arguments within [the lecture-narratives] should more strictly be called *arguings*, utterances made by individuals in concrete situations—wholly unlike the paradigmatic philosophical argument, which implicitly lays claim to a timeless, spaceless, subjectless condition as it pursues its logic. They are, that is, events staged within the event of the work; and they invite the reader's participation not just in the intellectual exercise of positions expounded and defended but in the human experience, and the human cost, of exposing convictions, beliefs, doubts, and fears in a public arena" (198). Fiction as a vehicle of knowing is not only critically different from philosophical modes of truth production; it also makes very different demands of its interlocutors. While philosophical arguments lend themselves to masterful reading practices, literary "arguings" must be engaged vulnerably, which is to say with an openness toward forms of "exposure" that may well upset the most rudimentary preconceptions of its interlocutors.

The tension between "truth" and "fiction" emerges everywhere in Amy Gutmann's introduction to *The Lives of Animals*, but also and more subtly throughout the multiple disciplinary "reflections" by Marjorie Garber, Peter Singer, Wendy Doniger, and Barbara Smuts that follow Coetzee's narrative. In her short response, Marjorie Garber—the literary critic invited to reflect on the text—reads the text through multiple registers: form and content, psychoanalysis, and gender studies. Although she engages the problem of "partitioning" bodies of knowledge and insists on reading the text from various vantage points, her conclusion is quite striking: "In those two elegant lectures we thought John Coetzee was talking about animals. Could it be, however, that all along he was really asking, 'What is the value of literature?'" (Garber 1999, 84). This closing inquiry implies that Coetzee uses the animal as a literary trope to speak about something *else*—that is, the status of literature. Literature reigns supreme for Garber at the end of the text, but this is certainly not so for the philosopher, the historian, or the anthropologist whose individual responses to the text derive from their own firmly entrenched relations to their individual disciplines.

This is all to say something quite obvious: interpretation and analysis are not freely flowing acts but rather are governed by specific intellectual currents. A disciplined scholar has authority by virtue of having "mastered" a body of knowledge and guards against the penetration of its mastered domain. In Garber's case, her discovery of literature at the end of a text that is already very clearly concerned with literature and its voice, its power, and its authenticity in the world beyond itself offers us an interpretation of the text that avoids the question of the animal in the name of literature. If the text is about *both*—the ethical problem of human–animal relations *and* the plight of literature in the moment of advanced capitalism—and we feel compelled to choose one over the other, we might very well miss the absolutely essential relation between them. By reading the animal strictly as a trope, as a nonliteral means of speaking about literature, we fail to understand how the text formulates a complex relation of dependency and struggle between the animal and literary studies. Rather than to subjugate the ethical question of animal liberation to literary studies, we might instead consider how the text relationally frames and negotiates animals and/as texts. To do so necessitates a willingness toward vulnerable reading, toward a reading practice by which we do not foreclose dependency and struggle among "subjects" but rather concede to the porousness of our disciplined ways of knowing. Recalling Animal's gesture of looking "into" Anjali's body and imagining therein a "nothingness" that creates "everything," perhaps through Coetzee's text we are offered a related invitation to risk seeing more than we are able to "know" concretely. Tailing Animal, what we risk is being dispossessed of our disciplinary mastery and the authority of our instantiated ways of knowing.

Costello's Wounded Humanimality

In "Force of Law" (2001), Derrida argues: "In *our* culture, carnivorous sacrifice is fundamental, dominant, regulated by the highest industrial technology, as is biological experimentation on animals—so vital to our modernity. . . . Carnivorous sacrifice is essential to the structure of subjectivity, which is to say to the founding of the intentional subject" (247). The unquestioned ability to inflict violence against animals is, for Derrida as for Costello, a structural aspect of Western subjectivity. There is no way then to challenge human mastery over animals without first calling this subjectivity into question. But how might we accomplish this from within it? The aging Costello relies on "seven decades of life experience" to argue that reason looks to her "suspiciously . . . like the being of one tendency in human thought" (Coetzee 1999, 23). Like the acts of vulnerable reading and writing, Costello opens herself to an experimental mode of knowing across experience and through language. In a crucially postcolonial gesture, she insists that reason partitions thought by forcefully policing its specious (and species) borders.

Costello begins her first lecture by evoking Red Peter, Kafka's fictional ape from "A Report to an Academy" (1971).[4] In the story, the educated ape recounts to the academy his ascent from life as a beast in the jungle and his postcapture emergence as a thoughtful being whose ability to speak intelligently renders him *almost* human.[5] In order to gain human status and rights, however, Red Peter must perform particular tasks in a disciplined manner to satisfy his audience. Like the scholar who works to master her field and forget what lies beyond her intellectual terrain in order to be validated by disciplinary interlocutors, the captive animal must in turn captivate his intellectual audience by proving his human likeness. Collapsing the distinction between herself and Red Peter as she stands before her audience, Costello declares: "Now that I am here . . . in my tuxedo and bow tie and my black pants with a hole cut in the seat for my tail to poke through (I keep it turned away from you, you do not see it), now that I am here, what is there for me to do? Do I in fact have a choice? If I do not subject my discourse to reason, whatever that is, what is left for me but to gibber and emote and knock over my water glass and generally make a monkey of myself?" (Coetzee 1999, 23). Costello posits herself here *as* an animal who, like Red Peter, stands before intellectuals and is expected to conceal her "tail" (her animality) by submitting her "tale" (her lecture) to the discourse of reason. Without a disciplined engagement with Western rational discourse, she will—like her animal double—remain unheard and dismissed (even dehumanized) by her audience. "Becoming" animal in this moment, Costello in one sense plays on the fact that as an aging woman she is already in some sense less than fully human. But there is also a fascinating and doubled gender switch at play here, since Coetzee "becomes" the female Costello, who herself "becomes" the male ape, Red Peter. There is something provocative about these ambiguous masquerades that persistently co-implicate sex with species. This returns us to Animal, whose overactive sexual impulses situate him paradoxically as "animal" (he cannot control himself) and as a "proper" heterosexual man who desires intercourse with women. Undoubtedly, Costello's willingness to "become" an animal is vitally different from Animal's, not least because his radical humanimality is staged from within the Indian slum as a geopolitical space of dispossession, while Costello's is literally performed on the stage of the Western academy. Despite their radically uneven material lives and the critical distinctions between them, these figures of difference share a mutual willingness to inhabit the break between the human and the animal.

Unlike Red Peter, who struggles as an ape to validate his entrance into the human world, Costello moves in reverse as a human toward an embrace of her animality. By drawing on forms of *thinking-feeling* that exceed reason, she attempts to speak for the animal *as* an animal—one that identifies itself as wounded within and by its human capture: "I am not a philosopher of mind but an animal exhibiting, yet not exhibiting, to a gathering of scholars, a wound, which I cover up under my clothes but touch on in every word I speak" (Coetzee 1999, 26). While her "tail" pokes through her clothing but is not seen by her audience, this ambiguous "wound"—a branding of sexual and species difference—is concealed beneath her clothing but "touched on" through speech. As if in sympathetic response to Costello's "wound," Butler mobilizes the concept of woundedness as an opening toward the Other. She writes: "I am wounded, and I find that the wound itself testifies to the fact that I am impressionable, given over to the Other in ways that I cannot fully predict or control. I cannot think the question of responsibility alone, in isolation from the Other; if I do, I have taken myself out of the relational bind that frames the problem of responsibility from the start" (Butler 2004, 46). While Butler's is a wound that implicates the Other as human, Costello opens the borders of the wound, urging us toward animal others. If for Butler the wound enables us to see our otherwise disavowed impressionability in relation to other humans, Costello affirms the wound as an opening toward animal others, including those that we already are. By affirmatively "touching on" her own humanimal wound, Costello calls for a radical expansion of our ethical horizons.

Vulnerable Listening

During the brief question and answer period following her public lecture, Costello is asked by a well-intentioned but perplexed audience member to clarify her thesis: Is she advocating for the mass closure of factory farms?

Does she want to convert her audience to vegetarianism? Does she want more humane treatment for animals, or to stop testing on them? To this request for clarification, Costello replies: "I was hoping not to have to enunciate principles. . . . If principles are what you want to take away from this talk, I would have to respond, open your heart and listen to what your heart says" (Coetzee 1999, 37). Costello's response is wholly inadequate to the context and no doubt strikes her audience as an evasion and a sign that she lacks a strong thesis. Indeed, it does both of these things, but it also does more. Implicit in her response is an assertion that the act of *listening* (to which I will return in the coda to this book) has greater ethical potential than speaking. Declarative speech is tied to the proscriptive, to the realm of law, which like reason is tautological and justifies its own ends. It is through a practice of *vulnerable listening* that Costello imagines we might hear something not merely spoken but felt. Recall here the discussion in the previous chapter of Singh's howl, which he cannot finally utter. Or Cassie's howl—one that I could hear but stubbornly could not read during the sudden onset of her blindness. What is at stake for Costello is not a reasonable claim about animals but a practice of learning to encounter animals vulnerably, including the wounded animal that she is. That we all are.

In her response to Coetzee's text, religious historian Wendy Doniger (1999) challenges Costello's position on animal silence by suggesting that far from confronting us with silence, the animal repeatedly speaks a language we simply refuse to hear. It is through this language—through the voice that is not heard precisely because another voice disables or refuses its recognition—that we can critically consider the productive potential of silent engagement. In Jean-Luc Nancy's formulation of the philosopher, he tells us that the philosopher is one who "cannot listen," who "neutralizes listening within himself, so he can philosophize" (2007, 1). To exceed philosophy, then, we must press on listening to those voices that appear voiceless in order to produce new forms of engaged entanglement with and beyond ourselves. The potential of vulnerable listening resides in an exchange between (animal) "silence" and (human) listening, an exchange that exceeds the didactic clamor of disciplinarity by crossing the borders of reason. To Doniger's mind, the question is not whether the animal *has* language but about the human refusal to hear its "silences."

Doniger extends Costello's formulation of animal language to include not only voice but also gesture, gaze, and so on. Like Costello, she posits the act of listening as absolutely central to understanding. Recall that Costello urges her audience members to "listen to their hearts" rather than to be governed by the didactic structure of the lecture form. Listening—even when we struggle profoundly to hear—is therefore absolutely fundamental to a becoming with the Other. As Doniger suggests, these other languages are forms of communication that must be not only heard but also interpreted. "This is the language we must learn to read," she insists. Like the human languages I discussed in chapter 2, animal languages will likewise continue to defy our will toward mastery over them. Yet since the act of reading (most broadly defined) is in all cases an imaginative and interpretive one, it is also therefore an act through which we might radically reconceive our responsibilities toward and as others. The voices of "barbarians," natives, and slaves were, after all, once similarly voices not worthy of being heard by the colonial ear. Both Costello and Doniger imply that by listening to those voices that have been forced to submit, voices that are so "foreign" that they have remained unheard, a radical reconceptualization of subjectivity itself can emerge. While this reconceptualization of vulnerable listening informs relations among humans, both Costello and Doniger insist that it necessitates a wholly new sense of being with/as animals.

Future Humanimalities

Rather than to articulate the animal as a figure for the oppression of more worthy human subjects, as anticolonial discourse has been wont to do,[6] Costello's commitment to sympathetic imaginings and practices of cultivated listening enables her to posit the animal as subject and her own subject-position as animal. In doing so, she urges us toward what I call the *future humanimalities*. Once we begin to take seriously the animality of the human, we must rethink the reach and methods—as well as the subjects and objects—of the humanities. Traditional humanities have taken for granted the human as an empirical object of study (as I discussed in different contexts in chapters 2 and 3) and have understood their importance as a pedagogical act of humanizing certain (human) subjects. Once we deconstruct the presupposed differences between humans and animals, the disciplinary division erected on that distinction will begin to crumble. To cultivate the future humanimalities, we might first ask how our already existing skills as scholars can move us beyond the masterful human enclosures of disciplinarity. Through her attention to metaphorical language, Costello enables us to begin to imagine how a future engagement with humanimal literary studies could dispossess us from our entrenched subjectivities and cultivate us otherwise. This future humanimalities will be, remembering José Esteban Muñoz (2009), a utopic one in the sense that it will be a practice that is forever dawning, never quite here.

Costello appeals to her academic audience to engage what she calls the "sympathetic imagination," a term that has gained attention in Coetzee scholarship (Durrant 2006). It is her own imagination of human characters, she reminds us, that has earned her an invitation to speak at a prestigious American university. Costello's magnum opus is a 1960s feminist rewriting of James Joyce's *Ulysses* from the perspective of Leopold Bloom's wife, Molly. Therein, Costello has created a world and a subject position for the fictional Molly Bloom, a character for whom Costello's readership reveres her. By imagining and articulating the world of Molly Bloom—literally a figment of Joyce's imagination made accessible to the world through Costello (who is herself literally a figment of Coeztee's imagination)—she has given rise to a character that her readers sympathize with and indeed love. She uses this example to illustrate the unlimited human potential for imaginative sympathy: "there is no limit to the extent to which we can think ourselves into the being of another. There are no bounds to the sympathetic imagination" (Coetzee 1999, 35). Costello submits to a romanticized sense of literary potential, and in so doing, denies the notion of ideology. She suggests that writers (and by extension readers) have the capacity to think beyond the discourses in which they operate. If we can imaginatively sympathize with a fictional character like Molly Bloom, she contends, we must certainly be capable of thinking our way into the real lives of animals. She dares us, in other words, to blur our engagements with the real and the fictional. Unlike Molly Bloom, after all, animals are living beings whose lives are not bound to the page but are physically among us: "If I can think my way into the existence of a being who has never existed," Costello declares, "then I can think my way into the existence of a bat or a chimpanzee or an oyster, a being with whom I share the substrate of life" (35).

Her academic audience is unsurprisingly puzzled by the romanticism of this appeal. The term "sympathetic imagination" is from the start under suspicion within an institution founded on objective inquiry and rational thought. If knowledge is something pursued in order to be mastered, the sympathetic imagination defies this mastery by extending itself to that which thought cannot foreclose. (Think again of Animal's wonder at the "empty space" that was nothing and everything all at once.) Despite the inevitable failure of her appeal, Costello insists that everyone—most urgently perhaps academics by virtue of being custodians of knowledge—must move beyond empirical knowledge into a form of thinking that implicates feeling. Picking up on this failure of imagination (of feeling and sympathy) within the academy and far beyond, Sam Durrant (2006) argues that *The Lives of Animals* is a text that continuously rehearses the failure of the sympathetic imagination in order to make way for a more effective relation toward the Other. For Durrant, this failure is "a precondition for a new kind of ethical and literary relation, a relation grounded in the acknowledgment of one's ignorance of the other, on the recognition of the other's fundamental alterity" (120).

Humanimal Metaphorics

There is arguably no more contentious moment in *The Lives of Animals* than Coetzee's turn toward the Holocaust, where the future humanimalities as a politics of dispossession comes into view. If ignorance of the Other is indeed always necessary, and as Durrant argues perhaps even productively so, Costello attempts to move her interlocutors toward a practice of responsible ignorance. Such a practice stands in contrast to the ignorance enacted during the Holocaust, during which people living near the camps ignored the practices of extermination that were so clearly signaled around them. This ignorance, Costello declares, situates those citizens imbued with full humanity as complicit with Holocaust executioners. Like the executioners, she provocatively claims, they refused to imagine themselves in the place of those being tortured and killed. In this way, the Holocaust represents a collective failure of the sympathetic imagination (Coetzee 1999, 34). This is the juncture at which Costello links the politics of Holocaust complicity to Western culture at large, which overwhelmingly ignores the mass torture and slaughter of factory-farmed animals. In each case, the failure to imagine oneself in the (horrific) position of the Other is a collective failure. She reminds her audience that "sympathy has everything to do with the subject and little to do with the object" (34–35). This call to imagine oneself in the place of the Other might seem to risk the same collapse of difference in the name of empathy that I criticized in the preceding chapter. But I want to suggest that Costello is in fact recommending something different. This is because she insists that the sympathetic subject is in no sense bounded—or limited—by the object toward which it reaches. Imagining oneself *in the place of* the Other does not require that we imagine ourselves to be *the same as* the Other. It is not, in other words, a lack within the Other that produces the Holocaust victim or the factory-farmed animal. In Levinasian terms, it is not the Other's lack of a face that signals its alterity but, as Matthew Calarco (2008) has argued, it is the turning away of our own faces that constitutes the Other's alterity for us. This marks the paradox of Hegel's master/slave dialectic; it is, after all, the master who is lacking, and not the subjugated slave. Costello points us toward the delicate maneuver between reckoning with our ignorance of the Other (there is a space between us and the Other that we cannot close) and the fact that we still bear responsibility for the Other. Our ignorance cannot justify ignoring their plight.

Costello insists on language as a locus for social change (and in this sense, she preaches to a literary choir). Her arguments press on language as that which reveals the unconscious and often conflicted tendencies in human thought. The rhetoric of the Holocaust is a prime example of this, illuminating the animal's function as the most crucial figure through which to evoke the atrocities of the Holocaust: "'They went like sheep to the slaughter.' 'They died like animals.' 'The Nazi butchers killed them.' Denunciation of the camps reverberates so fully with the language of the stockyard and slaughterhouse that it is barely necessary for me to prepare the ground for the comparison I am about to make. The crime of the Third Reich, says the voice of accusation, was to treat people like animals" (Coetzee 1999, 20). The animal as simile for the murdered human works to convey the sheer barbarity of the Holocaust. The Nazis were "butchers," and the victims suffered and died as though they were nothing more than "animals." In this metaphorical configuration, the Jew as animal deserves our deepest sympathy. Yet perversely, while the animal has become the most poignant simile for the Holocaust victim, it simultaneously also best describes the brutality of the executioners: "In our chosen metaphorics, it was they and not their victims who were the beasts. By treating fellow human beings, beings created in the image of God, like beasts, they had themselves become beasts. The human victims of the holocaust were treated *like* animals, but those who did the killing *are* animals" (21). As simile, the animal is a disposable object that is likened to the Holocaust victim as tortured subject. As metaphor, however, the animal is loathed by virtue of its violent nature. Our language reveals an ambivalent need to claim and decry the animal, to make it evoke both innocence and evil.

If for Costello poetic language offers us a crucial "feel" for the animal's experience of the world (Coetzee 1999, 30), it is also the figure of the poet in *The Lives of Animals* that refuses outright her attempts from within language to move us toward a humanimal politics. The respected (fictional) poet Abraham Stern is, like Costello, invested in language, form, and function. But he categorically refuses her use of rhetoric to develop her case for an animal ethics. Responding in written form to her analogy between concentration camps and slaughterhouses, between the slaughtered Jews and factory-farmed animals, Stern writes to Costello:

> You took over for your own purposes the familiar comparison between the murdered Jews of Europe and the slaughtered cattle. The Jews died like cattle, therefore cattle die like Jews, you say. That is a trick with words which I will not accept. You misunderstand the nature of likeness; I would even say you misunderstand willfully, to the point of blasphemy. Man is made in the likeness of God but God does not have the likeness of man. If Jews were treated like cattle, it does not follow that cattle are treated like Jews. The inversion insults the memory of the dead. It also trades on the horrors of the camps in a cheap way. (49–50)

It is not Costello's desire to rethink the animal that affronts Stern but rather that she relegates Holocaust victims to animal status in the service of her argument. He is not so much "against animals" as he is invested in the preservation of the exalted humanity of Holocaust victims. Here God guarantees the unidirectional movement of the simile; Stern must leave behind the language of poetry for the preservation of religious and cultural identity. Yet his refusal of rhetorical language to invert the "familiar" simile between Jews and slaughtered cattle reveals more than his position as an affronted Jew. As with the enormous chasm between animal similes and metaphors in Holocaust rhetoric, language poses a vital interpretive problem. For Stern, the reversal of the simile—from Jew treated as animal to animal treated as Jew—bears down on memory, history, and the murdered Jew. Describing the Holocaust victim as one sacrificed *like* an animal therefore signals the force and horror of the act. To reverse the simile threatens reason by issuing a comparison that renders the Jew as disposable as livestock. Stern's subject position—imbued with a profoundly traumatic history and invested with a desire to cling to the Jew's exceptional character—makes Costello's "trick with words" not merely difficult to digest but absolutely unpalatable. Paradoxically, while language provides for Costello the means to engage the sympathetic imagination, it is also her drive to toy with it that prevents Stern from sympathizing with animals.

This ideo-linguistic tension elicits Michael Rothberg's critique of "competitive memory"—the process by which two or more histories collide in a competition for historical supremacy and thus contemporary resources. Rothberg calls instead for a thinking of "multidirectional memory," wherein historical events as distinct as the Holocaust and decolonization struggles "coexist with complex acts of solidarity in which historical memory serves as a medium for the creation of new communal and political identities" (2009, 11). Multidirectional memory thus enables a noncompetitive coexistence between different traumatic pasts, enabling distinct histories such as the slave trade, the extermination of Jews and indigenous populations, and decolonization struggles to sound with each other rather than to compete in an economy of suffering. I want to suggest here that extending the concept of multidirectional memory to include the mass torture of animals can enable new conversations between Holocaust, postcolonial, literary, and animal studies rather than confirming a competitive hierarchy among them. It also allows us to reach toward a multidirectional sense of hum-animal being and to work through structures, histories, and languages of dehumanization toward a dehumanist politics.

While the animal may not remember its traumatic past in a conscious way (or does it?), it certainly continues to experience and be molded by its trauma. The absence of evidential animal memory in no way exonerates human populations from linking the modern violence done to the animal with other acts of violence enacted by and on humans (some remarkably similar in nature when we consider the striking resemblance between the extermination camp and the slaughterhouse). Rothberg argues that "a certain bracketing of empirical history and an openness to the possibility of strange political bedfellows are necessary in order for the imaginative links between different historical groups to come into view; these imaginative links are the substance of multidirectional memory. Comparison, like memory, should be thought as productive—as producing new objects and new lines of sight—and not simply as reproducing already given en- tities that either are or are not 'like' other already given entities" (2009, 18–19). Stern makes clear the problem of thinking the Holocaust victim and the factory-farmed animal as "bedfellows," since to his mind the link cannot help but to confirm the Nazi discourse that Jews were subhuman beings deserving of extermination. His resistance also signals the limits of decolonial thinking, which has, as I argued in the first half of this book, sought to redress the relegation of the colonized to animal status without accounting for the ways in which the human/animal distinction itself is deeply problematic within and beyond the human. Redressing the ways that humans have been rendered "animal" across time and space marks the limits of postcolonial thinking as much as it signals the limits of Stern's thought as affronted Jew. Both discourses remain limited by their political parameters and mired by unimaginative modes of comparison. In forget- ting the productive potential of acknowledging the animality of all humans, we abandon the urgent need to redress the human/animal distinction that makes possible the subjugation of *all* beings. Dehumanist readings of fic- tion can be a venue for Rothberg's necessary "bracketing of empirical his- tory," a venue through which we can begin to repoliticize animal metaphor- ics toward the liberation not only of particularly dispossessed humans but also of the animal as a sacrificial object. Recalling Animal's disarmingly productive insistence at the start of this chapter that he is both "just like" a human *and* "just like" his canine friend Jara, we might begin to assemble a politics that enables us—from within and beyond language—to be always both different from and proximate to those others to whom we are bound.

Toward a Dispossessed Humanimality

If humanist discourse has become instrumental to seeking rights and equality for those dehumanized by colonial force and its reverberations, it will seem to many counterintuitive, laughable, even an act of betrayal, that I engage postcolonial texts with an openness toward what I am calling a *humanimal ethics*. Yet by claiming the human—over and over again, across discrete historical moments and within particular political contexts—we have in this act of bringing some into the fold of humanity continued to produce others as abjectly outside. Anticolonial discourse has produced a series of human, dehumanized, and inhuman "remainders" through its claims to a universal human subject, a point I have laid stress on in chapter 1. Subsequently, I have explored how human rights discourse and humanitarian intervention have been represented in postcolonial literature as sites of violent erasure. Such critique—though vital—does not feel to me enough. I also feel compelled to experiment—in the Gandhian sense of experimentation, which entails a willingness to falter and an understanding that violence is inescapable—with other forms of discourse, intellectual practice, and embodied ethics that might become less harmful and exclusive than those we have to date been redeploying even in the name of "liberation." It may well be that literary and philosophical thinkers such as Matthew Calarco (2008), Mel Y. Chen (2012), Vanessa Lemm (2009), Susan McHugh (2011), and Cary Wolfe (2010) are already leading us toward a dispossessing of humanimalities to come. We do not have to be Animal, crippled by toxic exposure in the so-called Global South, nor do we have to be the white, aging female fiction writer of Coetzee's narrative in order to feel that there is something menacing about how the human has been claimed, performed, and enacted, or to desire more entangled forms of ethical becoming.

If a future humanimalities will enable—even require—a break from our disciplined trainings, it will also urge us toward more careful practices of dispossession, both in the sense of dispossessing ourselves from the humanist subjects that we have become and in the sense of producing more intimate ways of engaging those who have been forcefully dispossessed. From such grounds of dispossession, we might begin the work of sculpting ourselves as different kinds of beings. The future humanimalities offer us an impossible temporality in which we are learning from a future we have not yet reached; this is a utopian practice of learning how to break (in the now) from structures that have enabled us to turn away from the alterity of ourselves and others. If we have come to learn that our disciplines, like our subjectivities, are structured by violence—even (and perhaps especially?) those that have sought to humanize us—we can in response embrace the styles of thinking-being-performing together (with our disavowed "animalities" and with each other) that exist and are in the making, and that can revise the structures of subjectivity that have mapped us to date.

This is a scholarship that cannot be parsed from our mundane lives, a practice in which our "animal" aspects cannot be refused by the fully "human" work of intellectual inquiry. The dispossessions of this future humanimalities thus entail intimate acts of embracing and enfolding through which we call up the animals we have always been, and practice, along with Donna Haraway, new ways of becoming with the creatures we are, and the creatures that we live among. It is both a promise and a paradox of the future humanimalities that literature—a distinctively human form of communication/expression—may be one of the vital places where we can unteach and unlearn practices of the human.

CHAPTER 5

Cultivating Discomfort

I open this final chapter, about cultivation, discomfort, and the cultivation of discomfort, with an end that ushers us back toward a beginning. In the final sentence of Jamaica Kincaid's *My Garden (Book)* (1999), the Antiguan writer provocatively concludes her garden reveries by asserting, "I am in a state of constant discomfort and I like this state so much I would like to share it" (1999, 229). What is it about Kincaid's relation to her garden that produces this unabashed discomfort? Indeed, what is so enjoyable for her about discomfort, and how might we read and learn from her desire to "share" it? Kincaid's garden book—which explores her "attachment in adult life to the garden" (3) through colonial histories, botany, consumerism, mundane garden life, and exotic garden travels—is replete with sketches of bodily and psychic discomfort. Unlike the more romantic genre of gardening prose, Kincaid unearths her Vermont garden by contextualizing it within histories of colonization and their attendant human and botanical transplantations. In a similarly unromantic gesture, she also shares her own masterful fantasies through her garden meditations. Her fantasies of violence thus comingle across the text with the histories of colonialism from which she emerged as a subject.

In the earliest pages of *My Garden (Book)*, Kincaid narrates a scene in which she finds herself inexplicably digging up parts of her lawn into "the most peculiar ungardenlike shapes," until one day she realizes "that the garden I was making (and am still making and will always be making) resembled a map of the Caribbean and the sea that surrounds it" (1999, 7–8). For Kincaid, the garden is a repository of history, "an exercise in memory" that draws her back to uncontainable pasts both personal and political (8). Like those histories it elicits, the garden escapes and refuses the will of the gardener who desires mastery over it. Through Kincaid's discomfort,

5.1 Jamaica Kincaid watering her Vermont garden. *Jamaica Kincaid* by Annie
Leibovitz (1999).

we begin to learn the ecological stakes of human mastery and the critical
potentialities of feeling, recognizing, and inhabiting our own discomforts.

Throughout the text, she evokes the garden as a place rooted in memory and history and underscores the personal and political pasts—and the
forms of violence that constitute them—that grow into and through the
garden. It is a space in which the seeds of mastery continue, in more and
less subtle ways, to germinate through the gardener and her particular attachments. The discomforting turn of Kincaid's text also circles us back
to the very beginning of *Unthinking Mastery*, to the grounding claim that
while the rhetoric and activism of decolonialism have decried mastery in
its expressly colonial form, they have failed to account for the ways that
mastery has continued to propagate in other, but critically related, forms

and practices of both political and mundane life. The scale of dehumanist potentialities in the previous two chapters have moved us from intrahuman violence to the violence of humans over animals. In chapter 3, I considered through the figure of the humanitarian the complicity of liberal subjectivity with the systemic dehumanizing violence it wishes to amend, while in chapter 4 I broadened the horizon of this violence through a discomforting embrace of the human's animality and a critique of the human's masterful violence against animals. In this final chapter, we are turned ever more expansively toward dehumanist ecologies—and toward a practice of being uncomfortable in the world. A crucial part of this discomfort will come from having to reckon with the agency of nonhumans (the plants and animals who inhabit Kincaid's garden), since these other lives and agencies are caught up in a becoming with human agencies. When it comes to comfort, it is not only the human's that is at stake.

If comfort is, as Sara Ahmed reminds us, about "the fit between body and object" (2013, 425), discomfort allows us to pose the question of why some bodies can and cannot fit comfortably within particular spaces. I have discussed Ahmed already in chapter 2 in terms of her phenomenological reading of Fanon's embodiment of racial difference, but here I am interested in Ahmed's "Queer Feelings," in which she theorizes discomfort's generative potential. Ahmed argues that discomfort need not be read as strictly "constraining or negative" but rather can be transformative for normative social life: "To feel uncomfortable is precisely to be affected by that which persists in the shaping of bodies and lives. Discomfort is hence not about assimilation or resistance, *but about inhabiting norms differently.* The inhabitance is generative or productive insofar as it does not end with the failure of norms to be secured, but with possibilities of living that do not 'follow' these norms through" (2013, 430). It is not so much that discomfort becomes "radically" transformative by breaking away from norms completely but rather that discomfort shows us how to abide differently within those norms. But discomfort is also a *passage* through which we are moved by "a lack of ease with the available scripts for living and loving" toward other (perhaps no less discomforting) possibilities for collective life (425). Kincaid's garden prose cultivates discomfort, in part by showing us how within bourgeois life, according to Ahmed, one "can be made uncomfortable by one's own comforts" (425)—how even within the ease of relative affluence, discomfort can persist and proliferate. But Kincaid also shows us how this bourgeois discomfort leads back to other discomforting histories, such as those of colonial dispossession and theft, and the discomforts produced through the recognition of one's always failed mastery over the object in relation to which one seeks comfortable refuge. Crucially, Kincaid also makes her readers uncomfortable, by confronting us with her own violent fantasies and with her own perversely Orientalist representations of other dispossessed peoples (a topic to which I return in detail below). She thus writes her garden through relays of unease, offering discomfort as a politically fertile affect.

Transplanting Discomfort

For all the ways that discomfort can suddenly befall us, it is also an inheritance. In Derridian terms, we can call discomfort a hauntological affect that marks the present with a past, one that is in no sense easy to trace (Derrida 1994). Because so much of our discomfort—political, intergenerational, cultural, sexual—is inherited, and thus often unconscious, its potential to become an affective site of political resistance and reinvention requires a degree of psychic tilling. In her work on emotion and education, Megan Boler argues that a "pedagogy of discomfort" (1999, 196) may in fact be not only desirable but ethically imperative. For Boler, pedagogies of discomfort emphasize the bodies and materialities that both make life possible and differentiate (often radically) some lives from others. Practicing and teaching our discomforts can become acts of learning to live with the ambiguities and uncertainties of our complex ethical entanglements. Teaching discomfort, then, is an act of uprooting our deeply felt—but often deeply buried—discomforts. It is a way, in other words, of making discomfort conscious to those who embody it, as well as to those entangled with it in more and less complex ways. Yet when we learn discomfort unconsciously, we do so in ways that are complex and often difficult to articulate. This is at least in part because discomfort is often transmitted through composite networks of time and transplanted across generations and geographies. The site of the garden is a particularly fecund site through which to think discomfort precisely because it is a threshold space—often situated between the home and the world, between culture and nature.

The garden for me has always been a vexed space and the act of cultivation has been woven through with wonderment, confusion, and intense unease. Some of my earliest memories are of my mother at work in her garden, a space that seemed to flourish magically at her touch. In her famous essay "In Search of Our Mothers' Gardens" (1983), Alice Walker reminded feminist thinkers to look "low" rather than "high" to find the artful legacies embedded in women's work. Like Walker's, my mother's garden has always been a space of extraordinary beauty and bounty. It has been an open sanctuary for her across the stages of her adult life, one situated beyond (but importantly, adjacent to) a home marked by palpable forms of cross-cultural, gendered, and intergenerational discomforts over time. Similar to Kincaid's own emergence as a gardener, my mother's attachment to the garden began in the early stages of motherhood. The act of cultivating food seemed hand in hand with the act of raising humans (a deep immersion into growing wild things). My mother's gardening life began in a plot of a small community garden in central Canada, at the intersection of mourning and motherhood. Having moved from her beloved Montreal (a city to which she had once migrated by way of Belfast) to what then seemed to her a stark and hopeless prairie land, she found the city of Winnipeg had little to offer her beyond the conventions of married life for which she had moved.

My memories of my mother's garden do not stem from that community plot but rather are rooted two plots later in her magnificent garden behind 134 Westgate, where we were raised beneath a canopy of giant elm trees in a beige brick home that was, for most of my life, in a state of unrelenting restoration. Like the house itself, the garden was my mother's passion. But unlike the home, the garden was a sanctuary outside—in "nature"—that allowed her to separate herself off from the uneasy life that was unfurling within the home. If our home was tumultuously cleaved by cultural differences (my mother was a proudly disobedient feminist from Ireland who was a product of the Jewish diaspora, and my father—who hailed from India—was keen to have a "proper" family in an era when interracial families simply were not so), the garden for my mother was a refuge from the forms of physical and psychic discomfort proliferating within the home. But if her garden—in all its glory—was a space of refuge for my mother, it was also one into which the discomforts of the home spilled out into the earth. My mother used the garden as a repository of the political and personal forms of violence that had shaped and governed her life. The garden was also—and crucially—a space in which she did violence to herself, pushing her body beyond its limits and "beating the shit out of herself" (to quote a recurring yet unusually crass utterance of hers) in order to work out the impossible social dynamics that had made life inside intolerable. As a repository for violence and its fertile ground, my mother's garden was always a magnificent site of her discomfort—and a space within which I could not help but to share in it.

My mother's passion for the urban wild occupied an overwhelming degree of psychic space in my childhood. She was the founder of the Coalition to Save the Elms, a grassroots movement that proactively prevented the devastating effects of Dutch Elm Disease in Winnipeg. She battled against the Manitoba hog industry for its toxic environmental and social effects, prevented the demolition of countless historical buildings, and fought to save natural urban spaces from becoming sites of urban development. As a well-known environmental activist in our city, my mother held a certain acclaim as an ecofeminist renegade, so much so that a therapist of my youth once asked me in her presence whether I rather wished I was a tree, so that I could be assured of her absolute attention and unabated care.

It makes perfect psychoanalytic sense, then, that I would later come to work during my undergraduate summers as a tree planter in Northern Canada. For Canadians, tree planting is a fairly well-known subculture, comprised of mostly young, mostly white urbanites—often university students—who travel out to "the bush" to plant seedlings across clear-cut forests. By law, the logging industry of Canada is required to replant a percentage of the trees they cut, and planting companies bid for contracts to replant demolished forests. This results in a somewhat questionable net gain for the environment, since it promotes the regrowth of forests after they have been heavily logged. The culture of tree planting is one marked by brutal labor practices in which planters—with hundreds of saplings strapped to their bodies, sporting hard hats, steel-toed boots, and heavily duct-taped fingers—maneuver their way through logging debris in conditions ranging from snow to blistering sun. Planters are often swarmed by insects (black flies, deer flies, horse flies, etc.) as they pick their way across devastated geographies. The days are long, the repetitive motion of the work tolls on bodies, and there are days when the only sustenance a planter has for the workday is devoured by bears while planters look on helplessly at a distance. Planting is typically piecework, and most relatively skilled planters—conditions depending—plant thousands of saplings per day.

5.2 Collective labor: replanting saplings in the wreckage of clear-cut forests. Sarah Anne Johnson, *Planting Trees*, 2004. Chromogenic print, 11 × 14 in. Printed with permission of the artist.

For all its brutalities, tree-planting is also a coming-of-age experience for many young Canadians and a first attempt for most at communal living. This seamless relation between the intense rigors of planting life and the social bonds shaped through it are stunningly captured through Canadian artist Sarah Anne Johnson's exhibit *Tree Planting* (2005) (fig. 5.2). Moving between photography and still vignettes crafted through small clay figures and fabricated landscapes, Johnson's work charts the intensities, rigors, and passions of life in the bush. She captures the wildness of humans and the magic of flora and fauna that persist in and around intentional ecological catastrophe. In her piece *The Buffer Zone* (fig. 5.3), she represents from an aerial view a picturesque Canadian highway cutting through forest. Yet she reveals this forest to be an illusion crafted for highway passengers who cannot see that just beyond the tree line lies ecological devastation. Through an expanse of felled timber that extends beyond the borders of the image, Johnson exposes the hidden life of the clear-cut. Across her work, humans are represented both as extensions of the natural world and in stark contrast

5.3 The illusion of bountiful Canadian forests demystified through an aerial representation of the clear-cut. Sarah Anne Johnson, *The Buffer Zone*, 2003. Chromogenic print, 20 × 24 in. Printed with permission of the artist.

to it. If the clear-cut is itself devastation, so too are human bodies devastated within it. And if the clear-cut—despite its ruin—insists on life and beauty after its willed destruction, the damaged bodies of human planters and their solidarities likewise continue to vibrate and echo with utopian promise.

Tree-planting was my first experience of communal life, my first time being in an environment in which nudity was mundane, in which the taboo practices of urination and defecation became—often out of necessity—a public affair, and in which filth, wounds, and the body's return to uncultivated states were badges of extraordinary honor. The hardest work, the wildest parties, the closest to nature, the most intimate moments of collective life unfurled alongside—*and because of*—environmental devastation. If planting culture holds a radical social promise in its act of collective environmental repair, it is also haunted by those other socialities at the expense of which planting culture emerges. Clear-cut logging is very often—and often unbeknownst to planters—undertaken on unceded indigenous territory, with indigenous communities having scarce (if any) input about or benefit from the destruction of their lands. The commitment to practicing communal living and feeling (often brutally) utopic, in other words, comes at the cost of violent eradications both environmental and social. How can we think about such profound bonds formed through more and less conscious engagements with radical violence? Jodi Byrd's *The Transit of Empire: Indigenous Critiques of Colonialism* (2011) is a vital touchstone here, as she points to how settler colonialisms are "predicated on the very systems that propagate and maintain the dispossession of indigenous peoples for the common good of the world" (xix).[1] Here the questions of complicity and dispossession that framed the preceding two chapters surface again, summoning us to consider ways of inhabiting our own discomforting politics differently—of living alternatively within our contradictions rather than seeking to escape them.

It so happens that I was at my most poetically prolific in the clear-cut. Often miserably uncomfortable, driven to madness by swarms of bugs and the inescapability of penetrating sun or driving rain, I composed poems aloud in the trenches. This was art as salvation: poems became my way of *working through* the intolerable conditions of the labor. Without paper, ink, or free hands to capture them, these poems lived in the clear-cut as I worked—as though everyday language itself was being embedded in the earth along with thousands of saplings. Every once in a while a line will return to me, but most of them live in the clear-cuts that by now have become young forests again. If the language of those poems remains largely imprecise to me, what I remember of them is their tenor and tone, the ways they were always putting into language the urgent feelings of discomfort that came through me but also seemed to emerge from the clear-cut quiet of forests that once were. Without the precision of language, they sound to me now—from the distances of time and geography—like melancholic howls of hope. They took up the real and imagined histories of broadly conceived indigenous lives that had inhabited those desecrated forests and wrestled with the labor of piecework that I desired so much also to be *peace* work. They were poems that sought out complicity, that struggled not to extricate my labor from the forms of violence that enabled it but aimed instead at putting the present into conscious contact with histories—human and ecological—that had made possible my discomforting labor and communal bonds. Replete with failure and an uneasy awareness of complicity, these clear-cut poems took root in my own vital ambivalence, grasping at the queer promise of being exactly where I was and trying to inhabit the world otherwise there and then. *Here and now.*[2]

Vital Ambivalence

Kincaid's desire to "share" her discomfort and her often discomforting ecological prose become a way of locating her own violent entanglements and inescapable contradictions while bringing her readers into the folds of their own. She enacts *vital ambivalence*—a practice of representation that emphasizes, politicizes, and embraces the subject's contradictions and slippages. Kincaid stages her ambivalence through her attention to the living, agential space of the garden. Her vital ambivalence upturns the unthinking proliferation of masterful subjectivity by emphasizing the split subject that is at once masterful *and* oriented toward decolonization. Following R. Radhakrishnan's insistence that it is necessary for postcolonial studies not to read ambivalence as a sign of the postcolonial project's weakness but rather to "politicize this given ambivalence and produce it agentially" (2000, 37),[3] I read Kincaid's ambivalent gardening prose as an urgent and provocative call to return to the "seeds" of our cultivated subjectivities and to follow Kincaid's recognition within her garden of the "series of doubts upon series of doubts" (1999, 15) at root in our own subjectivities.

My contention here is that through the practices—linguistic and material—that shape her garden, Kincaid tends a decolonial ethics through split forms of self-representations that refuse modernity's insistence on a unified self.[4] Indeed, Kincaid herself engages a form of vulnerable writing in which she takes up the ecological by perverting genres and insisting on a form of self-narration that is not reducible to Enlightenment subjectivity. Her contradictions signal not a gap between conscious and unconscious drives or a Freudian version of contradiction and complexity but two kinds of consciousness at play in the subject. She is *both* a fierce and antagonistic critic of colonial domination *and*, as a bourgeois gardener, a willful participant in forms of dispossession that she ties back to histories of colonization. What her garden reveries make clear is that in order to mobilize feminist, ecocritical, and decolonial discourses, the foundational problem of mastery that underscores and binds them must be queried through the self-representation of the subject who is situated ambivalently in relation to Enlightenment thinking and its worldly manifestations.

While Kincaid queries "the relationship between gardening and conquest" (1999, 116), this relation remains expressly equivocal across her garden writing. She continuously sketches scenes, memories, and relations of violence that link the garden to more explicitly "political" forms of domination, coming to the realization that the garden is "a way of accommodating and making acceptable, comfortable, familiar, the wild, the strange" (44). And she shows us that part of this "strange" and "wild" nature springs precisely from within a version of the human itself, from the uncanny landscapes outside and inside the human. A case in point is the brilliant movement of discomfort across the concluding paragraph of *My Garden (Book)*. She begins with a return to an Edenic English garden after having traveled through Chinese landscapes in her ecotourist search for seeds to plant in her Vermont garden. Sitting at a dining table at Gravetye Manor in Sussex, once home of the famous English botanist and "inventor" of the English garden, William Robinson, Kincaid is struck with a violent fantasy. Amid the stunning beauty and reverence of Gravetye's famous gardens, Kincaid writes: "I had a delicious lunch in the dining room, and while eating I was struck with the desire to behead all of my fellow diners who were not traveling with me . . . because . . . because . . . because. Eden is like that, so rich in comfort, it tempts me to cause discomfort" (229). At Gravetye, with its soils rich in colonial histories of dispossession, Kincaid indulges both in the beauty of the place and in historically based fantasies of beheadings. Beauty, space, proximity, and temporality are entangled in this fantasy of execution, where (presumably white) strangers with whom she shares in Gravetye's indulgence become headless sacrificial bodies. In this fantasy, Kincaid as colonial subject holds sovereign power—but a power over undifferentiated subjects who are also critically *like* her by virtue of a shared passion for colonial English gardens.

Kincaid's ecological writings have been taken up to some extent by the recent surge of postcolonial ecocriticism, which seeks to map the vital connections between environmental and postcolonial studies.[5] This scholarship is founded on a core agreement that "what the postcolonial/ecocritical alliance brings out, above all, is the need for a broadly materialist understanding of the changing relationship between people, animals and environment—one that requires attention, in turn, to the cultural politics of representation" (Huggan and Tiffin 2010, 12). While highlighting the relations between economic power and environmental sustainability, postcolonial ecocriticism as a discursive field is also invested in how global narratives intervene in dominant formulations of the environment as an exploitable resource for certain human populations and how nondominant environmentalisms emerge through such narratives. Because in this discourse globalization is understood as a "latter-day colonialism based upon economic and cultural imperialism," postcolonial studies has become a critical way through which to read environmental crises and the narratives that represent them (Roos and Hunt 2010, 3).

Although Kincaid's ecological writings are familiar within this interdisciplinary turn, the emphasis has been on her explicit critiques of colonialism. In the introduction to their coedited volume, for instance, Elizabeth DeLoughrey and George B. Handley employ Kincaid's gardening prose to bolster an ecocritical critique of the "eighteenth-century homogenization of the natural world" (2011, 10). They argue that Kincaid becomes a crucial supplement to Michel Foucault's *The Order of Things* (1994), in which he dwells on the theory of natural history and the power of language to shape dominant ideologies. Unlike Foucault, who was not explicitly concerned with the *colonial* politics of "ordering,"[6] Kincaid emphasizes such politics through her critique of the (re)naming and classification of plant species during the colonial period. For her, "this naming of things is so crucial to possession—a spiritual padlock with the key thrown irretrievably away—that it is a murder, an erasing" (1999, 122). While ecocritical scholars have been quite right to see Kincaid as a crucial voice in environmental critiques of imperialism, the tendency in this scholarship is to cite her most direct critiques of the colonial enterprise without dwelling on the discomforting ambivalence of her prose—an ambivalence that I contend is absolutely crucial to politicizing her work beyond a straight critique of imperialism.

I use the term "straight" here to signal how queer theoretical trajectories can help to reorient Kincaid's work for and within postcolonial ecocritical scholarship. Jill Casid (2005) has pointed to the practice of relandscaping in colonial territories that was so vital to the imperial project. For Casid, looking back on the landscape of the West Indies as a colonial archive allows us to see the queer seeds of resistance that were always and from the outset germinating. Kincaid brings this history into the present, representing the postcolonial subject as one vitally and ambivalently tied to colonial force and the garden as a site of enduring colonial mastery. When Kincaid posits a relation between gardening and conquest, for instance, she queries whether we might cast the conqueror as a gardener and the one who works the fields as the conquered (1999, 116). Doing so, she recalls the slave plantation, putting it into discomforting relation with her own Vermont garden. Embedded in Kincaid's critique of colonial practices of mastery are the discontinuities and ambivalences of the postcolonial subject whose practices in relation to her garden often rehearse and subvert colonial modes and fantasies of mastery.

Recalling Halberstam's (2011) utopic summons to inhabit and embrace our failures, we can read Kincaid's always failed attempts at mastering her garden as a promise of stalling mastery. The vital ambivalence that she stages across her garden prose—always shifting between being the conqueror within her garden and being conquered (by colonists and by her garden), by casting herself as both Subject and Object—gestures toward Monique Allewaert's argument about personhood and colonialism in the American tropics. Allewaert contends that when we read across "artifacts" of the American tropics, we witness the emergence of human subjectivities that do not conform to the models of subjectivity made dominant through Enlightenment thought. Reading artifacts from the American tropics, Allewaert illustrates "the emergence of a disaggregated conception of the body that enables an understanding of the person that cannot be reduced to either of these periodizations' understandings of the human, nature, or politics" (2013, 9). Kincaid's vital ambivalence is attached but not reducible to the Enlightenment conception of the human, and her garden writing emphasizes a subject whose position in relation to the "natural" world remains haunted by both the force of Enlightenment thought and those other "conceptions" of subjectivity that it has repressed.

Wild Disruptions

In a fascinating discussion, Caribbean-born Vermont gardeners Kincaid and Kathleen M. Balutansky express their apprehensions about "colonizing" their gardens as territories already inhabited by other species. Balutansky explicitly links her gardening practice to the violent erasures and dispossessions of colonization. To this concern, Kincaid replies that "people with our history, when we give it some thought, we are very careful about the issue of displacing others" (Balutansky and Kincaid 2002, 795). She posits people of the tropics, in contrast to Europeans, as those who "live along with things" (795). Kincaid represents this tension in her garden prose, such as when an American botanist visits her garden and suggests the removal of certain trees from her property (1999, 34). Casting the trees as agents deserving apology, Kincaid is affronted by the audacity of the American who would not hesitate to destroy them. This commitment to living along with things, tied to colonial histories and the lessons wrought from them, posits Kincaid as a subject ethically formed by a violent past. This is an ethics that learns from colonization and reaches beyond the human consequences of colonial force by including "things" in her ethical frame.

All at once, and in a perfect play of her vital ambivalence, Kincaid tells Balutansky that in her garden she struggles endlessly to defend against wild invaders and to "keep things under control" (2002, 797). Kincaid acts repeatedly as a master of her garden. She enacts what Mick Smith calls "ecological sovereignty" (2011), which names the modern sovereign control over particular bounded spaces.[7] Straddling between self-representations that on the one hand pitch her as an ethical subject formed through colonization and on the other hand as yet another master emerging from the colonial encounter, Kincaid appears absolutely incongruous. Yet her narrative brilliance is rooted in this incongruity, through which she stages a critical disruption of the ways we imagine and sustain ourselves as bounded, coherent subjects.

If wild animals are under human threat in Kincaid's garden, they are also absolutely crucial to her garden reveries. At several moments in *My Garden (Book)*, she is disrupted by unexpected creatures that throw her off her narrative course. Wild animals tend to appear at moments in which Kincaid is dwelling on existential problems (how to live with the uncertainties of life, for example) or over a particular botanical species in her garden that will not conform to her desires. While Kincaid is grappling with her "fears" and her "responsibility toward others," for instance, a woodpecker begins suddenly to hammer at her house (1999, 25). This maddening interruption of her thought decenters the human focus of the text. Through its disruption (which is to say, its act of living), the woodpecker becomes entangled with Kincaid's fears and ethical queries. The wild becomes, in other words, folded into the narrative subject who wishes to deny it.

There are a series of similar vignettes in Kincaid's garden prose in which she violently fantasizes about killing animals. Of rabbits and woodchucks, she "plot(s) ways to kill them but can never bring myself to do it" (1999, 71), and when she captures a raccoon that she imagines to be "full of malice," she plans to drown it in a barrel of water before being halted by "the three whining pacifists I have somehow managed to find myself living with (my husband and our two children)" (50). Her explicit drive toward violence illustrates a radical break from the picture she paints of the Global South and practices of living along with other species. Her prose performs the exceptional status of the human while disrupting it, calling into crisis the product of European modernity by propping up and disabling its own fictions.

If for Kincaid the garden is "a way of accommodating and making acceptable, comfortable, familiar, the wild, the strange" (1999, 44), it is also a place in which that human comfort is always wildly disrupted. In her narration of a scene in which "one proper afternoon," as she is busy pondering the wisteria in her garden that will not conform to her desire, a fox appears and disorients her narrative trajectory (16). For Kincaid, the fox threatens the sovereign sanctity of her garden. (But this, we know already, is fantasmatic, since the misbehaving wisteria was already working to threaten her mastery.) If the fox breaks her from her mediation on the wisteria, it also gives rise to a fascinating psychological movement in which Kincaid first envisions the fox's coat as an ornamental object but turns abruptly to a radical inquiry into her own human subjectivity: "I believe I am in the human species, I am mostly ambivalent about this, but when I saw the fox I hoped my shriek sounded like something familiar to the fox, something human" (18). Kincaid's "hope" that the fox will recognize her shriek as issuing from a human is a hope that the fox will be scared away from her garden. Yet on another and crucial level, the fox is positioned to recognize (even confirm) for Kincaid a humanity about which she is both uncertain and "mostly ambivalent." The fox is thus *both* an unwelcomed animal intruder and, through the hope that it will recognize her voice, one that might call her *into* human being. Her response to the fox trails between fear and jealousy: "The way he would run away from me with his head turned toward me, watching me behind him as he propelled himself forward, was frightening. I could not do that. And then he disappeared into another part of the wild and I could not follow" (19). Kincaid's psychic play in the fox scene moves ambivalently from the complete objectification of the fox as "ornament," to a fear of its capacities, to a suspension of her own species being ("I believe I am in the human species"). Like Animal, who as we saw in the previous chapter emphasizes his own contingent humanity, here Kincaid likewise throws her relation to the human species into question. This sweepingly dehumanist movement takes us from the exterminating force of the modern subject, to the colonial question of who counts as human, and finally to the more primordial question of what the human *is* as a life form. Kincaid's dehumanism traffics between a human both familiar and strange, representing the human's complex adjacency to colonial history and to the animal in ways upsetting, unpredictable, and abidingly disruptive.

Garden-Variety Orientalism

What part of "the wild" does Kincaid inhabit? In her caustic travelogue *A Small Place* (1988), she writes to the white tourist (identified poignantly as "you") about the geographic, historical, architectural, and social lives of her Antiguan homeland. Positing the tourist as "an ugly human being" whose presence in Antigua echoes and extends colonialism, the book functions in part as a disinvitation to vacation on the island. The tourist industry, she explains, has supplanted colonialism, keeping Antiguans subservient to Western powers and desires. The tourist industry in Antigua, then, is a neo-colonialist enterprise with which those on vacation are critically entangled. Given her staunch critique of the tourist industry as an extension of colonialism, it comes as a surprise that in Kincaid's later garden writings she participates eagerly in "seed hunting" expeditions across China and Nepal. These ecotourist expeditions, aimed at collecting "exotic" seeds to cultivate in her Vermont garden, edge uncomfortably close to her fierce critiques of Western tourism in Antigua.

Kincaid's narrative self-location is expressly complex, straddling between an alliance with others "like me" who are subjects of colonial and neocolonial power and situating herself as part of the neocolonial "conquering class." In her garden travel prose, she slides between these conflicted modes of self-representation, rehearsing in often vexing ways the Orientalist travel practices and fantasies that cast her in the role of the "ugly" Western traveler. Her plant-hunting pursuits are first detailed toward the end of *My Garden (Book)*, when she travels to the Yunnan province in China, and later to Nepal in *Among Flowers*. It is in the latter text that she confesses, "I had no idea that places in the world could provide for me this particular kind of pleasure" (2005, 3–4). Unlike the ugly Western traveler of *A Small Place* (1988), who remains oblivious to the social conditions of Antigua and uses the place as a relaxing "escape" from real life, Kincaid's pleasures abroad are ones derived through repeated discomfort and unease produced through her foreign travel. But like the travels of other tourists, her journeys often neglect the lives of those who serve her. How should we think about this frustrating movement between Kincaid's staunch critique of tourism and the ways that she narratively celebrates her own complicities with it? I want to suggest that Kincaid's contradictions—far from being mere signs of her hypocrisy—reveal a postcolonial subject (in her case, a formerly dehumanized subject now imbued with Western bourgeois subjectivity) as one whose paradoxes upend the very foundations of Man. Kincaid in this sense harmonizes with Sylvia Wynter by emphasizing through her garden prose how the construction of particular narratives and the performance of particular versions of being human are intimately and inextricably linked. By exploiting the contradictions of the subject through narrative, Kincaid demonstrates an awareness of how the human is sociogenically produced. As though answering Wynter's call to produce new modes of being human, Kincaid's narrative plays with ambivalence and contradiction, emphasizing the cracks in postcolonial subjectivity and opening up the possibilities that may flourish from its fissures.

Kincaid's Rousseauean "walk" in Nepal is replete with reverie and reflection and situated precariously between a longing for full possession of the "rare" and "indigenous" that can be transplanted and cultivated "at home" and a discursive disavowal of this desire. Mimicking the language of colonial botanists, Kincaid states in no uncertain terms that "claiming . . . was the overriding aim of my journey" (2005, 71). She is often discomforted—if not disgusted—by the seemingly strange practices of the Chinese and Nepalese people whom she encounters during her seed hunts. Yet she tells her readers that her hunt in Nepal would "haunt many things in my life for a long while afterward, if not forever" (8). Kincaid moves—sometimes bewilderingly—between alliance with the Nepalese and radical difference from them. She grounds her alliance historically: "Because of my own personal history, every person I saw in this situation seemed familiar to me" (18). This "familiarity" (with those whose cultures are very different from her own) emerges again when she declares, "I only viewed everything I came upon with complete acceptance, as if I expected there to be no border between myself and what I was seeing before me, no border between myself and my day-to-day existence" (20).

Nevertheless, her difference from the Nepalese in *Among Flowers* is most forcefully articulated through the politics of naming, a politics she describes in the colonial context as a violent erasure in *My Garden (Book)*. In the latter text, through her reflections on the Swedish botanist Carl Linneaus, she ties European botanical practices to colonization through their mutual practice of renaming in the production of European knowledge. Like the colonial explorers who "emptied worlds of their names" (1999, 160), so too did the early botanists proclaim the names of species "not to fulfill curiosity but to possess" (156). Possession here is not merely claiming ownership over something but "a murder, an erasing" of the thing being (re) named. As in Genesis, where God gives humans dominion only after they have named the animals, the power to name precedes and extends itself toward mastery. The Canadian environmentalist David Suzuki emphasizes this power when he illustrates how naming shapes our orientations toward other things: "Calling a forest 'timber,' fish 'resources,' the wilderness 'raw material' licenses the treatment of them accordingly" (2007, 289). Suzuki emphasizes how destructive social practices become authorized through uses of language and the particular practice of renaming things in ways that legitimize their material exploitation.

The power to (re)name, then, comes to signal a mode of masterful relation in which the one who names is also the one who can bestow, classify, and possess. Kincaid's own acts of renaming signal particularly poignant forms of dehumanization that are overtly linked to colonial practice.[8] When Kincaid refuses to recognize the names of the Sherpas whose laboring bodies make possible her journey, she renames them through characteristics identifiable to her: the Sherpa who cooks her meals becomes "Cook"; the one who carries their dining table on his back is known to her and her fellow seed hunters as "Table"; and the Sherpa who speaks little English is named after the one phrase he knows—"I Love You" (2005, 26). Of the Sherpa she names Table, she declares, "I was appalled that someone had to carry this whole set of civility" (30). The point here is not simply that Kincaid—like Linnaeus and the colonists she critiques—engages the violence of renaming. There is a crucial continuity among the colonial, the botanical, and the ecotouristic in that they perform the possessive erasures of others, enforcing masterful world relations by naming others as if they exist for oneself. The Sherpa becomes Table not merely because the name describes the particularities of his work but because his work as a table carrier is oriented toward Kincaid's own comfort. The Himalayan seed hunt is a perversely neo-Orientalist undertaking—narrated through Kincaid's postcolonial and Western perspectives—that represents the Sherpa's labor as the only consequential aspect of his existence.

Of her nearly indiscriminate forgetting of the names of the Nepalese people who made possible her journey, Kincaid declares: "This is not at all a reflection of the relationship between power and powerlessness, the waiter and the diner, or anything that would resemble it. This was only a reflection of my own anxiety, my own unease, my own sense of ennui, my own personal fragility. I have never been so uncomfortable, so out of my own skin in my entire life, and yet not once did I wish to leave, not once did I regret being there" (2005, 27). The erasure of the Other thus becomes not about sheer power and the ability of the master to strip the slave of a world. Instead, Kincaid turns the erasure inward, signaling how her own "anxiety," "unease," "ennui," and "personal fragility" paves the way for the erasure of others. What Kincaid advances here is a list of feelings that align with Judith Butler's (2004) concept of "vulnerability," a state of reckoning with one's own unease and reliance while accepting without "regret" or defensiveness the fact of being in this position. In this instant, fragility is not something to be disavowed but something to embrace. At the same time, Kincaid's language also echoes the master/slave dialectic in fascinating ways. Writing from the narrative position of a postcolonial bourgeois subject, Kincaid reveals the uncanny continuity between the psychodynamics of the colonial master and the postcolonial subject that I have traced across this book. Indeed, she appears here to fulfill Fanon's theory that the postcolonial bourgeoisie would in turn come to reproduce the material disparities of the colonial moment if during decolonization a full proletariat revolution did not occur. And she knows this: Kincaid's explicit desire to eliminate others (like the fox) is turned inward to reveal her own profound discomforts; she effaces the Other because she is discomforted by alterity and because she herself fears effacement. What would it mean to stay with this vulnerability, to bear the familiarity of the Other, whose simultaneous likeness and difference are so profoundly distressing?

Wonderment and Time

There is a fascinating moment toward the end of *Among Flowers* in which Kincaid is inspired by the beauty of the Sacred Lake in Topke Gola. Gazing at this natural wonder, Kincaid is filled with "the joy of spectacle, the happiness that comes from the privilege of looking at something solely rare and solely uncomplicated. But the Sacred Lake plunged me into thinking of the unknowableness of other people" (2005, 151). From the privileged gaze rehearsed in the first sentence, Kincaid articulates a thoroughly anthropocentric view of the landscape as "solely uncomplicated." Yet she is then "plunged" by the lake, which surfaces as an agent that acts on her, immediately after which she declares "the unknowableness of other people." She moves from enjoying the extraordinariness of the foreign landscape to an assertion about how other people (like her garden) cannot be truly known, and this movement is prompted by a barely perceptible recognition of an agency that is radically Other. By reading Kincaid's contradictions vulnerably, her slippages between performing as a critic of neocolonialism and as a bourgeois postcolonial Orientalist, we witness the shadow of a nonmasterful subject, one that while still tied to structural modes of violence also allows itself to be "plunged" by others (both human and nonhuman) into other orientations. While it is abroad that her seed hunting narratives most glaringly expose the contradictions of the bourgeois subject, it is back "at home" in her American garden where this nonmasterful subject begins to take root and grow.

Ultimately, Kincaid's garden is one that nurtures unanswerable questions, emphasizes antagonisms, and germinates the masterful gardener's future disappearance. An integral part of the gardener's personality, Kincaid declares, is made up of that which is "to come" (1999, 85). As such, the gardener is one whose present activity is driven toward a futurity. But the garden is always also historical, haunted by gardeners past and by the possibilities of flourishing that have been historically stamped out: "Memory is a gardener's real palette; memory as it summons up the past, memory as it shapes the present, memory as it dictates the future" (218–19). As an intimate political space, the garden exists in a queer temporality. For Elizabeth Freeman, queer temporalities are "points of resistance" to normative temporal ordering, ones that "propose other possibilities for living in relation to indeterminately past, present, and future others: that is, of living historically" (2010, xxii). Against what Freeman calls "chrononomativity," which functions by organizing bodies to capitalize productive use, the queer time of the garden is one in which we can begin to "trail behind actually existing social possibilities: to be interested in the tail end of things, willing to be bathed in the fading light of whatever has been deemed useless" (xiii). Lingering in the queer temporalities of the garden—as a disruptive space that is always both historically haunted and future-oriented—we might ourselves become cultivated differently.

Seeking to define the complexity of the gardening subject and to describe its desires, Kincaid continuously shifts between her constitutive wonderment and fundamental hostility toward the garden. In *My Garden (Book)*, she writes: "Even after many years of gardening, I never believe a live plant will emerge from the seed I have put in the ground; I am always surprised, as if it had never happened to me before, as if every time were the first time" (1999, 49). Here, the garden produces something unbelievable for Kincaid, something bestowed with wonder precisely because the garden—the plants, the seeds, the soil, the perceptible and imperceptible beings that dwell therein—has an agency that is never reducible to the gardener's will. This experience of watching nature act always as though for the "first time," an experience that signals an engaged awareness of nature without intervening in its unfolding, is for Kincaid an essential part of the wonder of her garden. Yet in defining the desires of the gardener in the closing paragraph of the book, she explicitly casts the garden as a subjected adversary: "What does a gardener want? A gardener wants the garden to behave in the way she says, and when it does not, she will turn it out, abandon it, she will denounce the garden, not in general, only as it is particular to her, and we who come after will have to take some of what she loved and some of what she didn't love, and accept that there are some things we cannot take because we just don't understand them" (229). The gardener of the past relates to her garden as a possession, as that which can be abandoned and denounced when it does not "behave in the way she says." While the gardener remains a subject passionate about the garden as a concept, she deplores her "particular" garden for not reflecting and confirming her mastery. Yet Kincaid is also the gardener of the future— the "we who come after"—and in this spirit is willing to give up on the fantasy of mastery enacted by the earlier gardener, who may well be her own earlier self.

While Kincaid registers the continuities between her wonderment toward and desire to hold mastery over the garden, her prose also persistently attunes to the garden as an agential space. It is a space rife with uncontrollable and at times unwelcome life, and the recognition of this life—even when she explicitly disavows it—begins to upend the stability of the gardener as sovereign subject. It is the garden, and its unwelcome inhabitants, that reveal to the gardener the fantasmatic nature of the sovereign subject. It compels those engaged with the garden to consider their own psychic and bodily materialities. Melissa Orlie argues that "each of us is not only matter but impersonal matter; made of stuff over which nothing is master and whose entirety no one is in a position to know. It is precisely when this unpalatable fact is glimpsed that the ego is most likely to submit to delusions of sovereignty" (2010, 122). Orlie frames mastery as a delusion, an unrealizable fantasy most likely to appear at precisely the moment that the subject has to confront its vulnerability, its disavowed openness to the nonhuman and inhuman actors that materially and biologically give rise to and sustain human life, and to the lives and histories of other humans. Kincaid's garden—rife with unexpected visitors and "willful" species—reveals the entanglements of the past, present, and future as it uncovers not only the gardener's vulnerability but her fraught constitution as a porously bounded subject.

Always filled with thoughts of "doom" in her garden, of "thoughts of life beyond her own imagining" (1999, 61) that produce her discomfort, Kincaid returns the reader consistently to the unanswered refrain, "What to do?" (26). She sketches the agencies and historical trajectories of both garden and gardener, of colonization and its resulting transplantations, and in so doing asks us to weed through the tangled subjectivities of this postcolonial moment—a moment in which mastery is both the driving force of the modern subject and its anticipated ruin. Here, in the work of vital ambivalence and the vulnerable engagements it elicits, repressed conceptions of personhood linger and subjectivities straddle mastery and wonder. Through the radical unpredictability of inheritance and of precisely *not* knowing "what to do," Kincaid sustains a representation of the subject's incongruity and vital ambivalence. This ambivalence is the vital inheritance that leads us toward emergent conceptions of being. The queer hope of dehumanism is that we might uproot our masterful subjectivities, dwelling within our devastated landscapes alongside other dynamic agencies that are making up the future with us.

Coda

Surviving Mastery

Toward the end of Aimé Césaire's *A Tempest* (*Une Tempête*, 1969), an anti-colonial play that rewrites and restages Shakespeare's *The Tempest*, the slave-master Prospero articulates himself as a "prophetic scientist": "I am not in any ordinary sense a master, as this savage thinks, but rather the conductor of a boundless score: this isle, summoning voices, I alone, and mingling them at my pleasure, arranging out of confusion, one intelligible line. Without me, who would be able to draw music from all that? This isle is mute without me. My duty, thus, is here, and here I shall stay" (2002, 46). Against the experience of his "savage" slave Caliban, who characterizes him as a despotic colonial ruler, Prospero envisions himself to be engaged in extraordinary acts of magical mastery. He distinguishes his own practices from other "ordinary" forms of colonial mastery, casting his unusual masterful practices as works of art crafted from silence and chaos. Yet this exceptional mastery resounds with the more mainstream discourses of colonialism that likewise seek to replace "chaos" with something approaching (but always falling short of) civility. The violent occupation of the island and the enforcement of slavery become not merely the white man's burden but also an *artistic* act — a production of "one intelligible line" of music from voices that to him are otherwise "mute." To colonize for Prospero is to "mingle" for his own pleasure the forms of life that inhabit the island. His creative, magical mastery is for him not merely an act of domination but an act of *making sound* in ways that are pleasurable to and for him. Prospero is a self-designated artist whose artistic mode is enslavement, and what he needs is for his slave to understand — and to appreciate — his exceptional force.

In the final scene of *A Tempest*, after the other actors have departed,

Caliban and Prospero remain together on the now ostensibly "postcolonial" island. While no longer structurally master and slave, they remain firmly locked in the dynamics of mastery. Unrelentingly at odds and incapable of being together without coercion, their actions and sounds become mixed with the rest of the "natural" world that fully inhabits—physically and sonically—the island. If nature has always been living and sounding on the island, it is only now that we come to hear it as its own character, its own unfolding drama. A decaying Prospero, left only with the "magic" of his firearms, shoots arbitrarily into space as he impotently fights against the "unclean nature" that surrounds him, calling for Caliban to assist him (Césaire 2002, 65). Off set, the audience hears "snatches" of Caliban's ongoing freedom song, gleaned only "in the distance, above the sound of the surf and the chirping of birds" (66). Will the need for this song never cease? In this anticolonial restaging, Prospero has failed both to be master across the play and to relinquish his mastery at its end. So too has Caliban failed, having fought for a freedom that he still cannot feel or make Prospero recognize. Somewhere amid this decolonizing spectrum in which former masters and slaves remain locked in a struggle for recognition and power, we can envision the desiring liberal subjects of Mahasweta Devi and J. M. Coetzee, or the ambivalent autobiographical Jamaica Kincaid slipping between botanical awe and possessive desire. Somewhere therein we might also become able to position our own desires and pursuits, which often and despite ourselves remain deeply entrenched in a logic of domination we have yet to understand how to relinquish.

I am not uncritical of my recurring use of the term "we" across these pages, but it is one I cannot do without. At the start of *Unthinking Mastery*, Hélène Cixous's desire for unmasterful forms of being became entangled with my own, and these allied desires shaped a "we" that hoped toward antimasterful collectives. But "we" is not in any sense a given, nor is it exempt from its own masterful snares. Sara Ahmed, for example, sounds a cautionary note about the pronoun "we," which she persuasively argues remains bound to a Eurocentric collective construct that includes only via a process of violent exclusion (2006, 17). The Bush administration's rhetoric of "us" versus "them" in the aftermath of the attacks of September 11, 2001, for instance, illustrates how dangerous such conceptualizations become when they materialize against thousands of civilians whose maiming and deaths are the necessary by-products of this form of political inclusion. This "we" guards itself through particular dialectical political practices, ones that rely increasingly on mythical constructions of those-who-are-not-us, shaping whole worlds beyond us as dangerous and in need of submission.

But "we" is also necessary to collectivity, to imaginary and imagined futures in which "we" comes to include forms of being we have not yet learned to recognize, to hear, or to feel. Jeanne Vaccaro writes, " 'We' is an idea and a problem, a shape to ask after" (2015, 273). "We" is indeed a problem, one often marked by specific forms of human being and human inclusion. But it is, Vaccaro suggests, also a "shape" that we continue to question, to envision, to amend. In his framing of utopia, José Esteban Muñoz argues that "concrete utopias are relational to historically situated struggles, a collectivity that is actualized or potential" (2009, 3). While these utopias can be "daydream-like" and exist in the "realm of educated hope," they are guided by "the hopes of a collective, an emergent group, or even the solitary oddball who is the one who dreams for many" (3). Here we can see in Muñoz's formulation so many ways in which "we" moves between collectives and singularities, in which "we" is emerging and contingent rather than concrete and impenetrable. Gayatri Chakravorty Spivak reminds us in fact that the question "who are we" is part of the pedagogical exercise, one that cannot be answered in advance of its asking (2003, 25). My own "we" across *Unthinking Mastery* is a question as much as it is a hopeful summons to the (always imagined) future readers of this text who might be or might become invested in collective reorientations in the world. It is also fundamentally a dehumanist "we," one that arises not on the grounds of Western scientific discourse and humanist politics but from the promises of those subjugated and emergent worldviews that recognize life, feel energy, and hear rhythms where now there appear to be none.

This always inquisitive, always revising, always expansive "we" is as hopeful as it is necessary for survival. In the midst of global climate change, of vanishing rain forests and melting polar ice caps, of "natural" disasters across the globe, our masterful practices are perversely plowing the soils of our extinction. Mastery in this sense is a diagnosis of a certain form of human living that is—as *Unthinking Mastery* has sought to pressure— woven tightly into the fabric of our worldviews. Rather than to live by seeking out forms of mastery to correct damages done, or as though we have reached a palliative stage as a species, I am driven by a utopian hopefulness in the activities of unfolding mastery in all its aspects. To survive mastery, we must begin to deconstruct our own movements (intellectual, activist, corporeal) that remain entangled with the violent erasures of other lives, and of things we declare insensate. Survival depends on new forms of living together, gathered in collectives that promise to astonish us.

Unthinking Mastery has pointed toward twentieth- and twenty-first-century discourses that have aimed explicitly to disavow mastery and has illustrated how these discourses have often failed to theorize the absolutely vital links among these "historical" forms of mastery and those that continue to shape human subjectivities today. My aim has been to provoke a more detailed and sustained examination of mastery precisely in order to begin to understand the ways that, like Prospero, we engage unthinkingly in masterful acts that we firmly believe to be harmless, benevolent, or even works of art. Nonetheless, art can also open us toward forms of cohabitation and being with others that have been lost, suppressed, or have yet to be performed. The readings of postcolonial literary texts that I have offered across the book focus on a host of seemingly benevolent figures: the fictional writer's more-than-human ethics, the humanitarian aid worker, and the impassioned gardener and ecotourist. These are subjects that are invested in a politics of "the good" but have remained locked within their own impulses toward and pursuits of mastery.

Like those anticolonial thinkers in the first half of this book who took seriously mastery but continued to issue its force, and like the various fictional (and semifictional) characters that surfaced across the second half of this book, we are failures. We are failures both in our masterful pursuits ("nature" keeps having the last word) and, perhaps most urgently, in our current capacities to recognize our abiding desires for mastery even as we might renounce mastery politically. Kincaid's refrain from the previous chapter—"what to do?"—reminds us that we cannot rely on masterful proscriptions about ethics and politics, nor can we abdicate our responsibility to act even when we fear complicity and risk failure. In making the claim that we are failing in our "alternative" movements toward increasingly utopian worlds, I by no means wish to extinguish hope. On the contrary, I remain profoundly invested in envisioning and enacting utopias, through intimate and active imaginaries, in the work and wonder of even the most mundane and seemingly apolitical activities. I mean to suggest that in failure—and critically, in recognizing, reading, and becoming vulnerable to failure—we participate in new emergences, new possibilities for nonmasterful relations. Alongside Jack Halberstam, we might say that the undoing of masterful subjectivities can be located precisely in mastery's disappointments, in understanding failure as "a refusal of mastery" (2011, 11). The decolonial texts analyzed across *Unthinking Mastery* teach us that our "ways of inhabiting structures of knowing" are ways that obscure and legitimate the masterful fracturing of particular bodies, spaces, and things (12).

When we open ourselves to the ways that texts can teach us, what we begin to learn is our own undoing. If it is no longer au courant to claim as intellectuals our "mastery" over our disciplines (and I'm not sure that it is not), this change of language does not undo the drive to think of ourselves as the active subjects of reading and the texts we read as the inanimate objects that confirm our declarative knowledge. To distance ourselves from mastery is, first, an act of reframing our relations to *all* things, regardless of whether in the moment we bestow them with something currently called "life." From this point of departure, directionality becomes infinite and failure a process we might begin to meet with pedagogical delight.

Because our tendency has been to map history and time as and for the human (the histories of certain lives, certain collectivities, a certain "species"), we register only a shallow sense of embodiment and time. Edward Said (1979) and Antonio Gramsci (1971) mutually insist that we compile inventories of the infinite traces that history has left in us as subjects. Expanding Gramsci and Said, we must begin to understand that such "traces" far exceed human histories and the human subjectivities that history produces. While Fredric Jameson has famously urged us to "always historicize" (1981, 9), Christopher Breu compels us to look to histories far longer and more inclusively than we have done to date (2014, 28). The surface and deep traces that comprise us as beings are traces that entail not only other human lives that have touched ours but also and vitally the infinite forms of being that far predate and give rise to us as particularly formed subjects. At different moments across *Unthinking Mastery*, I have turned back to myself, sifting through some of those traces that comprise me. Those trees I have planted in clear-cut forests are still growing, amid words, affects, and footprints also left behind. I have also deposited traces in places I have never been, such as in the Arctic where polar ice caps are receding and through absence leaving behind their own devastated traces. Those traces left in me and those I leave behind constitute me as a subject. We live because we have deposited energy and matter into the world and because forces well beyond what we can see or hear or touch have embedded themselves in us and have enabled and sustained our existences. The impossible historical inventory to which we might aspire includes those ecological and material entities that underlie our individual and collective forms of being.

If the failures at the end of Césaire's play resound in Prospero's collapsing but relentless worldview, and in Caliban's as yet unachieved freedom, there is also extraordinary promise in engaging with and beyond this human deadlock. To be sure, the play's end signals the ongoing fight for decolonization, a battle that has become increasingly muted by the more insidious processes of globalization. If colonization is masterfully coextensive with liberal globalized life today, our task is to take stock of their abiding connections and to begin to untether them. The end of Césaire's play draws us through sound explicitly toward *other* voices—voices that have always been there but that (as readers, audiences, modern subjects) we have been untrained to hear. The background noise of the "natural" world becomes foreground, and the sounds of humans become sounds that comingle with other increasingly more dominant sounds. The sounds of nature at the play's end are always already with and among us. Listening to these voices, we might begin to hear other songs of survival, and to sound differently among them.

NOTES

Introduction

1 I capitalize "Man" in keeping with Sylvia Wynter's differentiation between Man and the human. For Wynter, Man designates the particularly Western, secular, imperial version of the human.

2 Some of the major thinkers within this stream of posthumanism insist that taking the human's animality seriously not only calls into question humanist traditions but also allows us to imagine alternative forms of political being. Jacques Derrida's *The Animal That Therefore I Am* (2008), for instance, which was originally a series of lectures in 1997, traces how a wide variety of philosophers, including Aristotle, René Descartes, Martin Heidegger, Jacques Lacan, and Emmanuel Levinas, all insist on the human difference from other animals (Derrida calls them *animots*, partly to call attention to the absurd flattening of difference enacted by the word "animals") by rehearsing some version of a distinction between reaction (which all animals can do) and response (which is supposedly reserved for humans). Although Derrida does pressure how humans, based on this dogmatic division, conceptualize animals, he is also interested in how this division has caused the human to misunderstand itself (downplaying, for example, how it also reacts more often than not). Donna Haraway's *When Species Meet* (2008) picks up on Mary Louise Pratt's (1992) concept of the "contact zone" to think about spaces (the scientific laboratory, the home where multiple species make mess mates, the dog show) where different species of animals come into contact, and about the politics and ethics that inhere in those contacts. Haraway insists that "people can stop looking for some single defining difference between them and everybody else and understand that they are in rich and largely uncharted, material-semiotic, flesh-to-flesh, and face-to-face connection with a host of significant others" (2008, 235). Brian Massumi's *What Animals Teach Us about Politics* (2014) turns to the animality of the human that is operative in play, drawing on the philosophies of Henri Bergson and Gilles Deleuze to see play—which is found among many animals—as the condition of possibility for language, art, and creative forms of political relation.

3 New materialisms tend to assert that matter is neither inert nor passive but rather active, agential, and, to use Jane Bennett's (2010) term, "vibrant." Mel Y. Chen builds on Bennett's general conception of vibrant matter in *Animacies:*

Biopolitics, Racial Mattering, and Queer Affect (2012), exploring how nonhuman agencies (of animals, rocks, and words) are deeply implicated in the human politics of race, gender, ability, and sexuality. William Connolly (2013) puts new materialist ontology to work in thinking about ecological politics within neo-liberal capitalism.

4 The term "queer inhumanisms" is the title of a 2015 special issue of GLQ edited by Dana Luciano and Mel Y. Chen in which Nyong'o's article appears.

5 See, for example, Timothy Brennan's *Wars of Position: The Cultural Politics of Left and Right* (2007), Neil Lazarus's *The Postcolonial Unconscious* (2011), and, most recently, Vivek Chibber's *Postcolonial Theory and the Specter of Capital* (2013).

6 In his review of Gayatri Spivak's *A Critique of Postcolonial Reason* (1999), Terry Eagleton suggests that "post-colonial theorists are often to be found agonising about the gap between their own intellectual discourse and the natives of whom they speak; but the gap might look rather less awesome if they did not speak a discourse which most intellectuals, too, find unintelligible" (1999, 3).

7 Giorgio Agamben's political philosophy is articulated around the concept of the "state of exception," which he elaborates from Schmitt's theories. For a sense of how far-reaching and influential Agamben's reworking of Schmitt has been, see *Politics, Metaphysics, and Death: Essays on Giorgio Agamben's "Homo Sacer"* (2005), edited by Andrew Norris.

8 For a more detailed account of the temporality of the master/slave dialectic, see Derrida's *Writing and Difference* (1978).

9 The asymmetry in recognition is the starting point for Glen Sean Coulthard's *Red Skin, White Masks: Rejecting the Colonial Politics of Recognition* (2014). There, Coulthard refuses recognition's snare, arguing that "instead of usher-ing in an era of peaceful coexistence grounded on the ideal of *reciprocity* or *mutual* recognition, the politics of recognition in its contemporary liberal form promises to reproduce the very configurations of colonialist, racist, patriarchal state power that Indigenous peoples' demands for recognition have historically sought to transcend" (3).

10 A postcolonial reading of Hegel will insist on a tension within this dialectical play, wherein the slave has always already been imagining a future in which he will become free.

11 Bernasconi writes: "Hegel was certainly justified in criticizing the travel liter-ature of his day for tantalizing readers by appearing 'incredible' and lacking 'a determinate image or principle' . . . but the manner in which he himself used that literature opens him to the charge of sensationalism as well. The accusation is sustained by the evidence of major and widespread distortion in his use of his sources" (1998, 45).

12 According to Hegel, Africans had a "sensuousness" developed through their geographic location that disabled them from a "fully developed mastery of reality," and they were thus excluded from the drama of world history (Berna-

sconi 1998, 52). It was Hegel's attempt, in fact, to prove that Africans had not yet reached a capacity for fixed objectivity.

Bernasconi explains, "Hegel's claim was not just that Africans lacked what 'we' call religion and the state, but also that one could not find among them a conception of God, the eternal, right, nature, or even of natural things. In consequence, Africans could be said to be in the condition of immediacy or unconsciousness. This is the basis on which Hegel characterized them as dominated by passion, savage, barbaric, and hence, most importantly for his discussion of history, at the first level" (52–53).

Such radically slanted declarations about "Africa," employed by Hegel in his choices to dramatize, selectively cite, and elide the cultural practices of Africans themselves, are what enable Bernasconi to declare that while Hegel may not have directly developed colonial practices, "he certainly contributed to the climate in which there was relatively little scrutiny of the conduct of Europeans in Africa" (62). Indeed, Bernasconi argues, Hegel's endorsement of African slavery did not hinge on an argument of their natural inferiority but rather on the fact that being subjected to slavery by European colonial powers would benefit Africans by bringing them into the fold of world history.

13 Between the fall of 1804 and the end of 1805, the journal *Minerva*, founded by the German publicist Johann Wilhelm von Archenholz, published a continuing series about the Haitian revolution "totaling more than a hundred pages, including source documents, news summaries, and eyewitness accounts, that informed its readers not only of the final struggle for independence of this French colony—under the banner Liberty or Death!—but of events over the past ten years as well" (Buck-Morss 2000, 838). While Archenholz was critical of the violence of the revolution, Buck-Morss argues that he came to appreciate the leadership and vision of Toussaint Louverture, and that there is evidence that Hegel was following this series. It is odd then that in Hegel scholarship "no one has dared to suggest that the idea for the dialectic of lordship and bondage came to Hegel in Jena in the years 1803–5 from reading the press—journals and newspapers" (Buck-Morss 2000, 843–44).

14 See Chen's *Animacies* (2012), which offers a new materialist account of the politics of objectification, dehumanization, and thingification through disability studies and queer of color critique. The GLQ special issue "Queer Inhumanisms" also makes this critical link between race and materiality through a series of persuasive articles.

15 The modern human understands itself by way of its mastery. Even Heidegger (1982) (via Friedrich Nietzsche) anticipated the moment in which the human as master of the world would come to crisis when our innovative technologies had advanced in ways we were not yet prepared to manage.

16 Radhakrishnan situates himself in opposition to scholars like Aijaz Ahmad, who argues, for instance, in his critique of Edward Said that Said's work is "self-divided . . . between a host of irreconcilable positions in cultural theory" (1992,

168–69). If we follow Ahmad's critique of Said as a selective thinker whose highly influential thought is founded on "irreconcilable positions," it is precisely here in these irreconcilabilities that we can begin to *read* rather than repudiate the subject and its ways of producing knowledge (to read Said himself, and to read the canon of Western literary history that Said reads with us).

I. Decolonizing Mastery

1 See especially Ann Pellegrini's chapter "Through the Looking Glass: Fanon's Double Vision" in *Performance Anxieties* (1997).

2 I discuss Robert Bernasconi's, Susan Buck-Morss's, and Caroline Rooney's work on Hegel's "reading" of Africa in detail in the introduction of this book.

3 Fanon offers definitive readings of white women's desire for black men in "The Man of Color and the White Woman" (1967e).

4 T. Denean Sharpley-Whiting's *Frantz Fanon: Conflicts and Feminisms* (1998) seeks to bridge Fanon and feminism by illustrating how to her mind the male revolutionary fight against racism and imperialism does not necessarily entail an antifeminist politics.

5 In his examination of the concept of the "proper" in Gandhian thought, Ajay Skaria argues that the Gujarati word *veshya* (prostitute) "marks the moment when a certain tension within *Hind Swaraj* over the question of the proper becomes especially fraught" (2007, 219).

6 For a more thorough gloss of the wider scope of Roy's book, see my review of *Alimentary Tracts* (Singh 2011). For a reading of Gandhi's vegetarianism as a student in England and his alliance with radical anti-Imperial groups in late nineteenth-century Europe, see Leela Gandhi's "Meat: A Short Cultural History of Animal Welfare at the Fin-de-Siècle" (2006).

7 Roy points to Swami Vivekananda's "prescription of 'beef, biceps, and Bahavadgita'" as the best known of India's curatives to the colonial characterizations of Indians as "feeble" and "effeminate" (2010, 79). Contexualizing his early draw toward carnivory, Gandhi tells his readers in the autobiography that "a doggerel of the Gujarati poet Narmad was in vogue amongst us schoolboys, as follows: 'Behold the mighty Englishman / He rules the Indian small, / Because being a meat-eater / He is five cubits tall'" (1993, 21).

8 Gandhi states that the force of satyagraha could be best translated as "love-force, soul-force, or more popularly but less accurately, passive resistance" (1997, 85).

9 Derrida builds from Søren Kierkegaard's reading of the story in *Fear and Trembling* (1983).

10 I have discussed Gandhi's "animal experiments" elsewhere (Singh 2015a), but for readers less familiar with Gandhi it may be useful to note here that his experimental practices were at the heart of this political action and included experiments with sexual abstinence and diet. Often, his experiments necessitated a

break with or modification of his commitments to ahimsa and to brahmacharya in order to sustain life or to create the least possible harm in a given situation. These experiments and modifications, Gandhi concedes, were not always successful in their aims, and he often invoked his failures and revised his actions according to them.

11 Desai and Vahed point to South African political figures like Nelson Mandela who have made a point of propping up the image of a South African Gandhi that ignore some of the more troubling historical facts about his time there (2016, 23–24).

12 Desai and Vahed's figures are from Jeff Guy's *Remembering the Rebellion: The Zulu Uprising of 1906* (2006, 170).

13 For a detailed history of this text, see the Cambridge edition of *Hind Swaraj* (1997, lxiii–lxiv).

14 Desai and Vahed (2016, 20) remind us that in the aftermath of his South African life, Gandhi would serve twice more as a stretcher-bearer for empire in 1914 at the start of World War I and again in 1918, revealing that Gandhi's commitment to empire could not be simply relegated to the South African part of his political career.

15 For a more detailed account of Gandhi's thinking of the animal in relation to abstinence, the formulation of hospitality in relation to animal consumption, and animal friendship, see "Gandhi's Animal Experiments" (Singh 2015a).

16 I dwell on the question of serving meat to carnivorous humans in more detail in "Gandhi's Animal Experiments" (Singh 2015a).

17 See Anurudha Ramanujan's "Violent Encounters: 'Stray' Dogs in Indian Cities" in *Cosmopolitan Animals* (2015).

18 Other men too—even Algerian men—are excluded from Fanon's bod(il)y politic of anticolonial liberation. Drawing on the biographical work of Irene Gendzier (1985), Fuss (1995, 161) considers how in 1953, when Fanon was appointed director of the hospital at Blida-Joinville (the largest psychiatric hospital in Algeria), his psychoanalytic practice required the use of Arabic and Kabyle translators to treat Algerian patients. I will return to this scene in the next chapter, where I attend specifically to language mastery in anticolonial politics, but here I want to note that these translators—educated Algerian men employed as nurses—are disabled from pursuing advanced medical degrees under colonial rule. They are instrumental to Fanon's practice (because he cannot understand his patients without them), and they are virtually erased from Fanon's own psychoanalytic accounts.

2. The Language of Mastery

1 See Jenny Sharpe's *Allegories of Empire: The Figure of Woman in the Colonial Text* (1993) for more on the discursive emphasis on colonized masculinities as perceived threats to white British women. Although Sharpe's study focuses on

the Indian context, she illustrates how the fantasy of dark-skinned male bodies as "dangers" to white women was a critical mechanism of colonial control in the colonies.

2 For an important Derridean account of Hindustani that takes up Gandhi's language politics, see Pritipuspa Mishra's "The Mortality of Hindustani" (2012).

3 As David Lelyveld illustrates, for Gandhi the name for this rashtrabhasha shifted across his writings, beginning with a declaration that the national language should be Hindi, which to Gandhi's early mind subsumed Urdu and thus included both Hindus and Muslims in its scope. Later, Gandhi would modify this to calling the rashtrabhasha "Hindi-Hindustani" to signal the inclusion of Persian or Arabic words, and finally he shifted the name to "Hindustani," moving away from Hindi altogether because the term "had become irretrievably bound up with hostility to Urdu" (Lelyveld 2001, 73).

4 This simplified account of the purity of the mother will come to be complicated through Melanie Klein's feminist psychoanalytic readings of the maternal relation, in which for her there is no "pure" relation between mother and child that is not always already caught up in destruction (1964). The aim for Klein, unlike Gandhi, is not to find a way out of this destruction but rather to understand that affection and aggression are not separable affects.

5 I return to this idea of the "aping" and being "like" the human in chapter 4 in my discussion of *Animal's People* (Sinha 2007) and *The Lives of Animals* (Coetzee 1999). There, we will see how being "like" becomes in *Animal's People* a critical and political generative difference, and how this "aping" gesture in *The Lives of Animals* becomes for the protagonist Costello an act of self-dispossession and a hopeful movement toward her animality.

6 Macaulay's famous "Minute on Indian Education," delivered to the British parliament in 1835, formulated language as a central problem in the goal of producing semicivilized colonial subjects. Macaulay argued that the dialects of India "contain neither literary nor scientific information, and are, moreover, so poor and rude that, until they are enriched from some other quarter, it will not be easy to translate any valuable work into them" (1835, 2). Here the ineptitude of the native language inhibits the transformation of the colonial subject into fruition as "a class of persons, Indian in blood and colour, but English in taste, in opinions, in morals, and in intellect" (8).

7 The mastery of languages is an explicitly stated goal in the 1965 Levin Report on the state of the field of comparative literature. While this language disappears in the 1993 Bernheimer Report, at least two of the respondents to this report—Michael Riffaterre and Elizabeth Fox-Genovese—take issue with the shift away from language mastery toward what they see as the encroachment of cultural studies. All these texts can be found in *Comparative Literature in the Age of Multiculturalism* (1995), edited by Charles Bernheimer.

3. Posthumanitarian Fictions

1   Indra Sinha's novel *Animal's People* (2007), to which I turn in the next chapter, can be read as posthumanitarian fiction. For my discussion of the novel in this frame, see Singh 2015b.

2   See Lisa Smirl's *Spaces of Aid: How Cars, Compounds and Hotels Shape Humanitarianism* (2015) for a nuanced account of the forces "in the field" that impede humanitarian aid practices. Smirl argues that "almost every aid worker comes to 'the field' with the intention to improve other people's lives. But as aid dollars become ever more scarce and aid workers are increasingly the target of violent attacks, a careful examination of why it seems so difficult to merely 'do good' is drastically needed" (xv). In the documentary *Assistance mortelle* (2013), the Haitian filmmaker Raoul Peck wades into the complexities of humanitarian efforts in the aftermath of the earthquake that devastated Haiti in 2010. Peck's film illustrates how workers, despite their best intentions and despite the record-breaking international aid funds sent to repair damages, quickly become ensnared in bureaucracies that render their work ineffective.

3   In *Complicities: The Intellectual and Apartheid* (2002), Sanders addresses the role of the intellectual in apartheid by theorizing complicity as that which is enfolded in every act and articulation of opposition. He therefore casts opposition as nondialectical.

4   In *Identification Papers* (1995), Diana Fuss charts the function of identification as a concept within psychoanalysis and identity politics, detailing how identification is simultaneously part of how a subject is *formed* and a crucial force that "calls . . . identity into question" (2). Lynn Hunt's (2007) account of the invention of human rights deploys a much less nuanced version of identification, attending only to the identity-building function of identification to think about what happens between readers and texts that generate the emotion she calls "empathy" (see especially chapter 1, "Torrents of Emotion").

5   Over and above this double identification produced by the form of these texts, in my own reading of "Little Ones" it becomes virtually impossible to ignore the uncanny repetition of Singh's name, which calls me into an uncomfortable proximity to the story's protagonist. His descent into madness at the end of the narrative thus compels me toward a radical revision of the narratives that have shaped me.

6   For an extended discussion of friendship and its relations to politics within Western philosophy (from Aristotle through Nietzsche via Michel de Montaigne), see Jacques Derrida's *Politics of Friendship* (1997). Derrida explores the tension between an "equality" among friends posited in what Aristotle calls "primary friendship" (23) and friendships, such as Nietzsche's "philosophers of the future," structured by certain kinds of dissymmetry (36) that are, nevertheless, characterized by forms of reciprocity or responsibility that are in no sense at play between the medical officer and his patient.

7 While the emphasis here is on how government programs and the actions of Singh and other bureaucrats are implicated in the distribution of resources that produces the differentiated bodies of Singh and the adivasi, Jane Bennett's *Vibrant Matter: A Political Ecology of Things* (2010) allows us to begin to consider the food *itself* as agential here: "Food, as a self-altering, dissipative materiality, is also a player. It enters into what we become. It is one of the many agencies operative in the moods, cognitive dissipations, and moral sensitivities that we bring to bear as we engage the questions of what to eat, how to eat, and when to stop" (51).

8 Agamben (1998) develops the concept of "bare life" (a phrase he borrows from Walter Benjamin) in order to account for what he calls, after Foucault, biopolitics. His theory depends on thresholds or "zones of indistinction" that separate the properly political from its outside. This zone of indistinction passes through the human itself: "There is politics because man is the living being who, in language, separates and opposes himself to his own bare life and, at the same time, maintains himself in relation to that bare life in an inclusive exclusion" (8). Agamben, following Arendt, principally builds his account of this "bare life" through analysis of concentration and refugee camps, where humans are reduced to being "bare life."

4. Humanimal Dispossessions

1 I am inspired by and indebted to the work of my extraordinary former student Kerry Boland, who in her evocative undergraduate senior thesis teased out the vital links between the novel's treatment of the human/animal and its queer sexual politics (Boland 2014).

2 The reading I offer of Coetzee's text here was originally published as "The Tail End of Disciplinarity" (Singh 2013).

3 In the preface to the first volume of Subaltern Studies, which would become a highly influential series across the social sciences and humanities, the South Asian historian Ranajit Guha begins with a declaration that the aim of the subaltern studies project is "to promote a systematic and informed discussion of subaltern themes in the field of South Asian studies, and thus help to rectify the elitist bias characteristic of much research and academic work in this particular area" (1982, vii).

4 It is important to note here that the dominant interpretation of the story has been one that reads the ape as a figure for the Jew. In this sense, Red Peter becomes a symbol of Kafka himself, as an intellectual whose Jewishness marginalizes him within the academy. This is precisely the kind of reading that obscures the other particularities of Red Peter, his animality, and our abilities as interlocutors to think/feel our way toward him as (another) animal.

5 Homi Bhabha's (1994) formulation of (post)colonial mimicry comes to bear explicitly here on animal studies. It is not simply that Red Peter "apes" his human

masters but that in the act of this aping he performs humanity in a style that begins to unfold the always performative aspects of humanity itself. We come to see the performativity of the human through the performance of the ape-as-human. In this sense, we become mimics of our own species.

6 See chapter 1, in which I illustrate through analyses of the language of Gandhi and Fanon how the animal emerges as a split, contestatory site in the framing of properly human subjectivities.

5. Cultivating Discomfort

1 I came to Jodi Byrd's *The Transit of Empire* (2011) in the late production stages of *Unthinking Mastery*. Her work is informed by indigenous perspectives as they challenge and redress settler colonial logics and postcolonial studies. Byrd emphasizes the concept of transit as it functions as a foundational settler erasure of indigenous peoples. I see her work as a vital site for unmasterful intellectual and political engagements, and as a sister text in the desire to redress and mobilize postcolonial discourse.

2 I am thinking here with the beautiful work of José Esteban Muñoz in *Cruising Utopia* (2009).

3 Radhakrishnan's work departs from a refutation of Aijaz Ahmad's (1992) critique of postcolonial studies, in which he reads ambivalence as a problem for the postcolonial project that registers its ineffectuality.

4 J. M. Coetzee's *Life & Times of Michael K* (1983) becomes an interesting novel to pair with Kincaid's garden prose. While at its surface Kincaid's bourgeois garden appears opposite to Coetzee's depiction of the abjection of the gardening subject under the force of apartheid, both offer "alternative" readings of the subject in relation to gardening practice that complicate the Eurocentric legacies of this subject. For a reading of Coetzee's novel in relation to ecocritical discourse, see Anthony Vital's "Toward an African Ecocriticism: Postcolonialism, Ecology and *Life & Times of Michael K*" (2008).

5 Recent critical works on the intersections between postcolonial studies and environmental politics include Graham Huggan and Helen Tiffin's *Postcolonial Ecocriticism: Literature, Animals, Environment* (2010); Bonnie Roos and Alex Hunt's *Postcolonial Green: Environmental Politics and World Narratives* (2010); Elizabeth DeLoughrey and George B. Handley's *Postcolonial Ecologies: Literatures of the Environment* (2011); and Rob Nixon's *Slow Violence and the Environmentalism of the Poor* (2011).

6 DeLoughrey and Handley's argument resonates with a body of literature looking to expand Foucault's project by pressuring his avoidance of the colonial project. See Ann Laura Stoler's *Race and the Education of Desire: Foucault's "History of Sexuality" and the Colonial Order of Things* (1995) and *Carnal Knowledge and Imperial Power: Race and the Intimate in Colonial Rule* (2002); Alexander G. Weheliye's *Habeus Viscus: Racializing Assemblages, Biopolitics, and Black Femi-*

nist Theories of the Human (2014); and Sylvia Wynter's "Unsettling the Coloniality of Being/Power/Truth/Freedom: Towards the Human, after Man, Its Overrepresentation—An Argument" (2003).

7 Thus "sovereignty is antiecological" (Smith 2011, xiii). Rejecting the common thought that "without sovereignty . . . nature cannot be preserved from being treated as a resource" (xiii), Smith turns to anarchist politics to think about an ecology that rejects territorial sovereignty.

8 Kincaid's critique of the imperial politics of naming rhymes with Jacques Derrida's (2008) critique of the French word "animaux," which forcibly erases differences between myriad animals into a single concept. Derrida's critique and his proposal of "*animot*" as a way to signal the violence of naming are discussed in chapter 4.

REFERENCES

Achebe, Chinua. 1965. "English and the African Writer." *Transition*, no. 18: 27–30.
———. (1958) 1994. *Things Fall Apart*. New York: Anchor Books.
Agamben, Giorgio. 1998. *Homo Sacer: Sovereign Power and Bare Life*. Translated by Daniel Heller-Roazen. Stanford, CA: Stanford University Press.
———. 2003. *The Open: Man and Animal*. Translated by Kevin Attell. Stanford, CA: Stanford University Press.
Ahmad, Aijaz. 1992. *In Theory: Classes, Nations, Literatures*. Oxford: Oxford University Press.
Ahmed, Sara. 2006. *Queer Phenomenology: Orientations, Objects, Others*. Durham, NC: Duke University Press.
———. 2013. "Queer Feelings." In *The Routledge Queer Studies Reader*, edited by Donald E. Hall, Annamarie Jagose, Andrea Bebell, and Susan Porter, 422–41. New York: Routledge.
Allewaert, Monique. 2013. *Ariel's Ecology: Plantations, Personhood, and Colonialism in the American Tropics*. Minneapolis: University of Minnesota Press.
Alter, Joseph. 1994. "Celibacy, Sexuality, and the Transformation of Gender into Nationalism in North India." *Journal of Asian Studies* 53 (1): 45–66.
Apter, Emily. 2005. *The Translation Zone: A New Comparative Literature*. Princeton, NJ: Princeton University Press.
Arendt, Hannah. 1976. *The Origins of Totalitarianism*. San Diego: Harvest Books.
Arnold, Matthew. 1993. *Culture and Anarchy and Other Writings*. Edited by Stephan Collini. Cambridge: Cambridge University Press.
Asad, Talal. 2007. *On Suicide Bombing*. New York: Columbia University Press.
Assistance mortelle. 2013. Directed by Raoul Peck. Paris: Arte France.
Attridge, Derek. 2004. *J. M. Coetzee and the Ethics of Reading*. Chicago: University of Chicago Press.
Balutansky, Kathleen M., and Jamaica Kincaid. 2002. "On Gardening." *Callaloo* 25 (3): 790–800.
Barad, Karen. 2007. *Meeting the Universe Halfway: Quantum Physics and the Entanglement of Matter and Meaning*. Durham, NC: Duke University Press.
Bennett, Jane. 2010. *Vibrant Matter: A Political Ecology of Things*. Durham, NC: Duke University Press.

Bergner, Gwen. 2005. *Taboo Subjects: Race, Sex, and Psychoanalysis*. Minneapolis: University of Minnesota Press.

Bernasconi, Robert. 1998. "Hegel at the Court of the Ashanti." In *Hegel after Derrida*, edited by Stuart Barnett, 41–63. New York: Routledge.

Bernheimer, Charles, ed. 1995. *Comparative Literature in the Age of Multiculturalism*. Baltimore: Johns Hopkins University Press.

Bernstein, Elizabeth. 2010. "Militarized Humanitarianism Meets Carceral Feminism: The Politics of Sex, Rights, and Freedom in Contemporary Antitrafficking Campaigns." *Signs* 36 (1): 45–72.

Bhabha, Homi. 1994. *The Location of Culture*. New York: Routledge.

Boland, Kerry. 2014. "Animal Allure: Postcolonial (Non) Human Sexuality in Indra Sinha's *Animal's People* and J. M. Coetzee's *Disgrace*." Honors thesis, University of Richmond.

Boler, Megan. 1999. *Feeling Power: Emotions and Education*. New York: Routledge.

Brennan, Timothy. 2007. *Wars of Position: The Cultural Politics of Left and Right*. New York: Columbia University Press.

Breu, Christopher. 2014. *Insistence of the Material: Literature in the Age of Biopolitics*. Minneapolis: University of Minnesota Press.

Buck-Morss, Susan. 2000. "Hegel and Haiti." *Critical Inquiry* 26 (4): 821–65.

Butler, Judith. 1990. *Gender Trouble: Feminism and the Subversion of Identity*. New York: Routledge.

———. 2004. *Precarious Life: The Powers of Mourning and Violence*. London: Verso.

———. 2015. *Notes toward a Performative Theory of Assembly*. Cambridge, MA: Harvard University Press.

Butler, Judith, and Athena Athanasiou. 2013. *Dispossession: The Performative in the Political*. Cambridge: Polity.

Byrd, Jodi A. 2011. *The Transit of Empire: Indigenous Critiques of Colonialism*. Minneapolis: University of Minnesota Press.

Calarco, Matthew. 2008. *Zoographies: The Question of the Animal from Heidegger to Derrida*. Chicago: University of Chicago Press.

Casid, Jill H. 2005. *Sowing Empire: Landscape and Colonization*. Minneapolis: University of Minnesota Press.

Césaire, Aimé. 2001. *Discourse on Colonialism*. Translated by Joan Pinkham. New York: Monthly Review Press.

———. 2002. *A Tempest*. Translated by Richard Miller. New York: TCG Translations.

Chakrabarty, Dipesh. 2007. *Provincializing Europe: Postcolonial Thought and Historical Difference*. Princeton, NJ: Princeton University Press.

———. 2009. "The Climate of History: Four Theses." *Critical Inquiry* 35 (2): 197–222.

Chatterjee, Partha. 1986. *Nationalist Thought and the Colonial World: A Derivative Discourse*. Minneapolis: University of Minnesota Press.

Chen, Mel Y. 2012. *Animacies: Biopolitics, Racial Mattering, and Queer Affect.* Durham, NC: Duke University Press.

Chibber, Vivek. 2013. *Postcolonial Theory and the Specter of Capital.* London: Verso.

Ch'ien, Evelyn Nien-Ming. 2005. *Weird English.* Cambridge, MA: Harvard University Press.

Cixous, Hélène. 1986. "Sorties: Out and Out: Attacks/Ways Out/Forays." Translated by Betsy Wing. In *The Newly Born Woman*, by Hélène Cixous and Catherine Clément, 63–132. Minneapolis: University of Minnesota Press.

Coetzee, J. M. 1983. *Life & Times of Michael K.* New York: Penguin Books.

———. 1999. *The Lives of Animals.* Edited by Amy Gutmann. Princeton, NJ: Princeton University Press.

———. 2003. *Elizabeth Costello.* New York: Penguin Books.

Coleridge, Samuel Taylor. (1798) 1951. "The Rime of the Ancient Mariner." In *Selected Poetry and Prose of Coleridge*, edited by Donald S. Stauffer, 6–24. New York: Modern Library.

Connolly, William E. 2013. *The Fragility of Things: Self-Organizing Processes, Neoliberal Fantasies, and Democratic Activism.* Durham, NC: Duke University Press.

Coole, Diana, and Samantha Frost, eds. 2010. *New Materialisms: Ontology, Agency, and Politics.* Durham, NC: Duke University Press.

Coulthard, Glen Sean. 2014. *Red Skin, White Masks: Rejecting the Colonial Politics of Recognition.* Minneapolis: University of Minnesota Press.

Damrosch, David. 2003. *What Is World Literature?* Princeton, NJ: Princeton University Press.

DeLoughrey, Elizabeth, and George B. Handley. 2011. *Postcolonial Ecologies: Literatures of the Environment.* Oxford: Oxford University Press.

Derrida, Jacques. 1978. *Writing and Difference.* Translated by Alan Bass. Chicago: University of Chicago Press.

———. 1988. "Signature Event Context." Translated by Alan Bass. In *Margins of Philosophy*, 307–30. Chicago: University of Chicago Press.

———. 1994. *Specters of Marx: The State of the Debt, the Work of Mourning, and the New International.* Translated by Peggy Kamuf. New York: Routledge.

———. 1995. *The Gift of Death.* Translated by David Wills. Chicago: University of Chicago Press.

———. 1997. *Politics of Friendship.* Translated by George Collins. London: Verso.

———. 1998. *Monolingualism of the Other, Or, The Prosthesis of Origin.* Translated by Patrick Mensah. Stanford, CA: Stanford University Press.

———. 2001. "Force of Law." Translated by Mary Quaintance. In *Acts of Religion*, edited by Gil Anidjar, 230–98. New York: Routledge.

———. 2008. *The Animal That Therefore I Am.* Translated by David Wills. New York: Fordham University Press.

Desai, Ashwin, and Goolam Vahed. 2016. *The South African Gandhi: Stretcher-Bearer of Empire.* Stanford, CA: Stanford University Press.

Devi, Mahasweta. 1998. "Little Ones." Translated by Ipsita Chanda. In *Bitter Soil*, 1–20. Calcutta: Seagull Books.

Devji, Faisal. 2012. *The Impossible Indian: Gandhi and the Temptation of Violence.* Cambridge, MA: Harvard University Press.

Doniger, Wendy. 1999. "Reflection." In J. M. Coetzee, *The Lives of Animals*, edited by Amy Gutmann, 93–106. Princeton, NJ: Princeton University Press.

Douzinas, Costas. 2007. "The Many Faces of Humanitarianism." *Parrhesia*, no. 2: 1–28.

Durrant, Sam. 2006. "J. M. Coetzee, Elizabeth Costello, and the Limits of the Sympathetic Imagination." In *J. M. Coetzee and the Idea of the Public Intellectual*, edited by Jane Poyer, 118–34. Athens: Ohio University Press.

Eagleton, Terry. 1999. "In the Gaudy Supermarket." *London Review of Books* 21 (10): 3–6.

Esposito, Roberto. 2008. *Bíos: Biopolitics and Philosophy.* Translated by Timothy Campbell. Minneapolis: University of Minnesota Press.

Fanon, Frantz. 1963. *The Wretched of the Earth.* Translated by Constance Farrington. New York: Grove Press.

———. 1965. "Algeria Unveiled." In *A Dying Colonialism*, 35–67. Translated by Haakon Chevalier. New York: Grove Press.

———. 1967a. *Black Skin, White Masks.* Translated by Charles Lam Markmann. New York: Grove Press.

———. 1967b. "By Way of Conclusion." In *Black Skin, White Masks*, 223–32.

———. 1967c. "The Fact of Blackness." In *Black Skin, White Masks*, 109–40.

———. 1967d. "Introduction." In *Black Skin, White Masks*, 7–14.

———. 1967e. "The Man of Color and the White Woman." In *Black Skin, White Masks*, 63–82.

———. 1967f. "The Negro and Language." In *Black Skin, White Masks*, 17–40.

———. 1967g. "The Negro and Psychopathology." In *Black Skin, White Masks*, 141–209.

———. 1967h. "The Woman of Color and the White Man." In *Black Skin, White Masks*, 41–62.

Foucault, Michel. 1990. *The History of Sexuality.* Vol. 1, *An Introduction.* Translated by Robert Hurley. New York: Vintage Books.

———. 1994. *The Order of Things: An Archaeology of the Human Sciences.* New York: Vintage Books.

Freeman, Elizabeth. 2010. *Time Binds: Queer Temporalities, Queer Histories.* Durham, NC: Duke University Press.

Freire, Paulo. 2000. *Pedagogy of the Oppressed.* Translated by Myra Bergman Ramos. New York: Bloomsbury.

Freud, Sigmund. (1962) 2000. *Three Essays on the Theory of Sexuality.* Translated by James Strachey. New York: Basic Books.

———. 2010. *Civilization and Its Discontents.* Translated by James Strachey. New York: W. W. Norton.

Fuss, Diana. 1995. *Identification Papers*. New York: Routledge.

Gandhi, Leela. 1998. *Postcolonial Theory: A Critical Introduction*. New York: Columbia University Press.

———. 2006. "Meat: A Short Cultural History of Animal Welfare at the Fin-de-Siècle." In *Affective Communities: Anticolonial Thought, Fin-de-Siècle Radicalism, and the Politics of Friendship*. Durham, NC: Duke University Press.

Gandhi, M. K. 1965. *Our Language Problem*. Edited by Anand T. Hingorani. Bombay: Bharatiya Vidya Bhavan.

———. 1976. *The Collected Works of Mahatma Gandhi*. 100 vols. Ahmedabad: Ministry of Information and Broadcasting, Government of India. https://www.gandhiheritageportal.org/the-collected-works-of-mahatma-gandhi.

———. 1993. *An Autobiography: The Story of My Experiments with Truth*. Translated by Mahadev Desai. Boston: Beacon.

———. 1997. *Hind Swaraj and Other Writings*. Edited by Anthony J. Parel. Cambridge: Cambridge University Press.

———. 1998. *Ashram Observances in Action*. Translated by Valji Govindji Desai. Ahmedabad: Navajivan Publishing House.

———. (1932) 2004. *From Yeravda Mandir: Ashram Observances*. Translated by Valji Govindji Desai. Ahmedabad: Navajivan Publishing House.

Garber, Marjorie. 1999. "Reflection." In J. M. Coetzee, *The Lives of Animals*, edited by Amy Gutmann, 73–84. Princeton, NJ: Princeton University Press.

Gendzier, Irene L. 1985. *Frantz Fanon: A Critical Study*. New York: Grove Press.

Ghazoul, Ferial J. 2006. "Comparative Literature in the Arab World." *Comparative Critical Studies* 3 (1–2): 113–24.

Gibson, Nigel C. 2003. *Fanon: The Postcolonial Imagination*. Cambridge: Polity.

Glissant, Edouard. 1989. *Caribbean Discourse: Selected Essays*. Translated by J. Michael Dash. Charlottesville: University of Virginia Press.

Goethe, Johann Wolfgang von. 1973. "Some Passages Pertaining to the Concept of World Literature." Translated by Joel E. Spingarn. In *Comparative Literature: The Early Years*, edited by Hans-Joachim Schulz and Phillip H. Rhein, 3–11. Chapel Hill: University of North Carolina Press.

Gramsci, Antonio. 1971. *Selections from the Prison Notebooks*. Edited and translated by Quentin Hoare and Geoffrey Nowell Smith. London: Lawrence and Wishart.

Guha, Ranajit, ed. 1982. *Writings on South Asian History and Society*. Subaltern Studies 1. Oxford: Oxford University Press.

Guy, Jeff. 2006. *Remembering the Rebellion: The Zulu Uprising of 1906*. Pietermaritzburg: University of KwaZulu-Natal Press.

Halberstam, Judith [Jack]. 2011. *The Queer Art of Failure*. Durham, NC: Duke University Press.

Haraway, Donna. 2008. *When Species Meet*. Minneapolis: University of Minnesota Press.

———. 2016. *Staying with the Trouble: Making Kin in the Chthulucene*. Durham, NC: Duke University Press.

Hardt, Michael, and Antonio Negri. 2004. *Multitude: War and Democracy in the Age of Empire*. New York: Penguin Books.

Hegel, G. W. F. 1977. *Phenomenology of Spirit*. Translated by A. V. Miller. Oxford: Oxford University Press.

Heidegger, Martin. 1975. *Poetry, Language, Thought*. Translated by Albert Hofstadter. New York: Harper Perennial.

———. 1982. *The Question Concerning Technology, and Other Essays*. Translated by William Lovitt. New York: Harper Torchbooks.

———. 1995. *The Fundamental Concepts of Metaphysics: World, Finitude, Solitude*. Translated by William McNeill and Nicholas Walker. Bloomington: Indiana University Press.

Home of the Brave. 1949. Directed by Mark Robson. Los Angeles, CA: Paramount Pictures.

Huggan, Graham, and Helen Tiffin, eds. 2010. *Postcolonial Ecocriticism: Literature, Animals, Environment*. New York: Routledge.

Hunt, Lynn. 2007. *Inventing Human Rights: A History*. New York: W. W. Norton.

Jameson, Fredric. 1981. *The Political Unconscious: Narrative as a Socially Symbolic Act*. Ithaca: Cornell University Press.

Jaspers, Karl. 2001. *The Question of German Guilt*. Translated by E. B. Ashton. New York: Fordham University Press.

Kafka, Franz. 1971. "A Report to an Academy." In *Franz Kafka: The Complete Stories*, edited by Nahum N. Glatzer, 250–62. New York: Schocken Books.

Kierkegaard, Søren. 1983. *Fear and Trembling/Repetition*. Translated by Howard V. Hong and Edna H. Hong. Princeton, NJ: Princeton University Press.

Kilito, Abdelfattah. 2008. *Thou Shalt Not Speak My Language*. Translated by Wail S. Hassan. Syracuse, NY: Syracuse University Press.

Kincaid, Jamaica. 1988. *A Small Place*. New York: Farrar, Straus and Giroux.

———. 1999. *My Garden (Book)*. New York: Farrar, Straus and Giroux.

———. 2005. *Among Flowers: A Walk in the Himalaya*. Washington, DC: National Geographic.

Kishwar, Madhu. 1985. "Gandhi on Women." *Economic and Political Weekly* 20 (40): 1691–1702.

Klein, Melanie. 1964. "Love, Guilt, and Reparation." In Melanie Klein and Joan Riviere, *Love, Hate, and Reparation*, 57–119. New York: W. W. Norton.

Kojève, Alexandre. 1980. *Introduction to the Reading of Hegel: Lectures on the Phenomenology of Spirit*. Translated by James H. Nichols Jr. Ithaca, NY: Cornell University Press.

Lazarus, Neil. 2011. *The Postcolonial Unconscious*. Cambridge: Cambridge University Press.

Lelyveld, David. 2001. "Words as Deeds: Gandhi and Language." *Journal of Urdu Studies*, no. 16: 64–75.

Lemm, Vanessa. 2009. *Nietzsche's Animal Philosophy: Culture, Politics, and the Animality of the Human Being*. New York: Fordham University Press.

Lorde, Audre. 1984. "The Master's Tools Can Never Dismantle the Master's House." In *Sister Outsider: Essays and Speeches*, 110–14. Berkeley, CA: Crossing Press.

Luciano, Dana, and Mel Y. Chen. 2015. "Introduction: Has the Queer Ever Been Human?" In "Queer Inhumanisms," special issue, *GLQ* 21 (2–3): 183–207.

Macaulay, Thomas Babington. 1835. "Macaulay's Minute on Indian Education." Accessed September 10, 2013. http://oldsite.english.ucsb.edu/faculty/rraley /research/english/macaulay.html.

Markovits, Claude. 2004. *The Un-Gandhian Gandhi: The Life and Afterlife of the Mahatma*. London: Anthem.

Marx, Karl. 1992. *Capital*. Vol. 1. Translated by Ben Fowkes. New York: Penguin Books.

Marx, Karl, and Friedrich Engels. 2002. *The Communist Manifesto*. Translated by Samuel Moore. New York: Penguin Books.

Massumi, Brian. 2014. *What Animals Teach Us about Politics*. Durham, NC: Duke University Press.

McHugh, Susan. 2011. *Animal Stories: Narrating across Species Lines*. Minneapolis: University of Minnesota Press.

Memmi, Albert. 1991. *The Colonizer and the Colonized*. Translated by Howard Greenfeld. Boston: Beacon.

Mishra, Pritipuspa. 2012. "The Mortality of Hindustani." *Parallax* 18 (3): 71–83.

Muñoz, José Esteban. 1999. *Disidentifications: Queers of Color and the Performance of Politics*. Minneapolis: University of Minnesota Press.

———. 2009. *Cruising Utopia: The Then and There of Queer Futurity*. New York: New York University Press.

———. 2015. "Theorizing Queer Inhumanisms: The Sense of Brownness." In "Queer Inhumanisms," special issue, *GLQ* 21 (2–3): 209–10.

Nancy, Jean-Luc. 2007. *On Listening*. Translated by Charlotte Mandell. New York: Fordham University Press.

Nandy, Ashis. 1983. *The Intimate Enemy: Loss and Recovery of the Self under Colonialism*. Oxford: Oxford University Press.

Ngũgĩ wa Thiong'o. 1973. "On the Abolition of the English Department." In *Homecoming: Essays on African and Caribbean Literature, Culture and Politics*, 145–50. New York: Lawrence Hill.

———. 1986. "The Language of African Literature." In *Decolonising the Mind: The Politics of Language in African Literature*, 4–33. Portsmouth, NH: Heinemann.

Nixon, Rob. 2011. *Slow Violence and the Environmentalism of the Poor*. Cambridge, MA: Harvard University Press.

Norris, Andrew, ed. 2005. *Politics, Metaphysics, and Death: Essays on Giorgio Agamben's "Homo Sacer."* Durham, NC: Duke University Press.

Nyong'o, Tavia. 2015. "Little Monsters: Race, Sovereignty, and Queer Inhumanism in *Beasts of the Southern Wild*." In "Queer Inhumanisms," special issue, *GLQ* 21 (2–3): 249–72.

Orlie, Melissa. 2010. "Impersonal Matter." In *New Materialisms: Ontology, Agency, and Politics*, edited by Diana Coole and Samantha Frost, 116–36. Durham, NC: Duke University Press.

Parry, Benita. 1998. "Speech and Silence in the Fictions of J. M. Coetzee." In *Writing South Africa: Literature, Apartheid, and Democracy, 1970–1995*, edited by Derek Attridge and Rosemary Jolly, 149–65. Cambridge: Cambridge University Press.

Pellegrini, Ann. 1997. *Performance Anxieties: Staging Psychoanalysis, Staging Race*. New York: Routledge.

Pettman, Dominic. 2011. *Human Error: Species-Being and Media Machines*. Minneapolis: University of Minnesota Press.

Prakash, Gyan, ed. 1995. *After Colonialism: Imperial Histories and Postcolonial Displacements*. Princeton, NJ: Princeton University Press.

Pratt, Mary Louise. 1992. *Imperial Eyes: Travel Writing and Transculturation*. New York: Routledge.

Radhakrishnan, R. 2000. "Postmodernism and the Rest of the World." In *The Preoccupation of Postcolonial Studies*, edited by Fawzia Afzal-Khan and Kalpana Seshadri-Crooks, 37–70. Durham, NC: Duke University Press.

Ramanujan, Anuradha. 2015. "Violent Encounters: 'Stray' Dogs in Indian Cities." In *Cosmopolitan Animals*, edited by Kaori Nagai, Karen Jones, Donna Landry, Monica Mattfeld, Caroline Rooney, and Charlotte Sleigh, 216–32. New York: Palgrave Macmillan.

Ramaswamy, Sumathi. 1997. *Passions of the Tongue: Language Devotion in Tamil India, 1891–1970*. Berkeley: University of California Press.

Rooney, Caroline. 2000. *African Literature, Animism and Politics*. New York: Routledge.

Roos, Bonnie, and Alex Hunt, eds. 2010. *Postcolonial Green: Environmental Politics and World Narratives*. Charlottesville: University of Virginia Press.

Rothberg, Michael. 2009. *Multidirectional Memory: Remembering the Holocaust in the Age of Decolonization*. Stanford, CA: Stanford University Press.

Roy, Parama. 2002. "Meat-Eating, Masculinity, and Renunciation: A Gandhian Grammar of Diet." *Gender and History* 14 (1): 62–91.

———. 2010. *Alimentary Tracts: Appetites, Aversions, and the Postcolonial*. Durham, NC: Duke University Press.

Said, Edward W. 1979. *Orientalism*. New York: Vintage Books.

———. 1994. *Culture and Imperialism*. New York: Vintage Books.

———. 2004. *Humanism and Democratic Criticism*. New York: Columbia University Press.

Sanders, Mark. 2002. *Complicities: The Intellectual and Apartheid*. Durham, NC: Duke University Press.

Saro-Wiwa, Ken. 1994. *Sozaboy*. New York: Longman African Writers.

Sartre, Jean-Paul. 1995. *Anti-Semite and Jew: An Exploration of the Etiology of Hate*. Translated by George J. Becker. New York: Schocken Books.

Schmitt, Carl. 2005. *Political Theology: Four Chapters on the Concept of Sovereignty*. Translated by George Schwab. Chicago: University of Chicago Press.

Serres, Michel. 2007. *The Parasite*. Translated by Lawrence R. Schehr. Minneapolis: University of Minnesota Press.

Seshadri-Crooks, Kalpana. 2002. "'I Am a Master': Terrorism, Masculinity, and Political Violence in Frantz Fanon." *Parallax* 8 (2): 84–98.

Sharpe, Jenny. 1993. *Allegories of Empire: The Figure of Woman in the Colonial Text*. Minneapolis: University of Minnesota Press.

Sharpley-Whiting, T. Denean. 1998. *Frantz Fanon: Conflicts and Feminisms*. Lanham, MD: Rowman and Littlefield.

Singh, Julietta. 2011. "Eat and Be Eaten: The Gastropolitics of the (Post) Colony." *Reviews in Cultural Theory* 2 (1): 38–41.

———. 2013. "The Tail End of Disciplinarity." *Journal of Postcolonial Writing* 49 (4): 470–82.

———. 2015a. "Gandhi's Animal Experiments." In *Cosmopolitan Animals*, edited by Kaori Nagai, Karen Jones, Donna Landry, Monica Mattfeld, Caroline Rooney, and Charlotte Sleigh, 120–32. New York: Palgrave Macmillan.

———. 2015b. "Post-Humanitarian Fictions." *Symploke* 23 (1–2): 137–52.

Sinha, Indra. 2007. *Animal's People*. New York: Simon and Schuster.

Skaria, Ajay. 2007. "Only One Word, Properly Altered: Gandhi and the Question of the Prostitute." *Postcolonial Studies* 10 (2): 219–37.

Slaughter, Joseph. 2007. *Human Rights Inc.: The World Novel, Narrative Form, and International Law*. New York: Fordham University Press.

Smirl, Lisa. 2008. "Building the Other, Constructing Ourselves: Spatial Dimensions of International Humanitarian Response." *International Political Sociology* 2 (3): 236–53.

———. 2015. *Spaces of Aid: How Cars, Compounds and Hotels Shape Humanitarianism*. London: Zed Books.

Smith, Mick. 2011. *Against Ecological Sovereignty: Ethics, Biopolitics, and Saving the Natural World*. Minneapolis: University of Minnesota Press.

Snaza, Nathan. 2013. "Bewildering Education." *Journal of Curriculum and Pedagogy* 10 (1): 38–54.

Spivak, Gayatri Chakravorty. 1988. "Can the Subaltern Speak?" In *Marxism and the Interpretation of Culture*, edited by Cary Nelson and Lawrence Grossberg, 271–313. Urbana: University of Illinois Press.

———. 1999. *A Critique of Postcolonial Reason: Toward a History of the Vanishing Present*. Cambridge, MA: Harvard University Press.

———. 2003. *Death of a Discipline*. New York: Columbia University Press.

Stoler, Ann Laura. 1995. *Race and the Education of Desire: Foucault's "History of Sexuality" and the Colonial Order of Things*. Durham, NC: Duke University Press.

———. 2012. *Carnal Knowledge and Imperial Power: Race and the Intimate in Colonial Rule*. Berkeley: University of California Press.

Suzuki, David. 2007. *The Sacred Balance: Rediscovering Our Place in Nature*. Vancouver, BC: Greystone Books.

Vaccaro, Jeanne. 2015. "Feelings and Fractals: Woolly Ecologies of Transgender Matter." In "Queer Inhumanisms," special issue, *GLQ* 21 (2–3): 273–93.

Viswanathan, Gauri. 1989. *Masks of Conquest: Literary Study and British Rule in India*. New York: Columbia University Press.

Vital, Anthony. 2008. "Toward an African Ecocriticism: Postcolonialism, Ecology and *Life & Times of Michael K*." *Research in African Literatures* 39 (1): 87–106.

Walker, Alice. 1983. "In Search of Our Mothers' Gardens." In *In Search of Our Mothers' Gardens: Womanist Prose*. New York: Harcourt, Brace, and Jovanovich.

Weheliye, Alexander G. 2014. *Habeas Viscus: Racializing Assemblages, Biopolitics, and Black Feminist Theories of the Human*. Durham, NC: Duke University Press.

Wolfe, Cary. 2010. *What Is Posthumanism?* Minneapolis: University of Minnesota Press.

Wood, Sarah. 2014. *Without Mastery: Reading and Other Forces*. Edinburgh: Edinburgh University Press.

Wynter, Sylvia. 1984. "The Ceremony Must Be Found: After Humanism." *boundary 2*, 12 (1)–13 (2): 19–70.

———. 2001. "Towards the Sociogenic Principle: Fanon, Identity, the Puzzle of Conscious Experience, and What It Is Like to Be 'Black.'" In *National Identities and Sociopolitical Changes in Latin America*, edited by Mercedes F. Durán-Cogan and Antonio Gómez-Moriana, 30–66. New York: Routledge.

———. 2003. "Unsettling the Coloniality of Being/Power/Truth/Freedom: Towards the Human, after Man, Its Overrepresentation—An Argument." *CR: The New Centennial Review* 3 (3): 257–337.

Wynter, Sylvia, and Katherine McKittrick. 2015. "Unparalleled Catastrophe for Our Species? Or, to Give Humanness a Different Future: Conversations." In *Sylvia Wynter: On Being Human as Praxis*, edited by Katherine McKittrick, 9–89. Durham, NC: Duke University Press.

INDEX

Achebe, Chinua, 84–85, 86, 87–88, 92
Africa, Hegel's relation to, 15–17, 34, 178–79n12, 180n2
Agamben, Giorgio, 19, 118, 178n7, 184n8
ahimsa, 31, 37, 41, 44–46, 49–51, 180–81n10
Ahmad, Aijaz, 179–80n16, 185n3
Ahmed, Sara, 53, 104–5, 151, 172
"Algeria Unveiled" (Fanon), 34–35
Alter, Joseph, 39
Among Flowers (Kincaid), 164–70
animality, 26, 122, 123–26, 137–38, 140–42, 184n4
Animal's People (Sinha), 26, 121, 123–26, 181n5, 183n1
animal studies, 4, 145, 184–85n5
anticolonial discourse, 2, 24–25, 29–64, 69–82, 122, 146–47, 174
anti-Semitism, 56–58
Apter, Emily, 89
Arendt, Hannah, 118, 184n8
Arnold, Matthew, 79
Asad, Talal, 7
Athanasiou, Athena, 122–23
Attridge, Derek, 134–35

Balutansky, Kathleen M., 161–62
Barad, Karen, 18
Bennett, Jane, 18, 20, 177n3, 184n7
Bergner, Gwen, 36
Bernasconi, Robert, 15, 178n11, 178–79n12, 180n2

Bernheimer, Charles, 182n7
Bernstein, Elizabeth, 103
Bhabha, Homi, 52, 58, 184–85n5
biopolitics, 3, 4, 11, 185–86n6
Black Skin, White Masks, 52, 53, 54–62, 63, 70–73
black studies, 3, 5
Boland, Kerry, 184n1
Boler, Megan, 152
Bramacharya, 31, 39, 42–43, 49, 181n10
Breu, Christopher, 20–21, 102, 175
Buck-Morss, Susan, 16–17, 179n13, 180n2
Butler, Judith, 11, 22–23, 122–23, 132, 138, 167
Byrd, Jodi, 157, 185n1

Calarco, Matthew, 147
Capécia, Mayotte, 36–37, 54
Casid, Jill, 160–61
Césaire, Aimé, 18, 25, 27, 82–83, 171–72, 176
Chakrabarty, Dipesh, 19, 93, 113
Chatterjee, Partha, 42
Chen, Mel Y., 20, 147, 177–78n3, 178n4, 179n14
Chibber, Vivek, 178n5
Ch'ien, Evelyn Nien-Ming, 78
Cixous, Hélène, 1, 3, 24, 172
Coetzee, J. M., 12, 25–26, 84, 97, 98–99, 105–6, 109–14, 131–46, 172, 181n5, 185n4
Coleridge, Samuel Taylor, 112

Haiti: Hegel's relation to, 16, 179n13; 2010 earthquake in, 183n2
Halberstam, Jack, 17, 21, 133–34, 161, 175
Handley, George B., 133, 160, 185n5, 185–86n6
Haraway, Donna, 2, 123, 148, 177n2
Hardt, Michael, 11
Hegel, G. W. F., 6, 13, 14, 15–17, 34, 54, 143, 178nn10–11
Heidegger, Martin, 65, 71, 89, 177n2, 179n15
Hind Swaraj (Gandhi), 37–38, 41–43, 46–48, 80, 181n13
Holocaust, 142–46
Home of the Brave (Robson), 60–62
Huggan, Graham, 133, 159, 185n5
humanitarianism, 96–100, 102–5, 118–19, 125
human rights, 100
Hunt, Lynn, 100, 183n4

Jameson, Fredric, 175
Jaspers, Karl, 118
Johnson, Sarah Anne, 155–57
Joyce, James, 141

Kafka, Franz, 137, 184n4
Kilito, Abdelfattah, 88–89, 90
Kincaid, Jamaica, 12, 26–27, 149–52, 158–70, 172, 174, 185n4
Kishwar, Madhu, 37, 39
Klein, Melanie, 182n4
Kójève, Alexandre, 14

Lazarus, Neil, 178n5
Lelyveld, David, 78, 182n3
Lemm, Vanessa, 147
Life & Times of Michael K (Coetzee), 26, 97, 98–99, 105–6, 109–14, 185n4
listening, 27, 138–40

"Little Ones" (Devi), 26, 97, 99, 106–8, 114–18, 122, 183n5
Lives of Animals (Coetzee), 12, 26, 84, 131–46, 181n5
Locke, John, 13
Lorde, Audre, 83

Macaulay, Thomas Babington, 81, 87, 182n6
Markovitz, Claude, 44
Marx, Karl, 6, 14, 91, 102
Marxism, 6
mastery: aspects of, 12–14; deconstructive mode, 3; Hegelian mode, 3, 13, 14, 15–18, 54, 143, 167; as intellectual practice, 8–10; of language, 68–69, 70–88, 89–94; mastering, 6; relation to academic discipline, 132–36, 175; relation to dominion, 12; relation to gardening, 168–70; relation to narrative, 17–21, 30, 97–98; relation to sovereignty, 10–11; relation to student protest, 65–68; remainders of, 30–31; of self, 13, 31, 41–43; ubiquity of, 1
Memmi, Albert, 25, 69, 70, 74–75, 77, 80
Mishra, Pritipupsa, 182n2
Muñoz, José Esteban, 5, 15, 30, 141, 173, 185n2
My Garden (Kincaid), 149–50, 158–64, 169–70

Nancy, Jean-Luc, 139
Nandy, Ashis, 41
narrative: relation to mastery, 17–21; relation to reading subject, 17–18, 99–101, 108–9
Negri, Antonio, 11
new materialisms, 4, 18, 20–21, 177–78n3
Ngũgĩ wa Thiong'o, 65, 84, 86–88, 92
Nietzsche, Friedrich, 93, 179n15, 183n6

nonhuman agency, 151, 161–64, 170, 184n7
Nyong'o, Tavia, 5

Orlie, Melissa, 170

Parry, Benita, 111
Partition of India, 12, 95
Peck, Raoul, 183n2
Pellegrini, Ann, 57–58, 73, 180n1
Pettman, Dominic, 19
postcolonial studies, 2, 3, 18, 21–22, 132–33, 159–60, 185n1; critiques of the field, 6–8
posthumanism, 4–5, 177n2
posthumanitarian fictions, 96–98, 99–105, 108–9, 118–20, 124
Prakash, Gyan, 29

queer inhumanisms, 5, 178n4, 179n14

Radhakrishnan, R., 21, 158, 179–80n16, 185n3
Ramaswamy, Sumathi, 76
rashtrabhasha, 76, 81, 182n3
Rhodes, Cecil John, 65
Riffaterre, Michael, 182n7
Rooney, Caroline, 15, 180n2
Rothberg, Michael, 145–46
Roy, Parama, 38–41, 44, 50, 115, 180nn6–7

sacrifice, 30, 39–41, 50–51, 85, 87
Said, Edward, 8, 89, 93, 132, 175, 179–80n16
Sanders, Mark, 98, 120, 183n3
Saro-Wiwa, Ken, 78
Sartre, Jean-Paul, 57
satyagraha, 31, 39, 43–45, 48–49, 83, 180n8
Schmitt, Carl, 10, 178n7
Serres, Michel, 10

Seshadri-Crooks, Kalpana, 32–33, 35–36
Sharpe, Jenny, 181–82n1
Sharpley-Whiting, T. Denean, 180n4
Singh, Julietta, 180–81n10, 181nn15–16, 183n1, 184n2
Sinha, Indra, 26, 121, 123–26, 181n5, 183n1
Skaria, Ajay, 38, 180n5
Slaughter, Joseph, 100
Smirl, Lisa, 103, 183n2
Smith, Mick, 12, 186n7
Smuts, Barbara, 135
Snaza, Nathan, 67
sociogeny, 54–55, 108–9
sovereignty, 3, 10–11, 35, 122, 162, 170, 186n7
Spivak, Gayatri Chakravorty, 22, 109, 173, 178n6
subaltern studies, 132, 184n3
Suzuki, David, 166
swaraj, 31, 37, 41–42, 43–48, 49, 75
sympathetic imagination, 141–42

Tempest, A (Césaire), 27, 171–72, 176
Tiffin, Helen, 133, 159, 185n5
translation, 46–47, 71–72, 181n18
tree planting, 154–58

utopian desire, 21, 27–28, 59, 173–74

Vaccaro, Jeanne, 173
Vaheed, Goolam, 45–46, 181nn11–12, 181n14
vegetarianism, 38, 40–41, 50, 139, 180n6
Viswanathan, Gauri, 68
Vital, Anthony, 111–12, 185n4
vital ambivalence, 26, 157, 158–61, 162, 170
vulnerable reading, 21–24, 63–64, 97, 101, 108–9, 119–20, 137, 168